Carter County, Tennessee

Minutes *of the* County Court

1826-1829

Works Projects Administration

1942

Please direct all correspondence and orders to:

SOUTHERN HISTORICAL PRESS, Inc.
PO BOX 1267
375 West Broad Street
Greenville, SC   29601
southernhistoricalpress@gmail.com

ISBN #0-89308-826-9

CARTER COUNTY

COURT MINUTES VOL 4
1826-1829

INDEX

Note: Page numbers in this index refer to those original volumn from which this copy was made. There numbers are carried in the body of the manuscript within parentheses.

Fulton, Samuel, 2, 70,
Furr, Sherrod, 309,
Fyffe, James, H, 67, 184,

Gamble, J. M. 26,
Gap, Creek, 110, 160,
Garland, David, 128, 175, 205
Garland, Ezekiel, 128,
Garland, Gutherage,(Gubtridge)
   128, 225,
Garland, Isaac, 330,
Garland, John, 117,
Garland, N. W. 308, 309,
Garland, Samuel, 275, 331, 338,
Garland, William, 12, 13, 24, 47
   70, 171, 101, 252, 275, 307,
   330, 331,
Gentry, Benja. Benjamin, 10, 24,
   267,
Gentry, David, 311
Gentry, Joseph, 30, 311,
George, Celia, 87,

Greenway, 118
Greenway, George, 19, 51, 111,
141, 157, 215, 222, 227,
228, 258, 259, 260, 269,
294, 299, 300, 306, 307,
316, 329, 346, 347, 349
Greenway, G. W. 270, 275, 320
335, 341,
Greenway, George, W. 125, 135,
156, 162, 165, 276, 287,
302, 321, 323, 336, 342,
Greer, John, 264
Greers, Richard, 17, 112, 169
Greer, Thomas, 328
Greer, Thomas, D. 135
Greer, William, 49, 221, 264
325
Grindstaff, 128
Grindstaff, Benjamin(Benja)
3, 25, 26, 27, 28, 29, 11
112, 128, 219, 226, 346
Grindstaff, Capt, 135
Grindstaff, Henry, 48, 87, 2
203, 204, 219, 226, 338
Grindstaff, John, 221, 246,
247, 263, 327,
Grindstaff, Nicholas, 36, 37,
113, 149, 158, 160
Groons, Creek, 289,
Guinn (Guin)(Gwinn) Able, 324
Guinn(Guin), 328,
Guinn(Gwinn), David, 45, 79,
90, 112, 145, 329,
Guinn, Isaac, 180
Guinn, James, 232
Guthrid, John, 167,

Hains,(Haines's) (Haynes),
David, 2, 26, 40, 43, 49,
65, 111, 241, 142, 143,
171, 172, 292, 328
Haines's George, (Geo.), 111,
142, 168, 172, 329
Haines's, Mill, 77
Hampton, H. B. 232,
Hampton, Hamelton, 302, 304
Hampton, Hamelton, B. 69
Hamptons, Jacob, 170
Hampton, James, 145
Hampton, J. 2, 11, 36, 37,

70, 75, 139, 173, 174,
222, 250, 268, 329, 257
Hampton, J. Senr. 269
Hampton, John, 138, 141,
158, 182, 287,
Hampton, Johnson, 1, 2,
12, 22, 45, 46, 52, 55
57, 59, 61, 86, 88, 89
126, 128, 129, 142, 166
170, 171, 192, 219, 224,
249, 250, 253, 280, 287
302, 304, 306, 326, 335
Hampton, Johnson, Senr.267
Hampton, Justice of Peace,
268
Hampton, Thomas, 182, 287
Hall, Joshua, 305,
Hall, William, 333
Harden, Elijah, 271, 221,
Harden, John, 2
Hardin, Levi, 305,
Hardin W. M. 119,
Harden (Hardin) William,
(Wm), 3, 54, 267, 297,
325,
Harley, James, 344,
Harley,(Harly), Nehemiah,
336, 337, 340, 342,
Harris, Benjamin, C. 24,
317
Harris, Elizabeth, 282,
Harris Carriger, Elizabeth
118
Harris, William, 282
Harris, William,(Wm.A.)
118, 138, 157, 160, 184,
213, 214,
Harrison,
Hart & Groves,(Grave), 4,
28,
Harts, Leonard, 292,
Harvy, James, 339, 348
Harvey, Wm. 320
Hatcher, John, 51, 113,
148, 157, 170,
Hatcher, Thomas, 112,
220
Hatcheway, E. 72,
Hatheway,(Hathaway),
Elijah, 87, 162, 226,

Howard, Isaac, 13,
Howard, John, 83, 85,
   101, 221
Howard, John, R. 163,
Howard, Samuel,(Saml.),
   25, 26, 27, 28,29,
   73, 83, 96, 106, 114,
   123, 128, 146, 150,
   151, 153, 272, 285,
   304,
Huffman, Moses, 112, I
   171, 192, 193, 194,
   234, 236,
Hughs, Caty, 202,
Hughs(Hughes),James, 7,
   83, 85, 114, 116,
   132, 133, 134, 184,
   214, 234, 238, 262,
Humphreys, Elisha,.6,
   8, 9, 239, 250, 256
   323,
Humphreys, Elizabeth,
   14, 144, 294, 295,
Humphreys, George, 323,
Humphreys, Jesse, 323,
Humphreys, John, 9,
Humphreys, Moses, 6, 8,
   24, 62, 65, 239, 250,
   256,
Humphreys, Polly, 323,
Hunt, Henson, 171,
Hunt, James, 292,
Hunt, Michael, 82
Hunt, Micheal Sr. 51
Hunt, Nancy, 135, 176,
Hunt, Peter, 47, 118,
   123, 135, 176,
Hunter, Jacob, 33,
Hutchens, Anderson, 241,
Huston,(Houston) Samuel,
   313, 314, 321,
Hyder, Benjamin,(Benja),
   310, 338, 343,
Hyders, Hampton, 119,
   167, 173, 287, 294,
Hyder, J. H. 222, 329,
Hyder, Jonathan(Jona)
   62, 64, 71, 230,
   238, 265,
Hyder, Johnathan, H.
   112,

Hyder,(Hider) Joseph,
   80, 119, 168, 170,
Hyder,(Hider),
   Michael,(Michl), 25,
   26, 42, 49, 119, 123,
   168, 185, 220, 267,
   277, 278, 279, 291,
Hyder, Michael Junr. 265
(Hider) Hyder(Mikel) 27,
   28, 29,

Indian, Creek, 169, 219,
   Ingran, Charles, 79,
Ingram, John, 170, 267,
   326,
Ingram, John, I. 143,
Ingram, William, 49
   168, 326
Inman, John, 62, 65, l
   168, 170, 293, 331,
   343,
Innmon(Inman), Lazarus,
   (Lazs.)83, 85, 196,
   297,
Inman(Innon)(Innman)
   Lazarus, G. 9, 145,
   191, 202, 217, 260,
   297, 327, 337,
Insor, John, 221, 342,
   343,
Insor, John K. 267, 271,
Insor, Thomas, P. 325,
(Illnoise), Illinoise,
   342, 343,
Irland,(Ireland),Thomas,
   158, 182,
Iron Mountain, 171, 264,
   288, 329,
Irwine,(Irwins)(Irvines),
   Samuel,(Saml.) 1,
   51, 65, 160, 169,
Irwin, Samuel, A. 192,
Isaac, Enos, 240,
Isaacs, Jesse, 76,
Island, Iselan, Creek,
   1, 30,

Jackson, Alfred, E. 42,
Jacksons, Cap't, 135,
   151, 153
Jackson, Stephen, 15,
Jackson, Jas. 67,

301, 307, 309, 308,
Laurel, Road, 50, 172,
Lewis, Abm. 163,
Lewis, C. 274, 317,
Lewis, Charles, 124, 294,
338
Lewis, Elisha, 163,
Lewis, Ephraim, 234, 236,
Lewis, H. 274,
Lewis, Howel, 274, 338,
Lewis, James, 181, 305,
Lewis, Lewis, 43,
Lewis, P. 274,
Lewis, Peter, 181, 338,
Lewis, Robert, 119, 124,
153,
Lewis, Stephen, 62, 63,
191, 253,
Lewis, Thos. J. 84,
Lewis, William, 51, 82, 83,
85, 92, 93, 94, 96, 266,
Lick, Creek, 116, 219, 285,
Limestone, Cove, 48, 79, 112
171, 209, 284, 329,
Lincoln County, 154, 155,
Lincoln, Mary, 30,
Linng, Reed, 47,
Lipps, Archibald, 159,
Lipps,(Lips),Jonathan, 24,
83, 85, 195, 229,
Lisenby, Charles, 220, 286,
327,
Little, Doe, 68, 102, 163,
172, 289, 304,
Little, Henry, 338,
Littleton, Smith, 22
Loudermilk, Adam, 325,
Loudermilk,(Lowdermilk),
Henry, 17,18, 31, 60,
307, 308, 309, 325, 327,
Lowdermilk, John, 170,
Love, Cleming, 323,
Love, Thomas, D. 3. 171, 3
327, 328,
Lovelace, Charles, 181, 191,
Lovelace, James, 174, 192,
233, 234, 308, 336,
Lovelace, Permeanas, 221,
Lovelace, Thomas, 196, 202,

211, 233, 234,
Lowe,(Loe), Abraham, 51, 82,
Lowe,(loe), Jacob, 190, 303,
Loyd, Absolem, 50, 261, 291.
295
Loyed, John, 143,
Lucky, John, 305,
Lusk, John,L. 209, 220, 291,
Lusk, Samuel, 48, 119, 150,
220, 291, 325,
Lyles, Allen, 18,
Lyons, Allen, 17,
Lyon, Ezekiel, 47, 169,
Lyon, John, 3, 169, 221,
269, 271,
Lyon, Michael, 80, 120, 293,
307,308, 309, 342, 343,

Maclin(Mclin), Robert,(Robt),
51, 58, 82, 142, 267, 302,
Maddin, John, 305,
Maddox, Mattox, Jesse, 142,
172, 292, 328,
Maddox, Wilson, 49, 113,
148, 157, 158,
Mark, Reeve& Sons, 38, 39,
40,
Markland, P.W. 202,
Massengale, Henry, 160,
Massengill's, Michael, 189,
212, 277,
Massengale, W. 138,
Massengill, William, 118,
Mast, Adam, 170, 176, 265,
Mast, J. 70
Mast, Jacob, 2, 89, 128,
129,
Mast, Reubin(Ruebin), 2,
129,
Masters, Katy, 37,
Maxwell, Samuel, 253, 278,
McBee & Rineheart, 119,
McCann, Michael, 61, 348,
McCullough, Joseph, 272,
McEfee, John, 297,
McFall, Francis, 196
McHenry, Andrew, 21, 98, 114,
126, 130, 142, 159, 160,
McHenry, Hugh, 21, 22, 98,
*145, 179, 294,

99, 103, 123, 126, 128,
130, 142, 158, 159, 160,
McHenry, Mary, 99,
McHenry, Margaret, 99, 130,
159,
McHenry, Nancy, 99, 130,
McHenry, Robert, 126,
McInturff, Adam, 144,
McInturf, Captain,(Capt)
48, 135, 161, 293, 332,
McInturff, Christian, 212,
McInturf, Christopher, 179,
292,
McInturf, Gabriel, 90, 95,
96,
McInturf, Israel, 142, 145,
McInturff, John, 82, 292,
308, 309, 315, 320, 328,
McInturf, John, Jr. 51
McInturff, Polly, 309,
McInturffes, Thomas, 49, 77,
111,112, 142, 172,
McInturf, William, 158,
McKenny, Samuel, 171,
McKenney, John, 224,
McKeehen, John, 119,
McKeehen, Samuel, 119, 327,
McKleyea,(McKelyea),Henry,
67, 308,
McLeod, A. 65, 319,
McLeod,(McLude), Abner,
(Abbnered),4, 28, 31, 60,
128, 150, 151, 153, 171,
192, 229, 245, 272, 277,
278, 279, 289, 318, 319,
McLeods, Captian, 319,
McNabb, 143,
McNabb, Alban, 209,
McNabb, Alfred, 328,
McNabb, Branch, 144,
McNabb, David, 21, 98, 150,
159, 260,
McNabb, Isaac, 72, 162,
McNabb, N. 315,
McNabb, Nathaniel,(Nathl.)
144, 291,
McNabb, Taylor, 203, 204,
205, 210, 327, 328,
McNabb, William, 21, 98,
159, 172, 173, 328,

(McQuen), McQueen, Isaac, 47,
McQueen, Samuel,(Saml), 47,
83, 65, 294,
McQueen, Samuel, E. 225, 287, 295
McQueen, Thomas,(Thos), 47,
50, 170, 289,
McQueen, William, 31, 50, 60,
(Wm) 62, 65, 170,
Merit, Edgecomb, 305, 312,
Messick,(Messeck), Wm, 129,
186, 248, 348,
Michael, William(Wm), 24, 47,
291, 310,
Mill, Creek, 100, 206, 207,
208, 289, 290,
Mill Road, 142,
Miller, Abraham,(Abrm), 111,
113, 142, 148, 157,
Miller, Bailes(Baylis)
(Bayles), 3, 22, 113,148,
170, 325,
Miller, George, 1, 36, 37, 74,
Miller, Isaac, 112,
Miller, Jacob, 24, 142, 267,
Miller, 326,
Miller, Jeremiah(Jerremiah),
4, 75, 265,
Miller, John, 36, 74,
Miller, Ruebin,(Rueben), 4, 60,
68, 75, 81, 164, 170, 219,
224, 257, 265, 283, 319,
320, 347,
Miller,(Wm) William, 49, 218,
Minks, John, 291
Mires, Peter, 56,
Molton, Henry, 210,
Moody, David, 171, 301,
Moody, David, C. 292,
Monroe, County, 21, 182, 323,
Montgomerys, 289,
Montgomery County, Virginia,
158,
Montgomery, Samuel(Saml). 80,
121, 221, 271,
Moor, G. 114, 173,
Moor, Green, 25, 26, 27, 28,
29, 47, 54, 142, 147, 148,
166, 178, 221, 261, 294,
300, 305,
Moor, George, 312

Smith, C, 10, 11, 41, 44,
Smith, Caleb, 9, 12, 22, 5,
  45, 52, 56, 58, 65, 69,
  145, 179, 196, 212, 261,
  271, 285, 325, 333, 334,
  335,
Smith, Daniel, 79, 87, 126,
  218, 293,
Smith, Elijah, 12, 85, 109,
  170, 264, 326,
Smith, Elisha, 108, 236,
  266, 289,
Smith, Ezekiel,(Ezl), 12,
  22, 45, 52, 58, 81,
  87, 126, 156, 166, 177,
  222, 225, 258, 259, 260,
  261, 262, 263, 265, 269,
  270, 275, 287, 294, 300,
  306, 312, 313, 335, 347,
Smith, George,(Geo.), 259,
  263, 267, 301, 307, 308,
  309,
Smith, Henry, 51, 327,
Smith, Hezekiah,(Hezekiah)
85, 224, 229, 236, 245,
Smith, Hiram, 47,
Smith, Isaac, 305,
Smith, Jacob, 51, 80, 83,
  87, 124, 171, 234, 236,
  239, 241, 242, 243, 244,
  245, 292, 325, 326,
Smith, Jacob, C. 218,
Smith, James, 112,
Smith, Jesse,(Jessie), 118,
  282,
Smith, John,(Jno.),43, 56,
  71, 83, 84, 88, 97, 116,
  123, 129, 139, 153, 158,
  160, 165, 190, 192, 195,
  196, 202, 211, 227, 241,
Smith, Joseph, 261, 285,
Smith, Carriger, Mary, 118,
Smith, Mrs. Mary, 143,
Smith, Mary, 173, 282,
Smith, Samuel(Saml), 79,
  267,

Smith, Sidny, 173,
Smith, Robert, 20

Smith, Solomon, 105,
Smith, **William**, (Wm.),187
  219, 293, 305,
Smith, Widow, 49, 292,
Smithson, Leuellen, 125,
Smitherman, Samuel, 117,
Smithpeters, Chatherine,
  37,
Smithpeter, George, 35,
  274, 277,
Smithpeter, M. 268,
SmithpeterMichael, 51, 80,
  81, 221,-
Snodgrass, Thomas, L. 169
Snodgrass, Thomas, 50,218
Snyder, Adam, 50, 218,
Snyder,(Snider), Christian,
  160, 170,
Snider,E. 310,
Snider, Fredrick, 27,
Snyder,(Geo),George, 50,
Snyder,(Snider), Isaac,
  22, 216, 292, 336,
Snyder,(Snider), Jacob,
  16, 170, 292, 326,
Snider, Michael, (Mickel),
  216, 292,
Snider, Snyder, Peter, 166,
  170,
Snider,William, (Wm.),16,
  31, 60, 170, 292, 327,
South, Carolina, 286,
Stalcup, Aaron, 15, 66,
  296, 302,
Stanfield, Samuel, 7, 71,
  92,
Stephen, Elizabeth, 109,
Sterret, Preston,
Stokes, Thomas, J. 288
Stoney, Creek, 47, 101,
  169, 221, 246, 247,
  252,
Stout, D. 269,
Stout,(Danl),Daniel, 3,
  171, 229, 235, 245,
  267, 301,
Stout, David, 51, 82,
Stout, Henry, 263,
Stout, J. 269,

Whaleys, Jeremiah, (Jerh)
   31, 60, 111, 143, 326,
Whaley, John, 31, 60,
Whaley, William, 293,
Webb, Nathan, 162,
West, Archibald, 111, 118,
   123,
West, J. C. 72,
West, Jesse, 73, 111, 217,
West, Joseph, C. 35, 74,
   93, 99, 140, 152, 183,
   213, 242,
White , Benjamin, 119, 282,
White, J.
White, L. 37, 51, 143, 299,
   329,
White, Lawson, 12, 22, 27,
   36, 52, 81, 125, 135,
   142, 225, 261, 266,
   267, 287, 294, 295,
   296, 300, 330, 335,
Whitall, Charles, 117,
Whitall, John, C. 117,
Whitall Maria, 117,
Whitall, Sarah, P. 117,
Whitehead, John, 2, 66,
   80, 121, 263, 322,
Whitehead, T. W. 69,
Wilcox, John, 173, 328,
Wilkerson, Thos. 34,
Wills, Lewis, 145, 179,
   212, 291,
Wills, Peter, 50, 80,
   123, 291, 325,
Williams, A. 315,
Williams, Archiblad,(Arch),
   25, 48, 150,171, 206,
   312, 313, 314, 315,
Williams, Archibald Jr. 82,
Williams, Archibald, Sr.
   51
Williams, A. W. 177,
Williams, Charles, 45,
William, Edmond, 171,
William, Elisha, 78, 161,
   191, 196, 202, 211,
   236, 271, 274,
Williams, Elkanah, D. 17,
Williams, G. 229,
Williams, George,(Geo.)

52, 74, 144, 150, 154,
   156, 174, 177, 227, 258,
   259, 260, 264, 26 9,
   290, 294, 305, 306, 321,
Williams, George, D. 25,
   150, 237,
Williams, Isaac, 345,
Williams, J. 327,
Williams, John, 61, 217,
   221, 299, 325, 327,
   328,
Williams, J. L. 174, 290,
Williams, John, L. 75, 98,
   108, 159, 166, 171, 173,
   261, 287, 291, 300, 306,
   307, 321, 325, 294
Williams, John, S. 12, 21,
   22, 135,
Williams, L. B. 97,
Williams, Mordaciai, 119,
   277, 278, 279,
Williams, Pleasent, 181,
Williams, Samuel, 237,
Williams, Saml. W. 25,
   80, 123, 230, 255, 272,
   286, 324,
Wilson, H. 328,
Wilson, A. L. 328,
Wilson, Alexander, 291, 310,
Wilson, Alexander, M. 170,
Wilson, A. M. Capt. 305,
Wilson, Andrew, 50, 51,
   68, 82, 170, 172, 267,
   274, 289, 300, 325,
Wilson, Andrew, L. 291,
   293, 331,
Wilson, Anna, 175,
Wilson, Benjamin,(Benjam.)
   171, 229, 245, 291,
Wilson, Epphen,(Eppen),
   48, 51, 171,
Wilson, Garland, 31, 60,
   170, 172, 302,
Wilson, George, 154, 180,
Wilson, Hugh, 92, 93, 94,
   95, 96, 158, 160, 218,
   266, 326,
Wilson, Isaac, 136, 137,
   182, 194,
Wilson, J. 173, 174,

Carter County

County Court Minutes Vol.4
1826 - 1829

(P.1)   Thursday November 16th 1826.
Court met according to adjournment present the worship-
ful
Johnson Hampton &   )   Esqr.
John Wright & Jesse Cole)

On motion of Alfred W. Taylor attorney A. appearing to
the court that the commissioner to make partitions of a
tract of land among the heirs of George Miller Decs'd
have failed to fix ꬰꬰꬰꬰ seals to thier signatures it
is tgerefore ordered that the return of Devision as
made to this court by said commissioners be sent back
to said commissioners for thier seals to be anexed to
the same returnable to next court.

Ordered by the court the court the order heretofore made
appointing a jury of view to examine the road & change
it from its present course so as to cross the Isleand
creek just above its mouth & then up Watauga river
to intersect the present road at or near A. M. Carters
brick Kiln be renewed & report to next court.

State   )
   Vs   )   In this case the defendent appeared
Samuel Irvine)   in open court & the attorney General
                    entered Noliproseqy & Thomas Nickols
innbehalf of the defendant assumed the costs it is therefore considered bythe court that the state recover
against the said Thomas the costs & that the said Thomas
be in mercy & & (P.2) Johnson Hampton vs Jacob Mast
continued on affidavit of plaintiff & orfered by the
court that a dedimus potistatum issue to some justice
of the peace Ash county North Carolinia to take the
depositions of Bedent Bear or Jordon countil Jr,
Holden Davis & John Hardin, giving defendent five days
notice or notice to Ruebin Mast his brother shall be
glad.

Hugh Boyd   )
   Vs   )   Declaration and Demurrer   continued
David Haynes)
David Watts
   Vs

David Waids   )
  Vs   )   Continued
Wm Carter   )
Jas Keys   )
J.Hampton   )
J.Campbell   )

Martin Kittsmiller)
  Vs   )   Plea over ruled & learn to
Thomas Nickols   ). amend plea & issue.

David Haynes   )
  Vs   )   Continued
William Brummet)

John Whitehead)
  Vs   )   Continued
Samuel Baily   )

Jacob Slimp   )
  Vs   )   Continued
Joseph Wilson   )

Joseph Wilson   )
  Vs   )   Continued
Jacob Slimp   )

William B. Carter   ).
  Vs   ). Continued
Andrew & Samuel Fulton)

(P.3) William Brown)
           Vs   ) An appeal from the judgement
       Thomas D. Love) of justice of the peace & new
atthis day came William Brown
by his attorney John Kenedy Esqr & the said Thomas D.
Love by his attorney James P. Taylor Esqr & thereupon
Came a jury (towit) Geo. P. Stout, Benjamin Grindstaff,
William Hardin Tobias Hendrix Baylis Waller John Lyon,
James Shuffield William Nave Abraham Nave David Bowers
Danl. Stout & Nath Campbell chosen elect tried & sworn
upon their oaths say do find for the defendant therefore
it is considered by the court that the defendant may go
hence without bail & it is further considered by the
court that the defendant recover against the plaintiff
his costs & charges put to and about his defence in this
behalf sustained & that the said William be in mercy
& & from which said judgement the said William by his
attorney aforesaid prays an appeal to our next circuit
court of law & Equity to be holden for Carter county
at the court house in Elizabethton on the third Mond-
day in March next & entered into bond with John Kenedy
his security of Washington county in the sum of one

hundred dollars sec bond which appeal is granted by
the court (P.4). Ruebin Willer &William Carter executors of the last will & testement of Jeremiah Miller
Decs'd returned in part & Inventory of the estate of
the decs'd & ordered to be recorded.

Abial C. Parkes)   And the defendant came into open
      Vs   )   court & confessed Judgement for
Joseph Cooper)   the sum of two hundred & thirty
                   six dollars therefore it is con-
sidered by the court that the plaintiff recover against
the defendant the aforesaid sum of two hundred & thirty
six dollars by him confessed & also his costs & charges
put to & about his suit in this behalf expended & that
the defendent may be in mercy & & stay execution three
months.

Richard Shakleford for the use of Hart & Groves
Hart & Groves)
      Vs   )   And the defendant being solemnly called
Abner McLeod) came not but made default therefore it is
                   considered by the court that the plain-
tiff ought to recover of the defendant but because
it is unknown to the court here what damage the plaintiff has sustained it is therefore ordered that a writ
of inquiry be awarded at next court.

For reasons appearing to the court it is ordered that
Golden Hicks be releas'd of his tax of forty nine cents
for the year 1826.

(P.5) F. Hodge   )
           Vs   )   The plaintiff having at a
        James W. Renfro) former time of this court
        Wm B. Carter   ) moved court for a judgement
        Wm Graham   ) against said Renfro & his
                          two securities an amount of
his default aconstitute & the said motion being continued over to this court & the plff having never failed
to prosecute success fully said motion it is considered
by the court that said motion be over ruled & that
the plff pay the costs it is therefore considered by
the court that the defendant recover of the plff their
costs about their defendant this behalf expended & &
the defendant in mercy & &

Thomas Berry   )
      Vs   )   Vincent Kelly constable retur-
Thomas Nickols)   ned an execution issued by a
                   justice of the peace in favors
of the plaintiff for six dollars twenty five cents
debt & fifty cents costs,search made in my county

for goods & chattles on which to levy this execution
& none found therefore levied the same on fifty acres
of land more or less where on said Nickols now lives
also his Moity of an entry of thirty five acres adjoining the same levied the 16th November 1826 & it
appearing to the satisfaction of the court from the
return of s'd constable that there is no goods & chattles of the defendant to be found it is therefore
ordered by the court that the sheriff sell said land
or so much thereof as shall be od value sufficient to
satisfy said executors & costs.

(P.6)   A. M. Carter   )
               Vs   )   William Carter Esqr
          Moses Humphrey   )   Sheriff by his deputy
          Elisha Humphrey   )   James I. Tipton returned
          John Scott   )   an execution issued by a
                                        Justice of the peace in
favor of the plaintiff for the sum of twenty five doll
ars & forty seven cents debt & fifty cents costs search
made & no goods & chattles found in my county levied &
this on the land where Elisha Humphrey now lives as the
property of said Elisha suposed to be three hundred acres more or less 16th November 1826 & it appearing to
the satisfaction of the court from the return of said
sheriff that there is no goods & chattles of the defendents to be found it is therefore ordered by the court
that the sheriff sell said land or so much thereof as
will be of value sufficient to satisfy the plaintiffs
debt & costs.

Vincent Kelly   )
               Vs   )   William Carter Esqr. Sheriffby
Thom as Nickols   )   his deputy James I. Tipton retur-
                              ned an execution Issued by a Just-
ice of the peace in favor of the plaintiff for the sum
of two dollars & fifty cents debt & fifty cents costs
search made & no goods & chattles found in my county
to levy this on levied this on the Interest that said
Nichols has in and to the land whereon he now lives
& all the interest that he sd. Nickols has to one
entry adjoining said Nickols of thirty five acres
November 16th 1826 & it appearing to the satisfaction
of the court from the return of sd sheriff that
there is no goods & chattles found it is therefore ordered by the court that tho sheriff sell said land or
so much thereof as will be of value sufficient to satisfy the plaintiffs debt & costs.
(P.7)

Samuel Stanfield)
               Vs   )   On Motion of plaintiff by his
Asiel Sharp   )   counsel & on argument of de-
                              fendent by his counsel it is
the opinion of the court that Asiel Sharp be called

to come into court to replevin the property attached
in the hands of John Ward Garnishee or his counsel &
the said Asiel Sharp being Solemnly called came notbut
made default therefore it is considered by the court
that the plaintiff ought to recover against the defendent but because it is unknown to the court what damage
the plaintiff has sustained a writ of enquiry is awarded
to the pl'ff at the next term of this court & that the
case lie open six months.

John Ward by attorney moved the court for permission
to plea but the same was overruled & defendent called
out & a deed of conveyance from William Carter Sheriff
to James Hughes for two hundred & sixty two acres of
land acknowledged in open court & admited to record let
it be registered (P.?)

(P.8) Dungan &Scruston)
                    Vs   )   Vincent Kelly constable
Thomas   Nickolas)   returned an execution
                                            issued by a justice of
the peace favoring the plaintiff for the sum of five
dollarsdebt & fifty cents cost I have made search
in my county for goods & chattles of Thomas Nickols
on which to levy this execution & none found on which
to levy it, therefore levied the same on fifty acres
of land more or less on which said Nickols now lives
also his interest of a moity of an entry of thirty
five acres adjoining the same levied the 11th November 1826 & it appearing to the satisfaction of the
court that there is no goods & chattles found it is
therefore ordered that the sheriff sell said lands
or so much thereof as shall be of value sufficient to
satisfy said execution debt & costs.

Jacob VanHuss)
            Vs   )
Moses Humphreys)   Vincent Kelly constable re-
Elisha Humphrys)   turned an execution issued
                                    by a justice of the peace
                                    favoring the plaintiff for
the sum of sixty three dollars &seventy two cents debt
& one dollar cost I have made search in my county for
goods & chattles on which to levy this execution &
none found therefore levid the same on three hundred
acres of land where said Humphreys now lives on levid
the 16th Nov. 1826 & it appearing to the satisfaction
of the court by return of said constable that there
are no goods & chattles found it is therefore ordered
that the sheriff sell said lands or so much thereof as
shall be of value sufficient to satisfy said debt &
costs

(P.9) Lazarus C Inmon)
         Vs   )   Vincent Kelly a
         John Humphreys &)   constable returned
         Elisha Humphreys)   an execution issued
                                 by a justice of the
peace favoring the plaintiff for the sum of seven dollars seventy one cents debt & fifty cents costs.
      I have made search in my county for goods & chattles
& can find none on which to levy this execution levied
the same on three hundred acres of land including the
place where said Humphrey now lives on Doe river levied
(levied) this the 16th November 1826 & it appearing
to the satisfaction of the court from the return of said
constable that there are no goods & chattles found it
is therefore ordered by the court that the sheriff sell
said lands or so much thereof as shall be of value so
sufficent to satisfy said debt & cost.

Gammon D, Crawford)
         Vs   )   David Waide constable returned
Elisha Humphreys)   an execution issued by a jus-
                         tice of the peace favoring
the plaintiff for the sum of thirteen dollars seventy &
three fourths cents debt & fifty cents costs search made
no goods or chattles found in my county to levy sd
executions on Levid the same on three hundred acres
of land lying on the waters of doe river adjoining caleb
Smith on the lower side & it appearing to the satisfaction of the court from the return of said constable that
there are no goods & chattles found it is therefore ordered that the Sheriff sell said land or so much thereof as shall be of value sufficient to satisfy said debt
& cost
(P.10)   Waugh & Tinly   )
           Vs   )   William Carter Esqr.
           Henry D. Johnson)   Sheriff by his de-
                                    puty James I Tipton
returned an execution Issued by a justice of the peace
favoring the plaintiff for the sum of ten dollars twenty
three cents & fifty cents costs search made no personal
property found in my county to levy this on levied on
fifty acres of land lying in said county adjoining the
land of Benjamin Gentry on the waters of little Doe of
Bones creek November 16th 1826 & it appearing to the
satisfaction of the court from the return of said depty
Sheriff there is no personal property found it is therefore ordered that the sheriff sell the said land or so
much thereof as shall be of value sufficient to satisfy
said execution debt & cost.

Waugh & Finley)
    Vs   )   William Carter Esqr. Sheriff
Henry D. Johnson)   by his deputy James I Tipton
                returned an execution issued by
a justice of the peace favoring the plaintiff for the
sum of fifty nine dollars fifty six cents debt search
made no personal property found in my county Levied
on fifty acres of land lying in said county adjoining
the land of Benjamin Gentry on the waters of little
doe of Roans creek November 16th 1826 & it appearing
to the satisfaction of the court from the return of
said deputy sheriff there are no goods & chattles found
it is therefore ordered that the sheriff sell said
land or so much thereof as shall be of value sufficent
to satisfy said executions debt & costs court adjourned
till tomorrow 8 oclock.
               W. B. Carter
               Jesse Cole
               C. Smith.

(P.11)   Friday 17th Nov'r 1826 Court met according
to adjournment Minutes read & signed & then adjourned
till court in course.
               W. B. Carter
               Jesse Cole
               C. Smith
               J. Hampton
               Justice C. Cty.

(P.12)   State of Tennessee)
          Carter county)) At A meeting of a
                    court of please &
Quarter sessions held for Carter county at the court
house in Elizabethton on the second Monday of Feby.
in the year of our Lord 1827 present the Worshipful,
        1 John Richardson
        2 George Emmert
        3 Jesse Cole
        4 William B. Carter
        5 Caleb Smith
        6 John S. Williams
        7 Lawson White
        8 Johnson Hampton
        9 Ezekiel Smith
      10 Jeremiah Campbell
      11 Julius Dugger.   Esquires.

Elijah Smith produced in open court the <u>scalf</u> of a
wolf adjudged by the court over four months old, &
the saidElijah Smith being sworn upon his oath, saith
that he killed the wolf in the county afore said since
the 1st day Janry 1811 & it appearing to the satisfaction of the court that the said E. Smith killed the wolf
in the county aforesaid it is, therefore ordered by the
court·that the said E. Smith be allowed three dollars
for killing said wolf to be paid out of the state
Treasure,

For reasons appearing to the court it is therefore
ordered that Leonard Bowers & Wm Garland be released
from attending as Jurors at this session.
(P.13) Ordered by the court that Thomas Heatherly Be
appointed constable who came into open court & entered
into bond with Wm Garland & Ewing Heatherly his securitys in the sum of one thousand Dollars with condition
Sec Bond & the said Tho. Heatherly took the several oaths
required by law for a constable & &.

Ordered by the court that Vincent Kelly be appointed
constable who came into open court & entered into bond
with Richard Kelly & William Carter his securities in
the sum of one thousand dollars with condition & & &
took the several oaths required by law for a constable
& &

Ordered by the court that Caroline Howard be bound
an apprentice to George Brown until said apprentice
shall attain to the age of eighteen years & the said
George Brown agrees to give said apprentice one years
schooling <u>betwen</u> twelve & fifteen years of age, a bed
& furniture two Suits of clothing & one fiting for
the Lords day.

Ordered by the court that Isaac Howard an orphan
now of the age of six years be bound an apprentice to
George Lacey untill said apprentice shall attain to
the age of twenty one years & the said George Lacey
agrees to give said apprentice a horse & saddle &
bridle of the value of one hundred dollars two suits
of clothes one fiting for the Lords day.

(P.14) Be it remembered that J. P Taylor Atty. Genl
in the presence of the court call'd on the clerk for
the reciept of the trustee of this county & of the
treasure of east Tennessee for the last year upon which
application the clerk produced to the court the trustees
reciept for the year 1826 in conformation with law
which was satisfactory to the court as to the reciept

of the Treasure the clerk satisfied the court sum was
not produced owing to the sudden depreciation of Nashville bank notes in consequence of which the treasure
would not recieve the money & which is provided for
by law passed at the last session as the court has been
informed & believe

Ordered by the court that Alford Ward an Orphan now
of the age of two years be bound an apprentice to Julius
Dugger untill said apprentice shall attain to the age
of twenty one years & the said Julius Dugger agrees to
Give said apprentice six months schooling and a horse,
saddle & bridle worth one hundred dollars & two suits
of clothes one fiting for the Lords day.

(P.15)   Ordered by the court that the clerk issue
a certificate for six months for the allowance made
at Augt   Session 1826 to Elizabeth Humphreys one of
the poor of this county.

(P.15)   Ordered by the court that James I Tipton
& George Lacey be appointed adm'rs of all & Singular
the goods & chattles rights & credits of Isaac Tipton
sen'r Deceased which were his at the time of his death
& the said James I Tipton & George Lacy come into open
court & entered into bon] with William B. Carter thier
security in the sum of one thousand dollars & & & were
qualified as the law directs as administrators.

Ordered by the court that Stephen Jackson be appointed
overseer of the public road in the room of Jacob Roberts
& have the same hands & bounds.
                                        Isd.

Ordered by the wourt that Tho. H. Johnson be appointed
overseer of the public road in the room of Aaron Stalcups
& have the same hands & bounds that Stalcup had & all
the hands as high up as George Crosswhite be the hands
to work on Said road.
                                        Isd.

Ordered by the court that the road laid off on the
south side of Watauga River from the widow Smiths to
Lawson Goodwins be & is hereby discontinued.

Ordered by the court that John Scott one of the
poor be allowed twenty dollars for his support & maintainance from Feby session 1826 up to Feby session 1827.

(P.16)   Where as John Wilson represents that the act
of North Carolina law opened a road from Toe river by
cranberry to the state line so as to avoid the yellow
Mountain , your petition states that a change in the

road on the Tennessee side so as to intersect the
North Carolina road will be of immense public advantage
for reasons appearing to the court it is therefore ordered that,

    1 John Shuffield
    2 Daniel Caleb
    3 Larkin S. Wilson
    4 Barnabas Oaks
    5 Wm Snider
    6 Jacob Snider &
    7 James Jones, or any five of them be

a jury of view proceed & examin the nearest & best
rout from the widow Smiths to intersect said North
Carolina road, with as little Prejicdice to plantat-
ions as may be & make report to next court.
                      Isd.
Ordered by the court that Edward Buckles be appointed
overseer of the public road in the room of Jesse Cole.

Ordered by the court that Lawson Goodwin & Allen
Goodwin be annexed to Abraham Whaleys hands who is
overseer of the public road from Duggers ford up to
Vanhooses.

(P17) Ordered by the court that Edward Hendry be
appointed overseer of the public road leading from said
Henry now lives to the ford of dry creek at Richard
Greers & that Jeremiah Cates, Skett Morgan, Calton
Morgan John Rowe, Abraham Rowe Thomas Rowe & hands
Joseph Rowe Elkanah D Williams John Hawn and William
Bowman be his hands.

Ordered by the court that John Dunlay be appointed overseer of the public road in the room of William Ellis
& have the same bounds & hands.

Ordered by the court that Henry Lowdermilk, Henry
Bogart, Andrew Taylor Senr Tho's P. Ensor Allen Lyons
Jona. Taylor & Andrew Taylor Jr be a jury to begin &
lay of a road at a bank then along so as to intersect
the old road & report to ne t court.

A plat & certificate of Survey from Samuel P Carter
by Alford M. Carter to Richard Kelly for thirty acres
of Land acknowledged in open court by the said Alfred
M. Carter.

A deed of conveyance from Samuel Headrick to Abraham
Haun for forty acres of land acknowledged in open court
by the maker thereof & admited to record let it be registered.

(P.18) A deed of conveyance from Henry Lowdermilk
to Allen Lyles for twenty three acres of land & 105

poles acknowledged in open by the maker thereof &
admited to record let it be registered.

A deed of conveyance from John Nave to Vina Ellis
& Solomon Ellis for ninety six acres of land acknowledged in open court by the maker thereof & admitted
to record let it be registered.

A deed of conveyance from John Nave to Levi Nave
for eighty four acres of land acknoledged in open court
by the maker thereof & admited to record let it be registered.

A deed of conveyance Levy Nave to Alfred M. Carter
for eighty four acres of land acknowledged in open court
& admited to record let it be registered.

A deed of conveyance from Solomon Ellis & Vina Ellis
to Alfred M. Carter for ninety six acres of land
acknowledged in open court by the makers thereof &
the said Vina Ellis wife of the said Solomon Ellis
being examined by the court seperate & apart from her
said Husband saith she executed the same freely voluntarily of her own accord without fear threat or persuation of her said husband andadmited to record let it
be registered.

(P.19) A deed of conveyance from John Robinson to
Richard Robinson for fifty acres of land provin in open
court by George Crosswhite one of the subscribing witnesses thereto & and ordered to be continued for the
probet of the other witness Thomas Johnson.

A deed of conveyancefrom Joseph Campbell to John
Peneger for one hundred acres of land proven in open
court by Jeremiah Campbell & Nathaniel Campbell two
Subscribing witnesses thereto & admitted to record
let it be registered.

A deed of conveyance from Godfrey Carriger & Chris-
tion Carriger executors of Godfrey Carriger Dec'd to
George Greenway for one hundred & thirty two acres of
land acknowledged in open court by the makers thereof
& admited to record let it be registered.

A bill of sale from Valentine Bowers to Godfrey
Nave for a negroe boy about twelve years of age a
slave for life adknowledged in open court by the
maker thereof & admited to record let it be registered.

A deed of conveyance from Jacob Nydever to Elisha
Cole for two hundred acres of land proven in open

court by john Royston one of the subscribing witness
thereto & ordered to be sent to the county of Sullivan for the probet of one of the other witnesses.

(P.20)   A deed of conveyance from Robert Smith
to George Emmert for forty two acres of land acknowledged in open court by the maker thereof & admited
to record let it be registered.

Ordered by the   court that a county contingant
tax be laid levied & collected for the year 1827
on each 100 acres of land -----12½
on each town lot ------------ 25
on each free poll------------- 12½
on each Slave----------------- 25
on each stud of Jack the season of one mare
on each Merchant-------------- 5
on each hawker or pedler -----250

Ordered by the court an additional tax be laid
levied & collected for the year 1827
on each 100 acres of land ----12½
on each town lott--------------- 37½
on each free poll -----------12½
on each slave ----------------25
on each stud of Jack --------25
on each Merchant----------2-50
on each Hawker or pedler-1-25

Ordered by the court that a poor tax be laid levied
& collected for the year 1827
on each 100 acres of land 18¾/4
on each town lott------- 37½
on each free poll--------18¾/4
on each slave----------37½

(P.21)   A power of atto. from Godfrey Carriger to
Tennessee Carriger to recieve   such conveyances or
assurances of land from Col. Jacob Tipton & James
Chisholm or to make to them or either of them such
conveyance or conveyances a I am bound to do to them
or either of them as the case may be for their part,
of two certain tracts or parcels of land located &
Entered by them in my name or otherwise to adjust the
matter or things with them acknowledged in open court
& admited to record.

A   power of atto. from James Edens to Preston
Sterret of Monroe county ---to sue for recover &
receive of & from all persons in Monroe county all
sum or sums of money debts & demands which are now

are may be hereafter due " to me acknowledged in open
court " admited to record.

A artikial of agreement between Andrew McHenry,
Hugh Mc Henry, John Williams, Wm McNabb, David McNabb,
James P. Taylor Acknowledged in open court by Hugh
McHenry John S, Williams " James P. Taylor " pooven in
open court by Alfred W. Taylor on the part of William
McNabb " David McNabb " admited to record.

(P.22)   Ordered by the court that William Carter
Sheriff be allowed five dollars for repaires done to
the Jail.

Ordered by the court that Sam'l Erwin Jr. James B.
Riley Littleton Smith, Joseph Paxton " Hugh McHenry
be allowed each one dollar for guarding Joseph Mullins,
& that Bailes Miller, be allowed two dollars for guarding & finding horse to carry said Mullins to the jail
for Washington county and that William Boren also be
allowed two dollars for guarding the said prisoner to
the jail aforesaid to be paid by the county of Carter
" that certificates issued therefore.

Whereas Isaac Snyder heretofore, produced to this court
a scalp of a wolf " the said Isaac having been sworn
upon his oath saith he has not redeved a certificate
for the same, It is therefore ordered that the clerk
issue a Certificate for the same to said Isaac.

The court proceeded to class themselves, Lawson
White Nol Tho. Johnson Do. Wm Peoples Do. Caleb Smith
Do. Julius Jugger No.2 Richd. Bonally Do. Jno.   *
Wilson Do. & Johnson Hampton - John S. Williams Do.
Ezeliel Smith, & J. Campbell 4 Wm. B. Carter, Jesse
Cole, John Richardson " Geo Emert. * 3rd John Wright

(P.23)   Ordered by the court that Lenor Briant
be bound an apprentice to John Wilson Junr. untill
Said apprentice shall attain to the age of twenty one
years, " the sd. John Wilson agrees to give sd.appren-
tice one horse & saddle of the value of one Hundred
dollars " six months Schooling " ".

Court adjourned until tomorrow nine oclock.

                              Jesse Cole
                              John J. Wilson
                              W. B. Carter.

Tuesday February the 13th 1827

Court met according to adjournment Present the Wors.
John Wilson, Richard Donally & William B. Carter Esquires.

Caswell C. Taylor)
        Vs   )   And the defendant came into
John Cook   )   open court & confessed Judg-
                           ment for one hundred & seven
dollars & fifty cents therefore it is considered by the
court that the said Caswell C. Taylor recover against
the said John Cook the said sum of one Hundred & seven
dollars & fifty cents by him confessed & also his costs
& charges put to & about his suit in that behalf expend -
ed & that the said John May be in Mercy & &.

(P.24)   State of Tennessee Carter county February
session, 1827 William Carter Esqr. returned the states
write of Ventrei Facias executed on Moses Rank, Jacob
Miller David Wolley, David Stuart, Jacob Range, Jonathan
Taylor Francis Rockhold, Benja. Gentry Frederick Shown,
John Stout Wm Michael Leonard Bowers Wm Nave Moses
Humphreys Wm Graham David Nave, Jona. Lipps, Wm Garland
Godfrey Carriger Wm Bunton Senr. Daniel Shell John Shull
Solomon Hendrix, Edward Hendry Thos.P. Ensor, & Samuel
Bogart of whome were drawn of dew form of law the fol-
lowing persons to serve a grand Jurors at this court.
Solomon Hendrix senr. forman.
Jacob Miller
Stephen Cooper
Jonathan Lipp
John Stout
Benjamin C. Harris
Moses Humphreys
Samuel Bogart
William Nave
John Shell John Keuehn
WilliamsDaniels
Vins Heatherly good & lawful men of whom the court ap-
pointed Soloman Hendrix foreman.

James Campbell cont. sworn to attend the grand jury.
(P.25)
Peter Parkes   )
        Vs   )   Jury Towit, Edward Henry, Jonathon
Saml. Bailey   )   Taylor, Isaac Tipton, Solomon Ellis
                      Michael Hyder, Thomas Gourley,Larkin
L. Wilson, William Adams, Saml, Howard, Green Moor,
Abraham Nave, Benj., Grindstaff & chosen Elected tried

& sworn upon their oaths & now at this day came the
parties aforesaid by their attornies on motion of the
plaintiff whereupon it is considered by the court that
a nonsuit be entered & it is considered by the court
that the defendant may go hence without day & the defendant recover agt. the plff. his costs & charges
put to & about his defence & that the said John
Whitehead may be in mercy & &.

A deed of conveyance from Archibald Williams to
Samuel W. Williams & George W. Williams for one
hundred & forty five acres of land acknowledged in
open court & admited to record let it be registered.

A bill of sale from Joseph Cooper to Solomon Hendrix
for a negroe boy named Dennes acknowledged in open
court & admited to record let it be registered.

(P.26)   David Haines   )
             Vs   )   And now at this
          James Blevins &   )   day came the par&
          John Scott   )   ties aforesaid
                                     by their atto. &
thereupon came a jury towit, Edward Hendry Jno. Taylor
Isaac Tipton, Sol Ellis, Michl. Fyder, Tho. Gourley,
Larkin L Wilson, William Adams, Saml. Howard, Green
Moore, Abrm. Nave & Benja. Grindstaff, chosen,Elected
tried & sworn upon their oaths say do find for the
plff & assess his damage to eighty dollars & thirty
cents, therefore it is considered by the court that
the plff recover agt. the deft the aforesaid sum of
Eighty Dollars & thirty cents & also his costs & charges put to & about his suit in that behalf expended &
that the deft may be in mercy & &.

    A deed of conveyance from Alfred M. Carter & John &
Stuart to J. P. Taylor for five hundred & sixty acres
of land was proven in open court by the oath of
William Carter & J. M. Gamble the subscribing witnesses
thereto & admitted to reccord let it be registered.

(P.27)   Martin Kittsmiller   )
             Vs   )   And now at this
          Thomas Nickols   )   day came the
                                     parties afore-
said by their attos. & thereupon came a jury,towit,
the same as in the foregoing case say do find for the
plff. & assess the plffs damage to sixty dollars &
ninety cents therefore it is considered by the court
that the plff recover agt the deft. his damage aforesaid by the jury aforesaid assessed & also his costs
& charges put to and about his suit in that behalf
expended & that the defts may be in Mercy & &.

Fredrick Snider)
   Vs)   This day came the parties
John Wilson)   by their attorny thereupon
Lawson White)   came a jury of good & lawful
men towit, Edward Hendy,
Jonathon Taylor, Isaac Tipton, Solleman Ellis, Mikel
Hider, Thos Gourley, Larking L. Willson, William Adams,
Saml. Howard, Green More, Abraham Nave &Benjamon,
Grinstaff sworn upon their oaths say do find upon their
oath say do find that the defendants have not paid the
debt in the plaintiffs declarations mentioned & by
reason of the detion thereof assess the plaintiffs damage (P.28) to thirteen dollars thirty seven cents &
five mill therefore it is considered by the court that
the plaintiff recovered against the defendants the debt
in the declaration mentioned an also his damage by the
jury aforesaid assess & also his costs & charges put
in about this suit in that behalf expended & that the
defendants may be in mercy &&.

Richard Shackleford for the use of hart & Grove)
   Vs   Now this day came the part-
Abhnerod McLeod)   ies by their attorny aforesaid an thereupon came a jury
of good & lawful men of the court of Carter towit,
Edward Hennory, Johnathan Taylor, Isaac Tipton Sollomon
Ellis, Mikel Hider,Thos. Gorley, Larkin L. Willson
William Adams, Samuel Howard, Green More, Abraham Nave,
Benjamon Grindstaff, good && sworn upon their oaths
say do find for the plaintiff & assess his damage to
one hundred & forty eight dollars & seventy five cents
therefore it is considered by the court that the plaintiff recover of the defendants the aforesaid sum of one
hundred & forty eight & seventy cents & also his costs
& charges put too in about this suit in that behalf expended & that the defendant be in mercy &&.

(P.29) William Brummit)
   Vs)   Now this day came the par-
  William Pain)   tes by the attoy. an
there upon came a jury
of good & lawful men of the county of Carter, towit,
Edward Henry, Jonathan Taylor, Isaac Tipton, Solomon
Ellis, Mikel Hider, Thos. Gorley, Lakin L Wilson,
William Adams, Samul Howard,Green More, abraham Nave
Benjamon Grindstaff, sworn upon there oaths say do
find for the defendant therefore it is considered by
the court that the defendant without day it is further
considered by the court that the defendant recover
against the plaintiff his costs & charges put to &
about his in that behalf expended & that the plaintiff
may be in mercy &&.

The assignment of a plat & certificet of servay from William Brown to Vria Banks for fifty acres of land acknowledged in open court by the maker thereof and admited to record.

The State   )
    Vs   )   The defendant being charged in the
Daniel Bradly)   bill of indicterent an he for plea
                        thereto by his att. saith that he
is guilty thereof therefore it is considered by the
court that the said Daniel be find fifty cents &
George Bradly assumes the cost therefore it is considered by the court that the state recover aganst
the defendant & George Bradly this security the fine
& costs of said prosecution.

(P.30)   State   )
             Vs   ).   And the defendant being
         George Bradly)   charge in the bill of of
                             Indietment thereto for
plea saith he is guilty thereof for it is considered
by the court that the defendant be fined twenty five
cents & pay the costs of said prosecution & may be
in mercy & &.

The state   )
    Vs   )   And the defendant being charged in
Benjamon Baker)   the bill of Inditement thereto for
                        plea saith he is guilty thereof
therefore it is considered by the court that the defendant be fined twenty five cents & pay the costs of
said prosecution & may be in mercy & &.

Ord by the court the road leading by from Elizabethton to Mary Lincolns be changed so as to cross the Island creek at or nare it mouth then up the Watauga
river & enter seck the old road at Alfred M Carters old
brick kiln and that the overseer be constructed to make
the alterations.

(P.31)   Ordered by the court that Moses Estept Evins
Hetherly Manuel, Jenkins, John (John) Blevins Carland
Wilson, John Whaley Phillip Shell, Jereriah Whealay
acknowledged Joel Cooper, John Feuohn Hennary Lowdermilk
Johnathan Pierce William McQuen Jacob Waggonar Abreham
Draek Joseph A. Briant George Lacey Ieter Emmit Abner
McLeod Jeams Clark Saml. Coorly Johnathan Range Richard
Denlapt William Snider Barnabas Oaks & David Brummit
Jurors to May session 1827.

A bill of sale from Wm B Blevins to Solomon Hendrix
for a negroe boy proven in open court by Wm Carter &

admited to record let it be registered.

State
 Vs   In this case the debt been called to
John Moreland)   come into court & answed the charge
                          of the state against him according to
his recognizance & James I. Tipton & Saml. T Boyed
his securities been call to bring in the body the said
John Moreland to answer some charge according to the
recognizance & the said John Moreland came not but
made default It is therefore considered by the court
that the state of Tennessee recover of said John
Moreland five hundred dollars the amount of his recognizance unless he show sufficient cause to the con-
trary at next court & that sci Fa issue accordingly
& it is further considered by the court that James
I Tipton & Samuel Boyed severlly forfeit & pay to the
state of Tennessee two hundred & fifty dollars each
the amount of thier recognizances unless they show
sufficient (P.32) cause to the contary at next court
& the Scirei facias respectively issue against each
of said defendants.

Court adjourned untill tomorrow nine oclock,

                                John I Wilson,
                                W. B. Carter,
                                J. Keyes.

                    Wednesday 14 Feb.1827
Court met according to adjournment present John I
Wilson, Wm B. Carter, James Keyes .

H. D. Johnson for   )
Elizabeth Carters use   )   Time is allowed deft to
J. B. Morely   )   declare untill next court
                                & deft have to plead at
August.

J. Taylor Assd.)
Wm Daniel   )   The deft being called to come
                          into court & defend the suit
& came not but made default it is therefore considered
by the court that plff recover of deft his damage but
because the same is uncertain it is ordered that a
jury come at next court & inquire of the damage.

A plat & certificate of Survey from William Vaun to
Uriah Banks for fifty acres of land acknowledged
in open court.

(P.33)   J. Taylor for alien use
                Vs

Wm Bridges ? Vaught Heaton
The defendant being calld. to come into court & defend
the suit came not but made default It is therefore
considered by the court that the plff recover of defendant his damage but because the same as uncertain
it is ordered by the court that a jury come at next
court to inquire of said damages & ?.

Leray Taylar)
   Vs)   The Demurrer of the plff
William & Isaac Stover)   to the pleas of the defen-
                     dants came on this day for
argument & the same being heard & fully understood it
is considered by the court that the demurrer be overruled & the plff be nonprosd. It is therefore considered
by the court that the defendants recover of the plff
thier costs about thier suit in this behalf expended
For which judgement the plff pray, an appeal to the
next circiut court for Carter county to be held at
Elizabethton on the 3 rd Monday of March next gave
bond & A . W. Taylor as security & the appeal is granted.

James Campbell constible proves two days attendance at
this court.

Jacob Hunter)
   Vs)   Plff dismisses his suit & deft
Barnibas Bowman)   assumes costs It is therefore
                     considered by the court that
plff recover of deft his costs about his suit in this
behalf expended & &

(P.34)   A. M. Carter)
            Vs.)   It this caus an
       Thos. Wilkerson)   attachment having
been obtaind by Alford M. Carter against the defendant for three hundred & thirteen dollars & sixty one
cents issued by John Richardson Esqr. & said attachment having come to the hands of Vincent Kelly one of
the constibles of said county was on the 5th of Feb-
rary 1827 levied upon two hundred bushels of corn
seventy eight cord of wood three head of horses two
silon watches some foder pots tin bucket, some tobacco
a coffee pot a pair of pot hooks & bridle with some
other articles which attachment was returned by said
Kelly to this court & the said deft being calld. to come
into court & defend the suit & replevy said property &
he having failed to do so & therein made default It is
considered by the court that said property so attachd.
be condemmd. for the satisfaction of said debt & because
of said default it is considered by the court that the

plff recover of the defendant the debt $313.61 in the
attachment & declaration mentond. together with the
costs of this suit & that erecution issue.

State   )
 Vs   )   In this case on motion of
Daniel Swinny)   Stephen Cooper the prosecutors
           father a sub-prosign is enter-
ed with this term of this court & the said Cooper assumed the costs It is therefore considered by the court that
the state of Stephen Cooper the costs*on this behalf
expended. * recover.

(P.35) State   )
     Vs   ) This being a Warrant
   Right Moreland) obtained by John
             Moreland against the
deft to keep the peace & he having appeard at this
court & the prosecutor having failed to appear & prosecute the same it is considered by the court that the
deft be discharged & that John Moreland pay the costs
of this suit the same being frivolous & Malicious
It is therefore considered by the court that the state
recover of the said John Moreland the costs of this
prosecution.

James Leyes Esqr. returnd a dist of taxable property.

Andrew Brummit)
  Vs   )   In this cause the plff mayd
Wm Doring   )   an appeal from the verdict
           rendered on yesterday enterd&
into bond & security & the same is granted to the next
circuit(court) to be held at the court house in Elizabethton, on the third Monday o' March next.

G. W. Rutledge)
  Vs   )   Ordered by the court that
Joseph C. West)   clerk issue -alias -

George Smithpeter)
  Vs   )   Plff being Solemnly calld.
Lawson Goodwin)   came not but made default
          & therefore it is considered
by the court that he be non prosd. & that deft recover
of plff his costs about his suit in this behalf expended.

(P.36) Where as John & George Miller Heirs of George
Miller declared at a former term of this court exhibited in court thier protition for an order of par-
tion of sixty acres of land among the Heirs of the

said George, lying on Roans creek in Carter county &
whereas said court appointed J. Hampton, Nickolas
Grindstaff, Lawson White, Lawson Goodwin & Thomas
Jones commissioners for said purpose together with
Andrew Taylor a Majority of Surveyor Whome have made
partition & made return thereof in the words & figures
following towit. It is therefore ordered by the court
that the same be recieved & recorded as follows.

State of Tennessee)
Carter county)   In of an order of court for
                                  the county aforesaid We commis-
                                  sioners appointed to make par-
tition of land among the heirs of George Miller deceased have completed said partitions as follows towit,
Polly Shell who intermarried Daniel Shell have lott no
first begining on a red oak the origional begining conner running east with the origional line sixty six poles
to a stake on said line thence north sixty eight poles
to a stake on the bank of Rones creek thence down the
Meanders of the creek to the begining containing fourteen acres & sixty poles.
    Lott no two John Miller begining at a stake conner
to lott no 1st. running with the origional east thirty
two poles to a stake & Blackoak pointers thence north
eighty five poles to sd. stake on the creek thence
down the creek with its Meanders thereof thirty four
poles to a (P.37) stake, thence South sixty eight
poles to the beginning containing fourteen acres &
sixty poles , lott no three George Miller Begining
on a stake & pointer a Black oak pointer at conner
to lott no two running thence east with the origional
line twenty seven poles to a stake thence north ninety
seven poles toa stake on the creek thence down the
creek with the Meanders thirty four poles to a stake
thence south eighty five poles to the begining containing fourteen acres. sixty poles. lott no four Katy
Masters Begining on a stake to lott no three thence
East with the origional twenty three & onehalf poles
to a stake & red oak pointer thence north ninety six
poles to stakes at the creek, thence down the creek
with the meanders thereof twenty five poles to a stake
thence South eighty five poles to the begining containing fourteen acres & sixty poles, lott no five
Chatherine Smithpeter begining on a stake conner to
lott no four runnung east with the origional line
twenty three & one half poles to a stake thence north
ninety six poles to a stake at the creek thence down
the creek with the Meanders there of a stake thence
south ninety six poles to the Begining containing
fourteen acres & sixty poles signed commissioners.

Nov. 11th 1826.

A. Taylor, Surveyor,
his
Nicholas X Grindstaff
mark
J. Hampton
L. White
L. Goodwin.

(L.3?)   Brown Guthary & Co.)
            Vs   )   On motion of plain-
         Mark Reeves & Sons   )   tiff by thier atto.
                                       John Aikin Esqr.
& it appearing to the satisfaction of the court that a
Ca Sa Issue from the county court of Sullivan county
against Mark Reeves & son for the sum of one hundred &
ten dollars fifty seven cents & five mills debt & costs
& the defendant having been arested on said Ca Sa &
they having given bond & security for thier appearance
at this court under the act of assembly requiring them
to pay the debt or take thebenefit of the Insolvent
debt act or to surrender property & it appearing they
have faild. to do so it is therefore considered by the
court that the plaintiff recover against the defendant
& thier security Nathen Birchfield the afore said sum
together with thier costs of this motion & that the
defendant be in mercy & &.

Brown Guthary & Co.   ))
            Vs   )   On motion of plain-
Mark Reeves & Sons   )   tiff of his atto.
                                       John Aikin Esqr.it
appearing to the satisfaction of the court that a Ca Sa
Issue from the county court of Sullevan county against
Mark Reeves & sons for for the sum of one hundred &
thirty four dollars Seventy six cents & five mills
debts & costs & the defendants being arrested on a Ca
Sa & they having given bond & security forthere ap-

pearence at this court under the act of assembly requiring them to pay the debt or surrender there property (P.39) or take the benefit of the Insolvent
debt or act & it appearing to the court they having
to do so it is therefore considered by the court that
they plaintiffs recover against the defendants & there
security Nathen Birchfield the aforesaid sum together
with thier costs of this motion & that the defendants
be in mercy & &.

Brown Cuthary & Co.)
Vs) On motion of plaintiff by Atto
Mark Reeves & son) John Aikins Esqr & it appearing to the satisfaction that
a Ca Sa Issue from the county court of Sullivan county
against the defendants for the sum of one hundred & &
eighty four dollars four cents & five mills debt & cost
& the defendants having been arrested then & they having given bond & security for there appearance at this
court under a act of assembly requiring them to pay
the debt surrender, property or take the benifit of
the Insalvent debt or act & it appearing to the court
the defendants having failed to do so it is there fore
considered by the court that the plaintiff recover
against the defendants & their security Nathan Birchfield the sum aforesaid together with there costs of
this motion & that they defendants be in mercy & &.

(P.40) Brown & Cuthary & Co.)
Vs) On motion of
Mark Reeves & Sons) plaintiff by
thier atto John
Aikin Esqr. & it appearing to the satisfaction of the
court that a Ca Sa issued from the county court of
Sullivan county against Mark Reeves & sons for the
sum of one hundred & ninety eight dollars nine & one
half cents debt & costs & the defendants having been
arrested there on & they having given bond for thier
appearance at this court under a act of assembly to pay
the debt or surrender property or take the benefit of
the Insolvent debt or act & it appearing they have failed to do so it is therefore considered by the court that
they plaintiffs recover against the defendants & thier
security Nathen Birchfield the sum aforesaid & costs f.
of this motion & that the defendents may be in mercy && .

David Hains)
Vs) In this case the defendant being calld
Wm Brummit) to come into court & defend this suit
came not but made default.
It is therefore considered by the court that the plff.
ought to recover his damage of defendant but because
it is uncertain It is ordered by the court that a
jury come at next court & enquire of the damages & &.

W. H. Robinson for Leonard Showns use)
          Vs   )   In this case
Thomas Paxton   )   the defendant
                                    being called
to come into court (P.41) & defend this suit came not
but made default.
   It is therefore considered by the plff ought to recover of defend his damages & &. But because it is uncertain It is ordered by the court that a jury come at
next court & inquire of the damage & &.

State   )
   Vs   )   Ordered by the court that
Negro Steph, Slave)   William Carter sheriff be
                    allowed fifteen dollars
seventy five cents for summoning a court & jury to
try said negro Slave out of any county moneys not
otherwise appropriated.
   Court adjourned untill tomorrow 9 oclock.

                              C. Smith,
                              Jee Emmert
                              W. B. Carter.

(P.42)   Thursday 15th 1827

Court met according to adjournment.

Micheal Hyder   )
    Vs   ) J. I . Tipton D. S. returned an Ca
Vaught Heaton) Sa issd. by a justice of the peace
                   in favor of Michael Hyder against
Vaught Heaton for the sum of sixty three dollars &
ninety cents debt & fifty cents costs, search made
and no goods nor chattles to be found in my county
to satisfy this Execution levied this on one tract
of land where Vaught Heaton now lives as the property of Vaught Heaton the quantity of acres not
known Feby. 3rd 1827 for which return appearing to
the court it is therefore ordered by the court that
the sheriff sell said land or so much thereof as shall
be of value Sufficient to satisfy said Execution &
costs of this motion.

A deed of conveyance from Benja Dunkin to Jacob Cameron for a town lot No 38. proven in open court by
Benjamin Brewer & Alfred E. Jackson two of the subscribing witnensses thereto and admitted to record let
it be registered.

(P.43)   Jas I. Tipton & George Lacy admins. Isaac
Tipton decd. returned an inventory of the goods &
chattles of said decd. as for as they new came to
there hands & ordered to be recorded.

Lewis Lewis)
    Vs   )   On the retetion of Lewis Lewis be-
John. Smith)   ing presented it is ordered by the
                   court that writs of certiairi & sup-
eridias issue according to law on bond & security
being given.

Hugh Royd   )
    Vs   )   Plaintiff in this case dismisses
David Haines)   this suit & assumes the costs
                   It is therefore considered by the
court that the deft recover of the plff his costs
about his suit in this behalf expended (P.44)
J. D. Morely)
    Vs   )   In this case a ca Sa Issued for
Benjamin Peters) plff against deft & he was arrested by J. I. Tipton, D. S. Isaac Stover began his
security according to act of assembly for the appearance of said Peters at this court to comply with the
act of assembly in such case made & provided & the
said Peters being calld. to come into court & com
p ly with said bond & the said Stover having been
calld. to bring into court said Peters to comply
with said bond & the said Stover having wholly faild.
to do It is therefore considered by the court that
the plff recover of the said Peters & Stover his security ten dollars & twenty one cents the amount
of the Ca Sa. with the sheriffs costs together with
the costs of this motion & that they be in mercy.

Court adjourned untill court in cause,

                              W. R. Carter,
                              Geo. Ermert,
                              C. Smith.

(P.45)   State of Tennessee)
             Carter county   )   At a meeting of
                                         a court of please
& Quarter sessions, Held for Carter county at the court
house in Elizabethton on the second Monday of May in
the year of our Lord 1827 present the Worshipful:
                    Caleb Smith
                    John Richardson
                    John Wright
                    William R. Carter
                    John Wilson
                    George Ermert

Ezekiel Smith
Richard Donally
William Peoples &
Jesse Cole, Esquires.

Ordered by the court that shff take into His care
Charles Williams the son of Nancy Hathhorn & have
him before the court at August session 1827 to be
bound out as an orphan.

Ordered by the court that Joseph Trusler an orphan
now of the age of fourteen years be bound an apprentice to David Gwinn untill said apprentice shall attain to the age of twenty one years, see Indenture.

This last will & testament of Samuel Wilson Decd.
proven in open court By Johnson Hampton & Ann Pearce
two subscribing witnesses there to & ordered to be
recorded (P.46) John Wilson Executors of the
last will & testament of Samuel Wilson Decd. entered
into bond with Johnson Hampton & Jeremiah Campbell
his securitys in the sum of one thousand dollars with
condition Sec. bond.

Ordered by the court that Tobias Hendrix be appointed
adminstrator of all & singular the goods & chattles
rights & credits of John Hendrix decd. & the said Tobias
Hendrix come into open court & entered into bond with
James P. Taylor his security in the sum of one hundred dollars & &. and is qualified as the law diricts.

William Buntin & James Buntin produced in open court
the scalps of two wolves adjudged by the court over
four months old and the said James being sworn upon
his oath saith that He said William Killd. one of the
wolves which one of the scalps came off & that he
killed the other himself in the county aforesaid
since the first day of January 1811 and it appearing
to the satisfaction of the court that the said William
& James killd. the wolves in the county aforesaid
It is therefore ordered by the court that the said William & James be allowed three dollars each to be paid
out of the state Treasury for killing said wolves.

(P.47) Ordered by the court that John Nave, Thomes
Ellis, George Morton, Godfrey Nave, William Garland,
Peter Hunt & Owen Edwards be appointed a jury to view
mark & lay off a public road begining between the
two fords of Stoney Creek form thence into the road
above John Richardsons & report to next court.

Ordered by the court that William O'Brian & Andrew Godsey be aded to his hands of Joseph O'Brien overseer of the public road.

Ordered by the court that William O'Brian & Andrew Godsey be aded to his hands of Joseph O'Brien overseer of the public road.

Ordered by the court that Isaac Musgrave & Aarron Musgrave be transfered from Greens Moore to John Taylor & work on the mountain road & Tapley Wilsons hands & William Davis be transfered from the mountain road & work under Green Moore & That Isaac McQuen Samuel McQueen, Hiram Smith Reed Linng at Thomas McQueens be transfered to work under said Moore untill the causway by John Wagners is completed.

Ordered by the court that Felix Brown & John Moorfield be transfered from Ezekiel Lyon to William Michael overseer & work under said Michael on the public road.

(P.4ᵒ) Ordered by the court that Thomas Rowe, Samuel E. Patton, Archibald Williams, Aaron Owens, James Gourly Reben Cox, John Rowe & Samuel Lusk be appointed a jury of View to examine & of practicable & of public utility to lay out & mark a road from James Gourleys by Thomas Rowes & Sarah Rowes and intersect the public road at Greers avoiding any injury to the Improvements on said rout & make report to next court.

Where as it has been made known to the satisfaction of the court that John Scott is one of the poor of Washington it is therefore ordered by the court that said Scott be stricken off the list of the poor of Carter county & the order made at last court be rescended.

William Peoples Esquire returned a list of the taxable property & polls in captian McInturf district for the year 1827.

Ordered by the court that the clerk furnish the sheriff with a list of the poor of Carter county and said sheriff is required to have the said poor persons brought to court at the next court then & there said poor persons to be let out to the lowest bider.

Ordered by the court that Henry Crindstaff, James Douglass John Cross, Solomon Cross, Moses Banks, William Banks, Eppen Wilson & William Baker be a

jury to view mark & lay of a road from some point
out of the Doe river road say Fisherseld Field of
there abouts passing through the Vally so as to intersect the road passing through the Limestone cove at
or near William Pakers & report to next court.

(P.49)   Ordered by the court that Daniel Caleb be
appointed overseer to cut & make a road from the
widow Smiths on Doe river by way of cramberry to meet
the North Carolina line & work the hands that worked
under William Miller & all the hands above William
Millers in the Crab orchard also John Potter & Peter
Potter be the hands to work said road.

Ordered by the court that William Baker, William Ingram Nathan Birchfield, John Kenner Robert Reeve, Willá-
iam Creer, Benjamin Hyder, John Hilton & Michael Hyder,
be appointed a jury of View to examine the mill road
Leading from Thomas McInkunf by William Peoples to
David Haines Mill and report it said road should be
altored and changed at said Peoples's farm to the next
court, and if the present road in thier openion should
be continued to assess the damages to said Peoples if
any.

Ordered by the court that Saml. Orford be appointed overseer of the public road from thewidow Smiths in the
Crab orchard to the state line & work the hands that
usually worked said road & open said road, & when the
same is opened the said Orford & hands return to the
cutting out the new road.

Exhibited and acknowledged in open court a deed of
coneyance from William Peoples to Wilson Maddox for
twenty four acres of land and admitted to Record
Let it be registered & &.
(P.50)   Exhibited and acknowledged in open court
a deed of conveyance from Isaac Campbell to James
Campbell and Daniel Campbell for two hundred & ten
acres and admitted to record let it be registered.

Ordered by the court that Mathias Vanhouse & Ely Mavoh
be added to William Cotts hands to work under said
Cott on the public road.

Ordered by the court that Adam Kryder be appointed
overseer of the public road from Jacob Wagners to
Showns X road & work the same hands that worked
under Geo. Snyder.

Ordered by the court that Andrew Arnold, Joseph
Jenkin's Thomas McQueen, Absolom Loyd, Peter Wills
Daniel Neal,William McQueen, Aron Rambeard be appointed a jury of view to examine and if practicable and
of public utility mark out a road of the third class
Begining at or near Andrew Wilsons dwelling house passing by Thomas McQueens & intersecting the Laurel road
near the widow Dorens & report to next court.

Exhibited & acknowledged in open court a deed of conveyance from Charles Bassenjine to John Crosswhite for one
hundred & six acres of land and admitted to record let
it be registered.

(P.51)   Ordered by the court that John McInturf,Jr.
Isaac Carroll, Peter Holt, Michael Hunt Sr. Andrew
Wilson, Jacob Smith, Zacheriah Campbell Jr. James Range
John Curtes, Thomas Gourley, Samuel Drake, Saml.
Irwin, Isaac Tipton, John Scott, David Stout, Andrew
Wilson, William Buntin, Elisha Rainbolt,Daniel Baker,
William Lewis, Abraham Low, Archibald Williams Sr.
Saml. W. H. Peoples, Joel Cooper, Joseph Taylor &
Robert Maclin, be appointed jurors to August session
1827.

Ordered by the court that Isaac Anderson, William
Vance, Eppy Wilson, John Hatches, Thomas Crow, Ruebin
Brooks, William Shown, James Blevins, Geo. Greenway,
Jacob Koon,Nathl. T. Eadens, Robert Stuart, Joseph
Renfro, Mathias Broyles, Saml. Tipton Jr. William Nave,
James Bradley,Casper Cable Jr. Charles Moorland,Henry
Smith, Leonard Shown, Isaac Reece, Michael Smithpeter,
James Gourley, William Ellis & Isaac Taylor Jr, be
jurors to the circuit court at September term 1827.

Court adjourned untill tomorrow nine oclock

                                     J. Richardson Esqr.
                                     W. B. Carter
                                     R. Donally
                                     John Wright
                                     Wm Peoples
                                     L. White
                                     Geo. Emmert
                                     Jesse Cole
                                     John L. Wilson.

(P.52)   Tuesday May the 18th court met according to
adjournment the Woeshipful,

                 Wm B. Carter
                 Richard Donally

John Wright
Lawson White
Ezekiel Smith
Caleb Smith
James Keys
Jesse Cole &
Johnson Hampton   Esquires.

Ordered by the court that Wm Carter Shff. be allowed
fifty dollars for his Ex officio services from May
Session 1826 up to May session 1827.

Ordered by the court that George Williams clerk be
allowed fifty dollars for his exofficio Services from
May Session 1826 up to May Session 1827.

State   )
  Vs   )   And the deft being charged
Elizabeth Heaton)   upon the bill of Indietment
                      & she for plea saith that
she is guilty thereof it is therefore considered by
the that the said E. Heaton be fined six & fourth cents
& that the state recover against sd. Elizabeth the fine
& costs of this prosecution & that the said Elizabeth
may be in mercy & &.

Ordered by the court that Hugh Jenkins be allowed twenty
dollars for the support &maintainance of a cherrokee
Indian three months.

Ordered by the court that Tho. Ellott allowed ten dollars for the support of & maintainance of Salley Musgrave
one of the poor six months.

(P.53)   State   )
            Vs   )   Basterdy Defendant
            Wilkerson Gifford)   maketh oath that
                                  justice requires
that an issue be made up in this case, it is therefore
ordered by the court that an Issue be made up in this
cause &cause & tried whether W. Gifford be the Reputed
father of an Illetigamate child born of the body
of Folly Reno. Whereupon for reasons appearing to the
court the proceedings aforesaid was continued on affidavit of deft.

Wilkerson Gifford, Alfred W. Taylor & William Gott
acknowledged themselves in Debt to the state that
is to say W. Gifford in the sum of two hundred dollars A. W. Taylor & Wm Gott in the sum of one hundred
dollars each to be levied of thier goods & chattles

lands & tenements & void on condition the sd.
Wilkerson Gifford appear before the justice of our
court of pleas & quarter sessions to be held for
Carter county at the court house in Elizabethton
on the second Monday of August next towit Tuesday
second day sd. cession then & there to answer to a
charge of the state for Basterdy & &.

Exhibited & acknowledged in open court a deed of re-
linquishment from Tho Elliott to the heirs of Michael
Carrigers for twenty seven acres of land admited to
record let it be registered.

Exhibited & acknowledged in open court a deed of re-
linquishments Tho. Elliott to the heirs of Michael
Carriger for twenty seven acres of land admited to
record let it be registered.

(P.54)   Ordered by the court that Geo Crosswhite,
Green Moore, George Brown, be judges at the Election
at Thos. Johnsons on little Doe & Wm. Harden Geo.
Lacey & Wm. Gott be judges of the Election at
Elizabethton at the next August Election agreeable
to act of assembly.

James P. Taylor for	)	
Obriens use	)	
Vs	)	The defendants came
Wm Bridges &	)	into open court & con-
Vaught Heaton	)	fessed Judgement for
		the sum of twenty five

dollars, therefore it is considered by the court that
thesaid pl'ffs recover of the defts. the sum of Seventy
five Dols. by them confessed and also his costs & charges put to and about his suit in that behalf expended
& that defts may be in mercy & &.

J. P. Taylor assigned	)	
Vs	)	The defendant came
Wm Daniel	)	into open court &
		confesses Judgement

for the sum of eighty two dollars therefore it is considered by the court the plff recover against the defendant the aforesaid sum of eighty two dollars for his
debt &als. his costs & charges put to and about His
suit in that behalf expended & that Defts may be in
mercy & &.

(P.55)   State   )
              Vs   )   The Deft being Charged
        Robert Bolen)   upon the bill of Indiet-
                             ment & He for plea there-
to saith that he is guilty, therefore it is considered
by the court that the deft be fined twenty five cents
pay the costs of this prosecution & in mercy & &c thereof
James B. Morley appointed constable who came into open
court & entered into bond with Richard Donally &
Johnson Hamton his securatys in the sum of one 1000
dollars with condition see bond & took the several oaths
required by law for a constable.

Wm Daniel appointed constable.

Abraham Tipton appointed constable who came into open
court & took the several oaths required by law & entered into bond with James I Tipton & Charles M. Gourley
his security in the sum of one thousand dollars see
bond.

Ordered by the court that the county Trustee by act of
assembly is dirdcted & bound to recieve a certain por-
tion of the taxes in Nashville Bank notes that sd trustee shall discharge said Nashville bank notes in payment of the claims against the county in proportion
the county in proportion to the amount of each claim
& in proportion of the Nashville bank notes legally
by him recieved.

(P.56)   Henry D. Johnson for)
        Elizabeth Carters use)   This cause by con-
                            sent of parties is
referd to the award of Alford W. Taylor and Caleb Smith
& if they cannot acree to choose an umpire and thier
award to be a rule of court, and it is agreed that Each
party may take deposation to be Red before the
arbritrators giving five days notice.

State   )
   Vs   )   Continued on affedavit of defendant,
John Smith)   and the defendant acknowledges him-
              self indebt to the state in the sum
of one Hundred dollars & Tho. Elliott in the sum of
fifty dollars to be levied of thier goods & chattles
lands & tenements & void on condition that John Smith
appear before the justice of our court of please &
quarter session to be held for Carter county at the
court house in Elizabethton on the second Monday of
August next towit, on Tuesday second day of said ses-
ion then & there to answer to a plea of the state.

John Smith   )
    Vs   )   Thi s cause by consent of
Evins Heatherly)   parties is refered to award
                       of Thomas Nickols and Peter
Mires if they cannot agree thay Shall chose an umpire
as to the costs of this suit each man is to pay half
of the corts the arbetrators to enquire only of the debt
& then award to be the Judgement of the court.

(P. 57)   Ordered by the court that Tennessee Carriger
and Godfrey Have be appointed administrators of all &
singular the goods & chattles rights & credits of
Godfrey Carrigers deceased which was his at the time
of his death and the said Tennessee Carriger & Godfrey
Have come into open court and entered into bond with
Christian Carriger, Johnson Hampton, James P. Taylor
& Thomas Crow thier securities in the sum of ten
thousand dollars & took the oaths prescribed by the
law for administrations and returned in part an Inventory of the goods & chattles of the deceased.

Ordered by the court that the meat & grain on hand at
the death of Godfrey Carriger be appropriated by Tennessee L. Carriger & Godfrey Have Administrators to the
support and maintainance of the family of the deceased
for the present year he having left no widow but sevral
infant children.
    The court then proceeded to elect a sheriff and on
counting the ballots it appeared that William Carter
Esquire was duley & constitutionally elected Sheriff
for and during the term of two years and the said William Carter come into open court & enterd into bond
with Benjamin Brewer, John L. Wilson & Johnson
Hampton his securities in the final sum of ten Thous-
and dollars with condition sec. bond.

(P. 58)   The court then proceeded to the election
of a Register & on counting the votes it appeard that
Benjamin Brewer was duly and constutionally elected
Register who came into open court & enterd into bond
with William Carter & James P. Taylor his securities
in the sum of five Thousand dollars with condition sec.
bond & took the several oaths required by law for a
public officer.

The court then proceeded to the selection of a county
Trustee and on counting the ballots it was found that
Ezikiel Smith was duly and constititionally elected
Trustee & entered into bond with James P. Taylor &
Caleb Smith his securities in the final sum of two
thousand dollars with condition sec. Bond

Ordered by the court that Robert Maclin be appointed to settle with the Entry taker of Carter county agreeable to act of assembly.

Ordered by the court that Wm. Gott & Geo W. Carter be appointed commissioners to settle with the clerks of the county & circuit court agreeable to act of assembly (P.59) William Carter Sheriff came into open court & entered into bond in the following words to wit,

State of Tennessee)
Carter county) Know all men these present
that we William Carter,
Benjamin Brewer, John L Wilson & Johnson Hampton are held & firmly bound unto William Carroll Govenor for the time being and his sucessor in office in the full & just sum of Five Thousand dollars to the which payment well & truly be made we bind ourselves our heirs Executors and administrators Jointly & severally Firmly by these present, signd sealed with our seals and dated this 15th day of May 1827 the condition of the above obligation is such that whereas the above bound William Carter is constituted & Elected Sheriff of Carter county for and during the term of two years from the day of the above date, now if therefore the said William Carter do & shall well & truly collect & recieve all the state & county taxes, for the year 1827 and 1828 and pay the state tax into the treasures office of East Tennessee & the county taxes into the county trustees office of the county on or before the last day of Decr. in each year aforesaid then the above obligation to be void & none effect Else to be and remain in full force & virture.

W. M. Carter,
Benja. Brewer,
John L. Wilson,
J. Hampton.

(P.60) State of Tennessee)
Carter county) May Session
1827 William
Carter shff returned the states writc of Venirci Facias executed on,
Moses Estep
Ewins Heatherly
Manuel Jenkins
John Blevins
Garland Wilson
John Whaley

Philip Shell
Jerh. Whaley
Joel Cooper
John Keuhn
Henry Lowdermilk
Jona. Pugh
Wm McQueen
Jacob Wagner
A. Drake
Joseph Obrin
Geo. Lacy
Peter Emirt
Abner McLeod
James Clark
Jona Range
Richd. dunlap
Wm. Snider
Barnebas Oaks
David Brumit , of whom weredrawn of
due form of law the following persons to serve as
Jurors towit,

The court appointed,
1 Jonathan Pugh   Forman,
2 Moses Estep
3 Philip Shell
4 Jacob Wagner
5 Richard Dunlap
6 Jerh. Whaly
7 Jona. Range
8 Geo. Lacy
9 Ewins Heatherly
10 John Keuhn
11 Jas Clark
12 Peter Emert &
Joel Cooper good lawful men of the court aforesaid Empaneled & Sworn to enquire for the body of the county
aforesaid.

Reuben Miller constable sworn to attend the grand Jury
& &.

(P.61)   Wm Carter Shff Elect came into open court
& took the several oaths required by law for a public
officer collector & &.

Johnson Hampton Esqr. returned a list of the taxable
property & poles in Capt. Clawsons District for 1827.

Court adjourned untill tomorrow nine oclock,

                    Juls. Dugger,
                    J. Hampton,
                    John L. Wilson.

Wednesday May the 16th 1827

Court met according to adjournment, Present the
Worshipful Julius Dugger,
Johnson Hampton &
John I. Wilson,   Esquires.

Ordered by the court that Henry Sailor be appointed
overseer of the public road from the branch by John
Williames old shop to the county line with the usual
hands to work.

On motion Michael McCann was qualified as an attorney
and admitted to practice & c.

(P.62)   State   )
               Vs   )   And the defendant being
            Thos Elliott)   charged upon the bill of
                               Indictment and he for plea
thereto saith that he is not Guilty thereof & puts him-
self on his country & J. P. Taylor atto. Genl. Who
prosecutes on behalf the state Doth the like where-
upon came a jury & the jurors of that jury towit.
Manuel Jenkins
John Blevins
William McQueen
Saml. Gourley
Barnabas Oaks
David Brumet
John C. Rolen
Jona. Hyder
Moses Humphreys
Lawson Goodwin
John Inman &:
Samuel Erwin chosen elected tried & sworn upon thier
oaths say do find the defendant not guilty on motion
& for reasons appearing to the court it is therefore
Ordered by the court that Lewis Lewis the prosecutor
taxed with costs Stephen Lewis assumes the costs it
is therefore considered by the court that the state
recover over against the said Lewis Lewis & Stephen
Lewis the costs of this prosecution & that the de-
fendant may be in mercy & c.

(P.63)   State   )
               Vs   )   Charged plea Guilty
            John Royston)   therefore it is consid-
                               ered by the court that
the said John Royston be fined one dollar pay the
costs of this prosecution & be in mercy & &.

State)
Vs) Warrant to keep the peace &
John Royston) the deft assumes costs & the
atto. Genl. by leave of the
courtenters a Noleprosequi therefore it is considered
by the court that the state recover against the defendant the costs of this prosecution & that the same may
be in mercy.

State)
Vs) And the deft being charged
Thomas Paxton) upon the bill of Inditement
and he for plea thereto saith
that he is guilty thereof it is considered by the court
that the defendent be fined fifty cents and that he be
in mercy & & and that the state recover his fine &
costs & &.

State)
Vs) And the defendent being charg-
Lewis Lewis) ed upon the bill of indictment
and he for plea thereto saith
that he is guilty there of it is considered by the court
that the defendant be fined fifty cents , Stephen Lewis
assumes fine & costs there fore it is considered that
the state recover of the defendant's the fine & costs of
this prosecution & that the defendants may be inmercy
& &.

(P.64) State)
Vs) Acknowledge them selves
Arthur Slone &) indebted to the state
Aaron Finch) Arthur Slone in the sum
of one hundred dollars
and Aaron Finch his bail in the sum of fifty dollars
to be levied of thier goods and chattles lands & Tenements Void on condition that the said Arthur Slone
appear before the justice of our court of pleas &
quarter sessions at a court to be hold for the county
of Carter at the court house in Elizabethton on the
second Monday of August next, towit Tuesday second day
of said term then & there to answer to a plea of the
state.

State)
Vs) The deft being charged upon
Abram. Tipton) the bill of Indictment saith
that he is guilty thereof
therefore it is considered by the court that the defendant be fined fifty cents pay the costs of this prosecution and be in mercy & & and that the state recover the
same & &.

Jas I Tipton)
    Vs   )   Judgement by default as t o
W. D. Johnson &) Bailey & write of inquiry
Saml. Bailey   )   of Damages awarded to be
                   inquired of at our next court..

Ordered by the court that Jonathan Hyder be fined five
dollars for swaring in contempt of court & reviling
against the Sheriff.

(P.65) David Waines
              Vs
          Wm Brumet

Tho. Ellott
A. McLeod
Manuel Jenkins
John Blevins
Wm McQueen
Saml. Gourley
Barnabas Oeks
John C. Rollens
Lawson Goodwin
John Inman
Saml. Irwin &
Moses Humphreys, chosen elec
Oaths say do find that the deft hath not kept and pre-
formed his covenant as in his Plea he hath alledged &
assess the plaintiff damage to one hundred & ten dollar-
ars therefore it is considered by the court that the
plff Recover agt. the deft his damages aforesaid by the
jury in manner &form aforesaid assessed and also his my
costs & charges put to and about his suit in that behalf Expended & that Deft may be in mercy & & costs
fer plff suit . By Wm B. Carter for 50-39 Cents.

Caleb Smith Resigns the office of a justice of the
peace in the following Words towit,"to the Honer-
able court of Carter county State of Tennessee greet-
ing your petitioner wishes to resign the office of
a justice of the peace I hope you will grant me my
request May 16th 1827 C. Smith".
    Which is accepted and ordered to be recorded,
(P.66) Ordered by the court the following be
added to the hands of Nathl. T Edens overseer towit,
Jas. C. Clark, Thos Gourley, Saml. Gourley, C. M. D.
Gourley & John Boyed & &.

Vencent Kelly constable returned an execution Issue
by a justice of the peace in favour of Tho.
Heatherly agt John Whitehead fore the sum of twelve
dols. & fifty cents debt and fifty cents costs

search made no goods & chattles found whereon to levy
this Execution then levied on the land where on the
said Whitehead no lived number acres not known also
Emtrys of fifty acres each adjoining the land of Aaron
Stalcup on the north side of Little Doe of rones creek,
it is therefore ordered by the court that the sheriff
sell said land or so much thereof as shall be of value
to satisfy said Executions & costs of this Motion.
(P.67) Vencent Kelly constable returned an execution issued by a Justice of the peace in favor of Jas.
H. Fiffe agt Jes Jackson for the sum of 21. D & cents
debt & costs search made no goods & chattles found
whereon to levy this Execution then levied on fifty
acres of land lying on the south scide of Rone creek
it being the land whereon Henry McIlCyea now lives, for
which return appearing to the court, it is therefore
ordered by the court that the shff sell said Lands or
so much thereof as shall be of Value sufficient to satisfy sd. Execution & costs of this motion & &.

Vincent Kelly cont. returned & Execution* by a Justice
of the peace in fayour of A. C. farks agt. V. Heaton
for the sum of 1.872/4 cents search made no property
found whereon to levy this Execution then levied on
the land whereon the sd. Heaton now lives, supposed
to be about three hundred & three acres lying on Little Doe of Rones creek, it is therefore ordered by
the court that the Sheriff sell said land or so much
thereof as shall be of Value sufficient to satisfy sd.
Execution & costs of this motion. * Isd.
(P.68) Vincent Kelley const. Returned an Execution
Issued by a Justice of the peace in favour of Charles
M. D. Gourley agt.V. Heaton for the sum of five dollars sixty 3/4 cents.
Search made no property found then levied on the
land whereon Vaught Heaton now lives supposed to be
about three hundred & three acres lying on little
Doe of Rones creek it is therefore ordered by the
court that the sheriff sell*land or so much thereof
as shall be of value Sufficent to satisfy sd. Execution and costs of this motion.* said

Reuben Miller const. returned an Executions Isd. by
a Justice of the peace in favor of Andrew Wilson agt.
Vaught Heaton for the sum of fifty dollars & thirty
seven cents, search made in my county no goods nor
chattles found but levied on land on the waters of
little Doe, The Quantity acres not known it is therefore considered by the court that the shff. Sell sd.
land or so much as shall be of value Sufficent to
satisfy sd. Executions & costs of this motion.

Jas. P. Taylor Atto. Genl. red the Clks Put for the
Treasuer for the year 1826 which is satisfactory to
the court. (P.69) Hamelton B. Hampton const returned & Execution Isd. by a justice of the peace
infavor of Wright Moorland agt T. W. Whitehead for
the sum of 25.37 Cents. no goods no chattles found
in mycounty of defts levied on a tract of land in
Carter county whereon the sd. Whitehead now lives num -
ber of acres not known it is therefore Ordered by the
court that the shff sell sd land or so much thereof
as shall be of value sufficient to satisfy sd Execution & costs this motion.

Hamelton B. Hampton const returned into court an execution issued by Caleb Smith favoring William B.
Carter Vs Vaught Heaton for twenty eight dollars &
eighty cents debt & fifty cents costs upon which he
returned that he had made search & could fond no
goods & chattles of defendants in said county &had
levied on a tract of land in Carter county whereon
the deft Heaton now lives number of acres not
known lying on little Doe of Hones creek adjoining
Daniel Stout & Godfrey D. Stouts lands March 7th
1827.
   It is therefore considered by the court that
said land be subject to the satisfaction of said
debt & that the same be sold by the Shff of Carter
county & that an order of s le issue or so much
thereof as shall be of value sufficient to satisfy said execution with the costs of this motion.

(P.70)

Wm B. Carter)
   Vs) Continued.
Andw. & Saml. Fulton)

Jas. Wilson)
   Vs) Plff dismisses his suit
Jab. Slimp) therefore it is considered
by the court that deft re-
cover agt. the plff his costs & charges put to and
a bout his defence & that plff may be in mercy & &.

Jacob Slimp)
   Vs) Plff dismisses his suit
Joseph Wilson) therefore it is considered
by the court that deft re-
cover agt. plff. his costs & charges put to and abowt
his defence & that plff may be in mercy & &.

David Waid)
    Vs) Continued
Wm Carter)
Jas. Keyes)
J. Hampton &)
J. Campbell)

J. Hampton)
    Vs) Contd. on rule & came as
J. Mast) heretofore.

(P.71)
Saml. Standfield)
    Vs.) Continued.
Azael Sharp)

Geo. Brown)
    Vs) Continued.
H. D. Johnson)

John Smith)
    Vs) Continued, Lucas Emert
Ewins Heatherly &) proved his atd: for 3
Tho. Heatherly) days as witness.

H. O. Johnson for)
E. Carters use)
    Vs) Referd see minutes
Jas. B. Moorley)

Wm H. Robertson for)
L. Showns use)
    Vs) Plff dismisses his suit
Thos. Paxton) & deft assumes costs
therefore it is considered
by the court that plff recover agt. the dept.

His costs & charges put to & about his suit in that
behalf expended & that deft may be in mercy & &.

John Smith)
    Vs) Rule to shew cause why the
Lewis Lewis) Certionari be dismissed.

Ordered by the court that the fine this day enterd
against Jonathan Hyder of five dollars be releasd.

(P.72)
Jesse Cobb   )
  Vs   )   Continued
J. C. West   )

A. M. Carter for)
B. Hatheways use)
   Vs   )   Issue
Isaac McNabb   )   plurius

Wm Graham   )
  Vs   )   Nor plea & Issue Joind contd.
L. Goodwin   )

Geo. W. Rutledge)
  Vs   )   Issue Plurius
J. C. West   )

Vaugh & Findley)
  Vs   )   Nor & Demeurrer contd.
Jas. I Tipton   )
Isaac Tipton   )

L. Goodwin   )
  Vs   )   Nor plea & Issue contd.
C. Freek   )

Peter Parsons   )
  Vs   )   Nor & Demurrer continued.
J. Stuart &   )
R. Stuart   )

(P. 73)
Saml. Tipton Senr)
  Vs   )   Nor plea & Issue.
Jesse Jones   )

Wm Adkins   )
  Vs   )   Time to declare.
A. Musgrave &   )
J. Wilson Senr   )

   A mortgage form Jesse West to James F. Taylor for
two open proven in open court by Wilkerson Gillford
and admited to record let it be registered.

Exhibited and proven in open court a mortage deed from
Vaught Heaton to Joseph Parkey for three hundred sixteen acres & a half land proven in open court and
ordered to be continued for the probet of the other
witness Turner C. Proffit.

A deed of conveyance from Vaught Heaton, William
Roberts & Theodocia Roberts his wife, Peter Rasor
& Easter his wife & Elizabeth Heaton to Samuel
Howard & George Brown was acknowledged in open court
by said Vaught Heaton,William Ro berts & Peter
Rason & Elizabeth Heaton & the said Theodocia
Roberts & Ester Rasor being examined by the court
seperate & apart from thier said husbands who
acknowledged that they signed & sealed the same
freely & Voluntarily without the threats persuasion
& coercion of thier said Husbands & thereupon the
same is admited to record & ordered to be certified
for registration as to the signature of said deed.

(P.74)
State   )
  Vs   )   Demur overruled & time to plead
J. Cooper   )   so as not to delay.

G. W. Rutledge)
    Vs   )   Plff by atty. dismisses his suit
Joseph C. West)   & assumes costs .
                   It is therefore considered by the
court that deft recover of Plff his costs about his
suit in this behalf expended & in mercy.

On motion of George Williams Clk. & Wm Carter Shff.
by J. P. Taylor depty it is ordered by the court
that the said clerk & shff recover the cost of a
division of land madebetween the heirs of George
Miller decd. of John & George Miller two of said heirs
& that execution issue & &.

James Campbell const. proved four days attendance as
a constitute at this court.

A statement of the sales of the property of Isaac
Tipton Decd. was returned by James I Tipton & Goor e
Lacey & Administrators.

(P.75)
Ordered by the court that William B . Carter, Jeremiah
Campbell, John L. Williams Esqr. be appointed commissioner to settle with William Carter & Rueben Miller
administrators with the bill annexd. of Jerremiah
Miller decd. & that they make report to our next
court.

Whereas on Monday it was considered by the court
that William Carter Shff. be allowed one hundred &
sixty dollars money,paid hyshim to David Have for

plastering the court house which order was omitted
to be entered on that day it is therefore now for
them ordered by the court that said Carter be allowd
said sum as producing to the trustee Waids recient
for the same and that it be paid out of any county
money not otherwise appropriated.

Court adjournd untill court in cause,
John L. Wilson,
J. Hampton,
W. B. Carter.

(P.76) tate of Tennessee Carter county.
At a meeting of a court of Please and quarter sess-
ion held for Carter county at the court house in Eliza-
bethton on the second Monday of August in the year of
our Lord 1827.
Present the Worshipful James Keys, George Emmert
Wm Peoples, John Wilson, W. B. Carter, Julius Dugar
Jeremiah Campbell and Jesse Cole. Esquires.

Ordered by the court as heretofore that the order requiring the Sheriff to have the poor persons of this
county at our next court of please & & and that the
Sheriff advertise Said poor persons will be let out
to the lowest bidder at next court & &.

Five Justices present Jesse Isaac produced in open
court the Scalps of three Wolves adjudges by the court
under four months old & the said Jesse Isaac being
Sworn upon his oath saith that he killed the wolves
that the Scalf came off on the county aforesaid
since the first day of January 1811 and it appearing
to the satisfaction of the court that the said
Jesse killed theWolves in the county aforesaid.
It is therefore ordered by the court that the said
Jesse be allowed the sum of six Dollars for killing
the aforesaid Wolves to be paid out of the state
treasury.

(P.77)
Whereas there has been heretofore a jury & the
Jurors appointed at last court has reported to this
court that the road from Thomas McInturff to Haines's
mill be and is here by confirmed to pass through the
land of William Peoples as heretofore laid off & by
us now laid off & that we conceive that said peoples
has now will recover no injury or damage in laying
off said road & it is ordered by the court that
Thomas McInturff be overseer of said Road with the
hands heretofore.

A notice to the said Thomas and that the said Will
iam/peeples have untill the 15th of November next to
gather in his crop &c.

Where as William Cassedy an orphan was heretofore
bound an apprentice to William Jones untill said apprentice shall attain to the age of 21 years & There as
Thomas Foxton, by his attorney A Finch moved the court
to have said apprentice liberated from the service of
the said Williams motion overruled.

(p.78) Ordered by the court that Julius Duncan be
allowed twenty dollars for the support & maintainence
of Alford Said an orphan child six months.

John Wright Esquire resigned the office and appointment of Justice of the Peace in the following words
(to wit) To the Worshipfull court of Please and Quarter
Session for Carter county I hereby as a justice of
the peace in your said county tender to you my resig-
nations with a request it may be entered of record.

                                        John Wright
Which is accepted by the court and to be recorded.

Ordered by the court that Daniel Shell be appointed
overseer of the public road in the room of Joseph
Rogers and have the same bounds and hands.

Ordered by the court that Elisha Williams be appointed
overseer of the public road in theroom of Hempser
Ritchy and have the same bounds & hands.

Ordered by the court that David Orumit be appointed
overseer of the public road in the room of James .
Clawson and have the same bounds & hands.

(P.79) Ordered by the court that Daniel Smith be
appointed overseer of the public road in the room of
George M. Pierce & have the same hands & bounds.

Ordered by the court that the report of the jury on
a piece of road leading from Fishers old field to
the Limestone Cove be confirmed & that David Quinn
be appointed overseer of said road & that William
Cross, Solomon Cross, Uriah Banks, Mosses Banks,
William Banks, James Moore, Eppen Woodby, William
Baker, William Garland, Harper Mosely, Charles
Ingram, Osborne Hill, Rueben Birchfield, Nathan
Birchfield, & Samuel Smith be the hands to work
said road.

Ordered by the court that William Stover be appointed
overseer of the public road in the room of William
Adams and have the same bounds & hands.

The assignment of a plat and Certificate of Survey
from John Sheilds Snr. to John Sheilds Jnr. for
one hundred acres of land acknowledged in open
court & admited to record.

(1.80) The assignment of a plat & certificate
of Survey from John Sheilds Senr. to John Sheilds
Jr. for one hundred and fifty acres of land acknowledged in open court and admited to record.

Ordered by the court that the following persons be
appointed Jurors to November sessions, 1827,
William Cross, William Jones, William Banks, Charles
Ferrels, Jas. Bunton, George Shuffield, John Potter
Jnr. Matthias Wargoner Sr. Joseph Waut, Daniel Ward,
Peter Wills, Isaac Shown, Joseph Gentry, William
Carrol Sr. William Brown, Abraham Hon Saml W.
Williams, John Ellis, Robert Morris, Peter Nave
Michael Lyon,Bethuel Puck, Jacob Poland, Samuel
Montgomery, Joseph Hider, Jesse Jinkins,

Ordered by the court that Michael Smithpeter be an
overseer of the public road in the stead of John Whitte-
head and have the same hands & bonds that Whitehead
had.

Ordered by the court that William Carter Sheriff bring
forward Rachel Werren an orphen child to the next court
of plea & & inorder that she may be bound out to some
suitable person.

(1.81)
Joseph Wilson   )
      Vs   )   Reuben Miller constable re-
Joseph Heaton   )   turned an execution Issued
                           by a justice of the peace in
favor of Joseph Wilson against Joseph Heaton for the
sum of twenty one dollars eighty five cents debt and
fifty cents costs, search made in my county no goods
nor Chattles found but levied on thirty two & a half
acres of Land on the Waters of Cobbs Creek adjoining
the land of Michael Smithpeter and others this this
twentieth of July 1827 and it appearing to the satisfaction of the court by the return of sd Constable,,
that he could find no goods nor Chattles of the deft.
to levy sd execution on it is there fore ordered by
the court that the Sheriff sell said Lands or so much
thereof as will be sufficient to satisfy said execution
and costs of this motion.

Court adjourned untill tomorrow 9 Oclock,

Jereh. Campbell,
J. Keyes,
J.L. Wilson.

Tuesday August 14th 1827

Court met according to adjournment present Jeremiah
Campbell, James Keyes, Ezeliel Smith and William B.
Carter, Esquires and Lawson White Esqr.

(P.82)
State of Tennessee)
Carter county   )   Be it remembered that on
this 14th day of August in the hear of Our Lord one
thousand eight hundred andtwenty seven, William
Carter sheriff of said County returned the States
Writs of Venire Facias executed which is in the
following, towit, State of Tennessee Carter county
to the sheriff of said county greetings.
     We command you to Summon John McInturff Jr.
Peter Holt Isaac Corrol Michael* Andrew Wilson
Jacob Smith Zachariah Campbell James Range John Curtis
Thos. Gouley Samuel Drakes Samuel Ervin Isaac Tipton
John Scot David Stout William Bunton Elisha Rainbolt
Daniel Baker William Lewis Abraham Loe Archibaod
Williams Jr. Samuel W. H. Peoples Joel Cooper &
Joseph Taylor and Robert McLin from whome good and
Lawful men of the county aforesaid were drawn in due
form of law grand Jurors of whome the court appointed.
     * Hunt
Archabald Williams foreman, Andrew Wilson Daniel
Baker Joseph Taylor Saml W. H. Peoples Elisha Rainbolt
James Range Joel Cooper Isaac Carrol John Curtis
Abraham Loe David Stout andIsaac Tipton who were qual-
ified and recieved thier charge and withdrew to con-
sider of thier presentments.

Charles M. D. Gourley a constable sworn to attend the
grand jury.

(P.83)   Five Justices present John Wilson produced
in open court a wolf scalp adjudged by the courts to
be over four months old and Jacob Smith being sworn
upon his oath saith that he killed the sd wolf in the
county aforesaid since the first day of January 1811
satisfaction of the court that the said Jacob killed
the said wolf in the county aforesaid it is therefore
ordered by the court that John Wilson be allowed three
dollars for killing the said wolf to be paid out of the
state treasury.

State   )
  Vs   )   And the Defendant being chargd on
John Smith)   the bill of Indictment and he for
                 plea thereto saith he is not guilty
thereof and put himself upon his Country and James
P. Taylor atto. Genl who prosecutes on behalf of
the State doth the like whereupon came   Jury and the
Jurors of that Jury towit, William Lewis Saml. Howard
James Strout Jonathan Ligs James Hughs John Howard
Lazs Inman Thomas Perry Solomon Ellis Zachariah Campbell
SamI McQueen and Joseph Wilson good and lawful men
of the county aforesaid chosen elected and tried and
sworn upon thier oaths say they do find the Defendant
guilty in manner and form as charged in the bill of
Indictment it is therefore considered by the court
that the defendant be fined one Dollar and pay the
costs of this prosecution and in mercy.

(I.S4) State Vs John Smith, Tobias Riddle and Thos.
J. Lewis prove thier attendance for three days each as
witnesses in this case.

State   )
  Vs   )   The Defendants comes into
Wilkinson Gifford)   open court and confesses
                        Judgement for the costs of
this prosecution. It is therefore considered by the
court that the state recover off the defendent the
costs of this prosecution and the deft in mercy &c.

State   )
  Vs   )   This case is continued on
Arthur Sloan   )   the atts of the Defendant
                     and Hedett & deft & Aaron
Finch his security came into open court and acknowledged themselves indebted to the State that is to say the
said Sloan in the sum of one Hundred Dollars & the sd.
Aaron in the sum of fifty dollars to be levied of thier
goods & chattles Lands and Tennement yet to be void on
condition the said Sloan appear before Justice of our
court of please & & on the second Monday of November
next towit on Tuesday the Second day of said term and
answer the charge of the State against him and not depart the court without leave first had and recd.

State   )
  Vs   )   John Royston prosecutor acknowledgeth
Arthur Sloan)   himself Indebted to the state in the
                     sum of one hundred dollars to be levied
off his goods and chattles lands & Tennements yet to

be void on condition the said Royston appear before
the justice of our court of please & & at the court
house in Elizabethton on the second Monday of November next (towit) on Tuesday the second day of said
term and prosecute and give evidence in this prosecution.

(P. 95)

State)
Vs) James Jones comes into open court &
Hezekiah Smith) being sworn upon his oath saith that
he is afraid that there will be done
him by the deft some great bodily harm & & and prays
the court that the deft may be bound to keep the peace
whereupon it is ordered by the court that the deft be
bound to keep the peace towit the good people of the
State of Tennessee and especially James Jones and the
deft comes into open court and Elijaha Smith bail acknowledges themselves indebt to the state is to say the
said Hezekiah in the sum of five hundred Dollars and
the sd Elijaha in the sum of two hundred & fifty dollars to be levied off thier goods and chattles lands
and Tennements yet to be void on condition the sd
Hezekiah Smith shall well and truly keep the peace of
the state to wards the good people of the state and
especially towards the said James Jones for the term
of twelve months.

State)
Vs) And the deft being charged
Hezekiah Smith) on the bill of Indictment
and he for plea thereto saith
he is not guilty thereof and puts himself upon his
country and James P Taylor atto. Genl who prosecutes
on behalf of the state doth the like whereupon came a
jury and the Jurors of that jury towit,
John Haun Joseph Paxton William Lewis James Stroud
Jonathan Lips James Hughes John Howard Lazs Inman
Solomon Ellis Zachariah Campbell Genl McQueen and
Joseph Wilson good and lawful men of the county afsd
chosen elected tried and sworn upon thier oaths say
the find the deft guilty in manner and form as charsd
in the bill of Indictment. It is therefore considered
by the court that the deft be fined twenty five cents
and that the state recover of the defendant the fine
aforesaid and the costs of this proseeution and the
deft in mercy & &.

(P.86)

Johnston Hampton)
    Vs   )   James Campell Constable re-
David R. Kinnick)   turned an Execution Issued
                       by a justice of the peace in
favor of the plaintiff against the deft for the sum of
of four dollars Fifty cents debt and one dollar costs
Search made in my county and no goods and chattles
found but levied the same on all the right title claim
and interest which the deft has in and to a twenty five
acre Entry which J. P. Taylor sold to Z. Hollers be-
wit, Marviel Hollow also an Entry of one hundred acres
adjoining the same in Taylors office also Joins James
Bradley, May 25th 1827, said last entry made by deft
from which return it appearing to the court no goods
and chattles of the deft to be found It is therefore
ordered by the court that the Sheriff sell said Lands
or so much thereof as will be sufficient to satisfy
said Execution and the costs of this motion.

Johnston Hampton)
    Vs   )   James Campbell constable re-
David R. Kinnick)   turned an Execution Issued
                       by a justice of the Peace
in favor of the plaintiff against the deft for the
sum of fifty Eight Dollars and thirty Four cents debt
and one dollar costs, search made in my county and
no goods nor chattles found but levied the same on
all the right, title claim and interest the deft has
in and to a twenty five acres entry which J. P. Taylor
sold to Z. Holler towit, Marvales Hollers also an
Entry of one hundred acres Joining the same in Taylors
office also joins James Bradley the said Entry made by
Dept May 26th 1827 and it appearing to the satisfaction
of the court by sd return that there is no goods &
chattles of the deft.
    It is therefore ordered by the court that the sheriff
sell said Lands or so much thereof as will be sufficient to satisfy said Execution and the costs of this
motion.

(P.87)

James Bradley)
    Vs   )   James Campbell constable re-
David R. Kinnick)   turned an Execution Issued
                   by a justice of the peace
for the sum of forty nine Dollars thirty Eight cents
debt and one Dollar costs in favor of the pleff
against the deft search made in My county & no goods
and chattles found but levied the same on all the
right title claim and Interest Deft has in and to

twenty five acres of land Entry which J.P. Taylor
sold to A. Holler to Marrial Hollow also oneentry
of one hundred acres joining the same in Taylors
office also joins James Bradely said Entry made by
Deft, May 20th 1827 for which return appearing return appearing to the satisfaction of the court
that there is no goods and chattles of the defendant
to be found.

It is therefore ordered by the court that the
Sheriff sell the said Lands or so much thereof as
will be sufficient to satisfy said execution together with the costs of this motion.

A relinqrisiment from Charles F. George and Celia
George wife of the said Charles heirs of Jacob Smith
decd come into open court and acknowledgedthey had
recd of Daniel Smith and Ezekiel Smith Executors of
the said Jacob six hundred Dollars in full satisfaction
of thier share of the Estate of the ad Jacob decd
which deed upon such acknowledgement was admitted
to record let it be registered.

Ordered by the court that Matthew Solts be appointed
constable who came into court enter into Bond with
Elijah Matheway and Henry Grindstaff his security
in the final sum of one thousand Dollars with condition see bond and took the several oaths required
by law for apublic officer (P.88) Mary Reno and
John Smith Wilkinson Gifford her securities come
into court and enter into bond in the final sum of
five hundred Dollars the condition whereof is that
the said Mary keep harmless the court of Please and
Quarter Session of Carter county from all Charges
and expences relative to the maintainance of an illi-
illimate child born of the body of the said Mary.

James Campbell comes into court and resigns the office and appointment of constable.

Court adjourned untill tomorrow 9 O;Clock,
            Jereh Campbell
            J. L. Wilson
            J. Hampton.

        Wednesday August 15th 1827

Court met according to adjournment present the
Worshipfull:
            Jeremiah Campbell
            Johnson Hampton
            John L. Wilson   Esqrs.

Lawson Goodwin)
    Vs)   This cause continued on
Christopher Frick)   affidavit of Deft.

(P.89)
Johnson Hampton)
    Vs)   Continued on afft of pla ff
Jacob Mast)   rule and commission to take
                     deposition as heretofore five
days notice.

State)
    Vs)   The Att'y General by leave
John Mourland) (Moreland) of the court enters a nole
                     Prosequi Thereupon the de-
fendant and James I Tipton his security came into court
and assum the cost It is therefore considered by the
court that the state recover of the Defendant and James
I. Tipton the costs of this prosecution and that the
Deft in Mercy & &.

State)
    Vs)   The attorney General with leave
John Mourland)   of the court enters a noleprose-
                     equi and the defendant and
James I. Tipton his security assume the cost.
    It is therefore considered by the court that the state
recover of the Deft and James I. Tipton the cost of
this prosecution and the deft in Mercy & &.

State)
    Vs)   The attorney General by leave
James I. Tipton)   of the court enters a nole
                     prosequi and James I. Tipton
assumes the cost. It is therefore considered by the
court that the State recover of the sd James I Tipton
the cost of this case and the eft in mercy

(P.90)
State
    Vs
Samuel T Boid bail of John Mourland (Moreland)
The attorney General with leave of the court enters a
nole prosequi and the sd James I. Tipton security
Samuel Boid assumes the costs it is therefore consider-
ed by the court that the state recover of the said
Samuel T. Boid & James I. Tipton the costs of this case
and the defendant in mercy & &.

State)
Vs) The Defendant being chargd
Gabriel McInturff) on the Bill of Indietment
pleads guilty and submits
to the court and it is considered by the court after
hearing Evidence the Defendant by fined twelve and a
half cents. It is further considered by the court that
the state recover of the defendant the fine aforesaid
and the costs of this prosecution and the deft in
Mercy & &.

State)
Vs) And the defendant being Solem-
Michael Slimp) nly called to come into court
to answer the charge of the
state came not but made default therefore it is consid-
erd by the court that the state recover against the
said Michael Slimp the sum of one hundred dollars the
amount of his recognizance and that Sci Fa Issue accordingly against the sd Michael to shew cause at our
next court of Please & & why execution may not Issue
therefore.

The assingment of a plat & certificate of servey of
fifty acres of land from David Guinn to William P.
Jones acknowledged in open court and admitted to record let it becertified to the register of the land
office that a Grant may Issue to the said Jones.

(P.91)
State)
Vs) And the said Eli Rasor being
Eli Rasor Bail) Solemnly called to bring
of Michael Slimp) into court the body of
Michael Slimp for whome he
was bail come not but made default it is therefore
considered by the court that the state recover of
said Eli Rasor the sum of fifty dollars the amount
of his recognizance and that Sci Fa Issue accordingly against the said Eli Rasor to shew cause at the
next term of our court of please & & Why Execution
may not Issue therefore.

State)
Vs) And the said Jacob Slimp
Jacob Slimp bail of) being solemnly called to
Michael Slimp) bring into court the body
of Michael Slimp for whom
he was bail came not but made default.
It is therefore considered by the court that the state

recover of the said Jacob Slimp Bail as aforesaid the
sum of fifty Dollars the amount of his recognizance
and that Sci Fa Issue against the said Jacob to shew
cause at the next term of the court of please & &.
Why Execution may not Issue therefore.

State   )
  Vs   )   And the Defendant being solemnly
John Jones   )   called to come into court and answer
                      the charge of the state came not but
made default It is therefore considered by the court
that the State recover of the Defendant the sum of
                      the amount of his recognizance and
that Sci Fa Issue against the said Jones to Shew cause
at our next court of please and quarter sessions why
Execution may not Issue therefore.

(4.92)
State   )
  Vs   )   and the said James
James W. Clawson Jr bail   )   W. Clawson Jun.
of John Jones   )   being solemnly
                                       called to bring
into court the body of John Jones whom for he was bail
came not but therein made It is therefore considered
by the court that the state recover of the sd James W
Clawson bail as aforesaid the sum of seventy five Dollars amount of his recognizance and that Sci Fa Issue
against the said Clawson to shew cause at the next term
of the court of please & &. Why Execution may not Issue
for the same.

State   )
  Vs   )   And the said James
James W. Clawson Senr.   )   W. Clawson Senr
                                  being Solemnly cal-
led to bring into court the body of the said John Jones
as he was bound to do came not but therein made default
It is therefore considered by the court that the said
James W. Clawson Sr. forfeit to the state the sum of
seventy five dollars the amount of his recognizance
and that Sci Fa Issue against him to shew cause at next
Term of the court of pleas & & Why Execution may not
issue against him for the same.

Samuel Stanfield)
      Vs   )   In this cause came the part-
A   Sharp   )   ies and thereupon came a
                        jury of good and lawful men
towit.

William Lewis James W. Renfroe John Royston Larkin
Jinkins Joseph Wilson Peter Rasor Thos. Crow Russell
Royston John C. Rollins Hugh Willson Lewis Lewis &
William Bridges who being elected tried and sworn the
truth to speak upon the issue joined between the parties on thier oath do say they find the defendant has
not kept and preformed his (P93) covenant as in pleading he alledged and asses the plaintiff damages to the
sum of one hundred and eighteen dollars seventy five
cents. It is therefore considered by the court that the
plaintiff recover of the deft the sum of one hundred
and eighteen Dollars & seventy five cents the damage
assessed as aforesaid by the jury aforesd together
with the costs about his suitin this behalf expended
and the deft & &.

Henry Ward   )
    Vs   )   In this cause came the part-
Joseph Cooper   )   ies by thier attorneys and
                               thereupon came a jury of
good and Lawful men towit, William Lewis James W.
Renfroe John Royston Larkin Jinkins Joseph Wilson
Peter Rasor Thos Crow Russell Royston John C. Rolling
Hugh Wilson Lewis Lewis and William Bridges.
    Who being elected tried and sworn the truth to
speak on the Issue Joined between the parties on thier
oath do say they find the defendant has not kept and
preformed his covenants as in Pleading he has alledged
and assess the plaintiffs damage to ninety three Dollars and twenty eight cents. It is therefore considered
by the court that the plff recover of the defendant
the sum of ninety three Dollars and twenty Eight cents
the damage assessed as aforesaid by the jury aforesaid
together with the costs about his suit in this behalf
expended and the deft &.

Jessee Cobb   )
    Vs   )   In this cause came the parties
Joseph G. West   )   by thier attorney and there-
                               upon came a jury of good and
lawful men towit, William Lewis James W. Renfroe
John Royston Larkin Jinkins Joseph Wilson Peter Rasor
Thomas Crow Russell Royston John C Rollins Hugh Wilson
Lewis Lewis &William Bridges who being elected (P.94)
tried and sworn the truth to speak upon the Issue
joined between the parties on thier oaths do say they
find the defendant has paid the debt in the plaintiffs
declaration mentioned except the sum of one hundred
and ninety two dollars and eighty three cents.
    It is therefore considered by the court that the
plaintiff recover of the defend't the sum of one hun-

dred and ninety two dollars & eighty three cents the
balance of the plaintiff's debt and the further sum
of eight dollars sixty seven cents the damage assessed
as aforesaid by the Jury aforesaid together with the
costs about his suit in this behalf expended and Deft
&c.

James I. Tipton)
    Vs (In this cause came the plff
Samuel Bailey)   by his attorney and thereupon
                 comes a jury of good and law-
ful men (towit) William Lewis James W. Renfroe John
Royston Larkin Jinkins Joseph Wilson Peter Rasor Thos
Crow Russell Royston John C. Rollins Hugh Wilson Lewis
Lewis and William Bridges who being elected tried and
sworn the truth to inquire of the plffs damage on
thier oath do say they find for the plff & assess the
plaintiffs damage to two hundred eighty four dollars
fifteen cents.
    It is therefore considered by the court that the
plaintiff recover of the deft the sum of two hundred
and eighty four dollars and fifteen cents the damage
assessedas afores'd by the jury aforesaid together
with his costs about his suit in this behalf expended
and the deft in &c.

(P.95)
William Graham)
    Vs)   Covenant In this cause came
Lawson Goodwin) the parties by thier attorneys
                and thereupon came a jury of
good and lawful men towit, Gabriel McInturf James W.
Renfroe John Royston Larkin Jinkin Joseph Wilson Peter
Rasor Thomas Crow Russell Royston John C. Rollins
Hugh Wilson Lewis William Bridges who being
elected tried and sworn the truth to speak on the
Issue joined between the parties on thier Oath do
say they find that the Defendant has not kept and perfor
med his covenant as in pleading he hath alledged and
assess the plaintiff's damage to eighty three dollars
and twenty cents. It is therefore considered by the
court that the plaintiff recover of the defendant the
sum of eighty three dollars and twenty cents the damage assessed as aforesaid by the jury aforesaid together with the costs about his suit in this behalf
expended & the Defendant in mercy.

Samuel Tipton Sr.)
    Vs   )   In this cause came the part-
Jessee Jones   )   ies by thier attorneys and·
thereupon came a jury of good
and lawful men towit, Gabriel McInturf James W. Renfroe
John Royston Larkin Jinkins Jos. Wilson Peter Rasor
Thomas Crow Russell Royston John C. Rollins Hugh Wilson
Lewis Lewis and William Bridges.
Who being elected tried and sworn the truth on the Issue
Joined between the parties on thier oath do say they
find that the defendant has not kept and preformed his
pleading he hath alledged and assess the plaintiffs
damage to one hundred and (P.95) eighty eight dollars and forty three conts. It is therefore considered
by the court that the Plaintiff recover of the defendant the sum of one hundred and eighty eight dollars
and forty three cents the damage assessed as aforesaid
by the jury aforesaid together with the costsabout his
suit in this behalf expended and the defendant &c.

William O'Brian   )
    Vs   )   The plaintiff comes into
Greenberry Delashmit)   court and dismisses his
suit and assumes upon
himself the costs it is therefore considered by
the court that the defendant recover of the plaintiff the costs about his defence in this behalf expended and the plaintif for his false clamor &c.
covenant.

Peter Rasor   )
    Vs   )   In this cause came the
Samuel Howard   )   parties by thier attorneys
George Brown   )   and thereupon came a jury
of good and lawful men,
towit William Lewis James W. Renfroe John Royston
Larkin Jinkins Joseph Wilson Thomas Crow Russell
Royston John C. Rollins Hugh Wilson Lewis Lewis
William Bridges Gabriel McInturf. Who being elected t&
tried and sworn the truth to speak upon the Issue
joined between the parties on thier oaths do say
they find that the defendant has not kept and preformed thier covenant as in pleading they have alledged and assess the plaintiffs damage to one hundred
and forty four dollars fifty five cents.
It is therefore considered by the court that the
plaintiff recover of the defendant the sum of one
hundred and forty four dollars & fifty five cents the
damage assessed together with the costs in this behalf expended and the defendants &c.
(P.97)
John Smith   )
    Vs   )
Lewis Lewis   )
Joseph Paxton &c)
James W. Clawson

Certioneri and now at this day came the said John and
Smith by his attorney James P. Taylor and Aaron Finch
and the said Lewis Lewis by his atto. L. B. Williams
who puts in his place John Allen Esqr. and on argument of counsel It is considered by the court that
the rule be sustained and that the plaintiff recover
of Lewis Lewis Deft and Joseph Paxton & James W.
Clawson his securities the sum of one dollar and
forty cents for his debt and also his costs and
charges about his suit in this behalf expended.

Godfrey Nave & Tennessee L. Carriger administrators
of Godfrey Carriger dec'd return an additional
Inventory of the personal Estate of Godfrey
Carriger dec'd and there upon ordered to be recorded

Godfrey Nave & Tennessee L Carriger administrators
& & of Godfrey Carriger, dec'd return an Inventory
of the sale of the personal Estate of Godfrey
Carriger dec'd and ordered to be recorded.

(P.98)

Thomas Paxton)
    Vs)   Thomas Paxton by his atto
William Jones)   A Finch comes into court &
               moves the court to Liberate
from the service of William Jones, William Cassoly
an orphen boy whome the court formerly bound unto
the said William Jones and an argrument of counsel
It is considered by the court that said motion of
the said Paxton be overruled and It is also considered by the court that the said William Jones recover of the said Paxton the costs incurred by said
motion.

James P. Taylor
    Vs
Hugh McHenry administrator of Andrew McHenry dec'd
and others.
Judgment having been obtained by the plff against the
defendant as administrator an John L. Williams, David
McNabb & William McNabb at the August session 1826
of this court for the sum of seventy two dollars and
cost & execution having according to act of assembly
been twelve months from administration granted on the
14th day of July 1827 execution was issued on said
judgement against the defendant and having now been
returned by the sheriff with this indorsement search
made & no goods & chattles of the deceas'd to be
found in the land of Hugh McHenry administrator on
which to levy said execution whereupon on motion of
James P. Taylor it is ordered by the court that

Joseph Cooper be appointed guardian pendents (P.99)
lite for the following named persons minor heirs of
the said Andrew McHenry deceas'd (towit) Lydia
Sullenberger, Archibald Kings, Lea Sheets Andrew Sheets
Polly Sheets Hugh Sheets Potsy Sheets, children of
Mary Sheets dec'd formerly Mary McHenry and thereupon
it is ordered by the court that scirei Facias issue
against the said Joseph Cooper guardian & &.
Hugh McHenry , Charles Hays & Nancy his wife formerly
Nancy McHenry & Margaret McHenry the other heirs of
Andrew McHenry dec'd returnable to our next court of
please & C for Carter county to show cause if any thay
can why pl'ff Should not have execution of his judgement
against the land of the deceased which descended to
them on the death of the said Andrew McHenry dec'd.

George W. Rutledge)
    Vs   )   The attachment obtained by the
Joseph C. West   )   Pl'ff having been return'd
                          by the sheriff levied upon
                          one negroe boynamed Isaac &
a negroe pannamed Billy and it appearing to the satisfaction of the court that said Joseph C. West is a
citizen of another state it is ordered by the court
that all further proceedings in this case be staid six
months in persuance to act of assembly & &.

(P.100)   A mortage from Jacob Slimp to Michael
Slimp for a four acre entry including the mouth of
mill creek & the head of the spring Jacob Slimp uses
water from water of Rones creek and assignment of his
interest in any recovery which he may may make in a
suit- Vs- Leonard Shoun David Waggoner & William P.
Carter was acknowledged in open court by said Slimp
and admitted to record let it be registered

A deed of conveyance from William Carter sheriff of
Carter county to James P. Taylor for one hundred and
thirty acres of land lying on south side of Watauga
river between the land of Isaac Tipton & James P. Taylor including the plea where David Stuart lived and
sold by said Carter as the property of John Stuart was
acknowledged in open court by said William Carter
sheriff and admitted to record let it be registered.

(P.101)

John U. Nelson   )
    Vs   )   Vincent Felly constable
Charles Rasendine)   returned an execution

issued by a justice of the peace in favour of the plaintiff against the said Bassendine for the sum of sixty
two dollars and twenty two cents debt & Fifty cents
costs search made in my county for goods & chattles on
which to levy this execution & & none found therefore
levied the same on ninety acres of land lying on both
sides of little Doe of Rones creek whereon said Bassendine now lives one track of Forty acres on both sides
of said creek & one other of Fifty acres on the south
side of said creek also his interest in a tract of land
& Forge thereof number of acres unknown, known by the
name of Carrigers Naves & Bassendines forge on stoney
creek all in Carter county and it appearing to the
satisfaction of the court by return of said constable
that no goods & chattles can be found to levy said execution upon. It is therefore ordered by the court
that the sheriff sell said land or so much thereof as
shall be of value sufficient to satisfy said execution
& costs of this motion.

Exhibited & acknowledged in open court a deed of conveyance from Joseph Heaton to John Howard for eighty
two acres of land and admited to record let it be registered.

(P.102)

George Morton) Vincent Kelly constable re-
　　Vs) turned an Execution Issued
Charles Bassendine) by a justice of the peace
in favor of Plaintiff against Defendant for the sum
of seventy three dollars eight cents debt and fifty
cents costs. Search made no personal property found
in my county then levied on ninety acres of land lying on both sides of little Doe of Rones creek whereon said Bassendine now lives one track of forty acres
on both sides of said creek one tract of fifty acres
on the south side of sd creek also s'd Bassendine interest in a tract of and forge thereon number of acres
not known lying on Stoney creek known by of Carriger
Naves and Bassendine forge Tract June 6th 1827 and
it appearing to the satisfaction of the court that
there is no personal property found It is therefore
Ordered by the court that the sheriff sell said lands
or so much thereof as will be sufficient to satisfy
said execution and the costs of this motion.

John C. Helm) Vincent Kelly Constable
　　Vs) returned into court an Execut-
Charles Bassendine) ion Issued by a justice

of the peace in favor of the Plaintiff against the
Defendant for the sum of fifty seven dollars sixty
Eight cents debt and fifty cents costs 6th June 1827
Search made no goods and chattles found then levied on
ninety acres of land lying on both sides of little
Doe of hones creek whereon said Bassendine now lives
one tract of forty acres on both sides of said creek
one other tract of fifty acres on the south side of
said creek also his Interest in a (P.103) tract of
land and forme thereon number of acres not known lying on stoney creek known by the name of Carriger
Naves and Bassendine forge tract and it appearing to
the satisfaction of the court by return of sd constable
that there was no goods and chattles found It is therefore ordered by the court that the sheriff sell said
Tracts of land or so much thereof as will be sufficient
to satisfy said Execution and also the costs of this
motion.   Hugh McHenry Vs Joseph Heaton

Vincent Kelly constable returned to court an Execution
Issued by a justice of the peace In favor of the Plaintiff against the defendant for the sum of twenty seven
dollars ninety one cents debts and fifty cents costs
June 21st 1827 Search made no property found in my
county then levied on forty four and a quarter acres
of land being the land whereon Joseph Heaton now lives
and it appearing to the satisfaction of the court from
said return of said constable that there was no goods
and chattles to be found It is therefore ordered by
the court that the sheriff sell said Tract of Land or
so much thereof as will be sufficient to satisfy said
Execution and also the costs of this motion.

(P.104)
John C. Helm)
    Vs)   Vincent Kelly constable return-
Aaron Musgrave)   ed into court an Execution issued by a justice of the peace in favor of the plaintiff
against the defendant for the sum of seventeen dollars
eighty five cents debt and one dollar costs.
Search made no property found levied on an entry of
twenty five acres of the waters of Roans creek on the
south side of the main road adjoining David Wagoners
land Including Isaac Osbourn & Joseph Osbourn tract no
734 Located the 6th February 1826 also a tract whereon
John Musgrave Jr now lives lying the main road middle
fork of Roans creek containing one hundred acres
June 25th 1827 and it appearing to the satisfaction
of the court from the return of said constable that
there is no goods and chattles of the deft found

It is therefore ordered by the court that the sheriff
sell the said Lands or so much thereof as will be sufficient to satisfy said Execution and also the costs
of this motion.

John & James Obrian   )
 ·   Vs   )   Vincent Kelly constable retur-
John O. Doughterty   )   ned into court an Execution
                            Issued by a Justice of the
peace for the sum of sixteen Dollars twenty two cents
costs in favor of the Plaintiff against the Defendant
Saerch made no property in my county then levied on a
lot in Elizabethton whereon said Dougherty now lives
No non quarterly not known July 19th 1827. debt and
    fifty cents
(P.105)   An It appearing to the satisfaction of the
court by return of said constable that there is no goods
nor Chattles found It is therefore ordered by the court
that the Sheriff sell said lot to satisfy said Judgement and also the costs of this motion.

Thomas Heatherly   )
 .Vs   )   In this case on the 14th
Solomon Smith   )   June 1827 a cause was Issued
                          by J. Richardson Esqr. against
deft for nine dollars & fifteen cents debt & fifty cents
costs an the interest & & which cash came to the hands
of Vincent Kelly constable who on the 14th June 1827
executed the same on the said Smith & he thereupon entered into bond with John Taylor security condition'd
as the law directs for the appearance of said Smith
at this court to comply with requisite of the act of
assembly & & and the said Sollomon Smith having failed to appear to comply with his said bond have on
motion of A. W. Taylor atty. it is considered by the
court that the Plff recover judge against the said
Sollomon Smith & John Taylor his security for his debt
& interest & costs together with the costs of this
motion towit nine dollars 15 cents debt with interest
and fifty cents costs & costs of this motion & they
in mercy.

(P.106)   Thursday 16th 1827

James I. Tipton   )
        Vs   )   It appearing to the satisfact-
John Moreland   )   ion of the court that James I.
                        Tipton as bail of John Moreland
had there judgement entered against him as security of
said Moreland on a former day of this court for the amount

of twenty nine dollars & seventy cents costs the said
there cases It is therefore on motion of J. Taylor
considered by the court that the said James I Tipton
recover of the said John Moreland the said Sum of
twenty nine dollars & seventy cents the amount for
which the said Tipton is liable as security for said
Moreland together with costs of this motion & Deft
in mercy.

A deed of conveyance from Vaught Heaton, Wm Roberts,
Theodotia Roberts Peter Rasor, Easter Rasor Elizabeth
Heaton & Joseph Heaton to Samuel Howard & George Brown
for three acres of land acknowledged in open court by
Joseph Heaton and admited to record let it be register-
ed

(P.107)
Saml Boyd &
J.I. Tipton
  Vs
John Moreland   It appearing to the satis-
            faction of the court that
            said Boyed & J. I. Tipton
as the security of the said Moreland have on yesterday had judgementrendered against them for eight
dollars & ninety cents the costs of Sci Fa against
said Boyd as bail of said Moreland.
  It is therefore on motion of J. P. Taylor att'y
considered by the court that Plff recover of the
defendant the said sum of eight dollars and ninety
cents for which they are liable together with the
costs of this motion.

Court adjourned untill courtin cause,
             Jereh Campbell.

(P.108)   State of Tennessee)
       Carter county   )   At a meeting of
                 a court of please
and quarter session Held for Carter county at the court
house in Elizabethton on the second Monday of November
in the year of our Lord 1827 Present the Worshipful
         John I. Wilson
         George Emmert
         John Richardson
         William Peoples
         Jessee Cole,
         John L Williams   and Esquires.

For reasons appearing to the court it is therefore
ordered by the court that Wm Cross & William Jones
be released from attending as jurors at this session

Ordered by the court that Martha Helton wife & ralike
of Moses Helton be appointed administratrex of all
and Singular the goods and chattles rights & credits
of Moses Helton Deceased and the said Martha Helton
come into open court and Entered into bond with Aaron
Finch her security in the sum of five hundred dollars
with condition see bond.

Elisha Smith appointed constable came into open court
and entered into bond in the sum of one thousand dollars with John L. Wilson and James I. Tipton his securities & took the Several oaths required by law for a
constable.

(P.109)   Ordered by the court that Elijah Smith be
allowed ten dollars seven & a half cents for articles
heretofore furnished Elizabeth Stephens one of the
poor of this county to be taken out of the allowance
heretofore made for said pauper she having Died at
six months after allowance.

Ordered by the court that Caty Colbough one of the
poor be allowed twenty five dollars for her support
& mantainance from May session 1826 up to May session
1827.

Ordered by the court that Dianna Sizemore be allowed
fourteen Dollars & ninety two cents & a half the
ballance due Elizabeth Stephen her mother one of the
poor of this county up to her death.

Ordered by the court that John Shavour be allowed
fifty Dollars for the Support and mantainance of
Omey Heatherly one of the poor of this county
for the year ending at this court.

Ordered by the court that James P. Taylor atto.
General be allowed fifty dollars for His Exofficio
Services from November session 1826 up to Novr.
Session 1827.

(P.110)   William Arnold produced in open court
the scalp of three Wolvs adjudged by the court one
over four months old and two under and the said
William Arnold being sworn upon his oath saith he
killed the wolves in the county aforesaid since the
first day Jany. 1811 and it appearing to the Satisfaction of the court that said Wm Arnold killed said

wolves in the county aforesaid it is therefore ordered
that the sd Wm Arnold be allowed seven Dollars for
killing sd wolves to be paid out of the state treasury.

Ordered by the court that Matthias Keen one of the
poor be allowed fifty five Dollars for his support and
maintainance from November session 1825 up to Novr.
session 1826.

Ordered by the court that Matthias Keen one of the poor
be allowed fifty five Dollars for his support and maintainance from November session 1826 up to Novr. session 1827.

Ordered by the court that Julius D. Arnold be fined two
Dollars for swearing in presence and in contempt of
court and threatining one of the court and be in custody of the sheriff untill fine and costs be paid.

(P.111)   Ordered by the court that Peter Holt
overseer of the public road from David Haines'sfence
to the county line hence the following hands,
Wm B. Holt Silas Helton Alexr. Vance Isaac Carroll
Abrm Miller Tho McInturff Wm Carroll Tho Gillis
Cavender Brumet John Wright Elezar Watson Wilson
Maddox and the hands on George Haines's farm to be
the hands to work on said road.

Ordered by the court that George Geenway Be appointed overseer of the public road in the room of Archibald
West and that the Hands fomerly under West be the
hands to work on said road under Greenway & &.

Ordered by the court that George Lacey be appointed
overseer of the public road in the Room of Abial C.
Parker and have the Same hands & bound that Parker
had

Ordered by the court that Lucas Emmert be appointed
overseer of the public road in the room of Jesse
West and have the same hands & bound that West had.

Ordered by the court that Jeremiah Whaley Be appointed
overseer of the public road in the room of Abraham
Whaley & have the same Hands and bounds that Abrm.
Whely had.

(P.112)   Ordered by the court that Nathn. Burchfield
overseer of the public road in the Limestone cove.
Have the following hands to work on said Road towit

Isam Morris, John Morris Nathn. Burchfield Jr. Reuben
Burchfield Wm Gourley & James Smith.

Ordered by the court that the following hands be attached
to the former hands of David Gwinn towit Henry Gourley,
Samuel Gourley Benja. Hyder James Dugless Jas. Carpenter
Isaac Miller Benja Grindstaff & Henry Simmerly.

Ordered by the court that the following persons be sum-
moned a jurors to the March Term of 1828.
Solomon Hendrix Jacob Range Richard Kelly Joseph Obrian
Valuntine Bowers Campbell Crow Moses Huffman Thomas
Gourley Jonathan H. Hyder Joseph W. Renfroe Richard
Greer Jonathan Pugh Thomas Hatcher Joseph Combs Wm Baker
Robert Reave Thos McInturf Christian Carriger John Nave
Owen Edwards Saml. Oxford John Shuffield Elisha Rainbolt
Jacob Vanhuse Joel Dugger

(P.113)   Ordered by the court that the following
persons be summoned as jurors to serve at theFebruary
session of the court 1828   (Viz)
William Crow Solomon Cross Thos Crow John Hatcher
Jenkins Emanuel Patton, Saml. E. Joseph Rowe Lewis
Morgin Thos H. Johnston Andrew Shoun Wm Jones Boyles
Miller Jonathan Poland Saml. Erwin Larkin Thompson
Leonard Bowers George Lacy Abraham Nave Thomas Buck
Wilson Maddox Abraham Miller Wm B. Holt William Doran
Nickolas Grindstaff Joseph robinson Aaron Owen.

Ordered by the court that David Prise and Mathias
Waggoner be appointed overseers of the Road in the
Rume   and Stead of Joseph Ausbourn and Joseph Shoun
Resigned & have the same bounds & hands that Ausburn
& Shoun had.

Exhibited and acknowledged in open court a power of
atto. from Martha Helton widow Ralikes & Admrx. of
Moses Helton Decsd. to John Blair Esqr. to recieve
from the proper office of the United States the
amount of monthly & Extra pay & & due and owing
her interstate or whatsoever may be due her inter -
state & admited to record & &.

(P.114) A deed of conveyance from Andrew McHenry
to Samuel Howard for one hundred acres of land proven
in open court Andrew Baker A subscribing witness and
ordered to becontinues for the probet of one of the
other witnesses

John Sander's)
    Vs   )   Godfrey Carriger & Christian
John Stuart)   Carriger Execr. Vs John Stuart
                  and John Carriger Vs John

Stuart. In their causes James Hughes was summond to attend as a Guarnishe and disclose accordingly who JohnStuart
is endebted to him by Execution which amounted in whole
costs Interest and primciple to one hundred and sixty
dollars or thereabout under these executions his property was lately sold and I bought two sets of Blacksmith
tools for forty one dollars which is to be credited
unless John Stuart should pay me my bid and then I will
let him have the tools again. being first sworn statesthat
To secure these debts John Stuart gave me a note on
Obrian Gott and Obrian for twelve hundred and fifty
dollars in Iron at one hundred and fifty dollars pr
ton payable at their Forge on Doe River due the first
day of January one thousand eight hundred and twenty
Eight for which note I gave his my reciept in which
I acknowledged I hold said note to secure the payment
of the said four judgements which I have against the
said Stuart until he payes me the debts if paid before
the note is due and if not I am to receive the Iron
and hold that without Interest till he satisfies the
debt then I am bound to pay over the note on Iron to the
holder of my reciept my Execution ran at Stuarts request and had them levied on his property and I hold
the note and Blacksmith tools untill I get (P115)
my money and my reciepts his corn and household furniture was sold at the same time under Renfros Executions my executions levied on the ballance of his property to satisfy them to be sold next Friday.
I did not direct my Execution to run myself but
Stuart wished it done & I told him he might do as he
pleased and some how or other they were reused and
levied & &. He knows of no body else indebted to him
and who has effects in his hands & & He says he is not
endebted to him Stuart and that he has no effects of h
his unless as before stated. This note I have fild
since las t spring.

Court adjourned untill tomorrow till nine O'Clock,

                              John I. Wilson,
                              Geo. Emmert
                              John Richardson.

November 13th 1827 Court met according to adjournment.
present , John Richardson, John I Wilson George Emmert
J. Campbell.

(P. 116)

William Dixon	)
Vs	)
Mark Reeves	)
Casper Reeve W.	)
Robert Reeve	)
Whitte Reeve	)
Clayton Reeve	)

In this cause the Defendant
came onto open court and con-
fess judgement for the sum Ɖ
of one Hundred and fifty four
dollars & twenty two cents.
It is therefore considered by
the court that the plaintiff
recover of the defendant the sum of one hundred and
fifty four dollars and twenty two cents the sum confessed as aforesaid together with the costs which he hath
in this behalf expended and that the Defendants be in
mercy & & Stay Execution two months.

John Smith Executor & &	)
Vs	)
Joseph Scott	)
Samuel Scott	)
Isaac Scott	)
William Scott	)

William Carter Shff returned
an Execution Issued by a justice of the peace in favor Ɖ
of the plaintiff against the
Deft's for the sum of Seventy
one dollars and twenty Eight
cents and a fourth of a cent Debt, and one Dollars and
seventy five cents costs search made no goods and
chattles found in my county to levy said execution on
but levied on one hundred acres of land in Carter county as the property of Isaac & William, Joseph and
Samuel Scott living in Carter county on Lick creek
adjoining James Hughes and others the sixth day of
November eighteen Hundred and twenty seven

W. Carter Shff. and it appearing to the satisfaction
of the court by the return of sd. Sheriff that (that)
there (P.117) is no goods and chattles of the defendants to be found. It is therefore ordered by the
court that the sheriff sell said lands of so much as
shall be of value suffucient to satisfy said Executions
and costs of this motion

A Power of Attorney from Casper W. Reeve J. White
Reeve Clayton Reeve Hannah Ann Reeve and Sarah W.
Reeve to Benjamin Davis of the county of Burlington
and State of New Jersey to settle with Sarah P. Whitall
administratrix of John G. Whitall deceased and with
Charles Whitall who with the said John. G. Whitall both

of Gloucester county State of New Jersey adminstrators
of Sarah Reeve dec'd and of the estate of Maria Whitall
dec'd the said John G. Whitall having departed this
life before a full settlement hath been made with the
said Sarah Reeve Maria Whitall has been left his widow
Sarah P. Whitall sole Executrix of his Estate and to
receive from them all money goods & property of ever
description to which we are either of us may be in-
titled as heirs or distributees of the said Sarah Reeves
our Grand mother and of the said Maria Whitall her
daughter and to give legal and Sufficient acquitances
and to do all acts which may be requisite on proper fp,
for the recovery of said money or property was proven
inopen court by Samuel Smitherman and John Garland and
admited to record.

Ordered by the court that Robert Reeve be appointed
Guardian to Rebecca T Reeve and thesaid Robert Reeve
came into open court and entered into Bond in the
final sum of two thounsad dollars for the faithful
preformance of his Gaurdinship .

(P.118)   Ordered by the court that Jonathan
Poland be appointed overseer of the public road in
the room of Archibald West and the former order be
resinded as to Greenway and the said Poland have
the same hands and bounds that said West had.

Ordered by the court that Casper G able be appointed
overseer of the public road in the room of James Bunton
and have the same bounds and hands that Bunton had.

A bill of sale from William Massengill to Solomon G.
Ward for one negro man Slave aged about fifty named
Jack and one negro woman aged about thirty five named Joice and one male child named Dick aged about six
months was acknowledged in open court & admitted to
record let it be registered.

A deed of conveyance from Peter Hunt to Benjamin
Cole for seventy five acres of land acknowledged
in open court by the maker thereof and admited to
record Let it be registered.

A deed of conveyance from Jesse Smith & Mary his
wife formerly Mary Carriger Caleb B. Cox and Anna
formerly Anna Carriger and William A Harris and
Elizabeth his wife formerly Elizabeth Carriger to
Samuel Crawford for one hundred acres acknowledged
in open court by Caleb B. Cox and Anna Cox his wife
being examined separately and apart from her said
husband by the court touching her free consent of
*and fifty

signing sealing and delivering the same saith that
She executed the same freely voluntarily and of her
oun accord without fear threat or persuasion of her
said husband admitted to record on the part of the
said Caleb B. Cox and Anna his wife and continued for
the acknowledgement of probit of the other obligors.

Ordered by the court that William Simerly be appointed
overseer of the public road by way of Gap creek from
the top of the deviding ridge between Doe river cove
and Gap creek to the end of the lane Boyds old farm
and work the hands of Michael Hyders farms on Gap
creek and Joseph Hyders farm and Hampton Hyders farm
Saml Peoples (Peples) farm and Jhon Emmon farm widow
Overbees farm Samuel Lusks farm John McKeehen farm
Samuel McKeehen farm Elijah Elkins farm.

An article of agreement between Godfrey Carriger dec'd
and the subscribers towit, Henry Nave John Taylor
Christian Carriger Mordicai Williams David Nave
William Allen Christian Nave Robert Blevins Caleb B.
Cox John T. Bowers John T. Allen William Bishop John
Nave Junr. Benjamin White Andrew Emmerd William Taylor
Jeremiah Cannon Israel Cole Sr. Levi Nave and W. N.
ardin for a donation of land to build a shool or
meeting house on proven in oben court by William
Allen and Caleb B. Cox and admited to record let it
be registere d.

McBee & Rineheart   )
       Vs   )   And the defend' having been
Robert Lewis   )   arrested on a Ca Sa Issued
                             by a justice of the peace
and the said Robert Lewis came into open court and took
the insolvent debtors oath and filed in court the following schedule of his property towit McBee and Rineheart
 Vs Robert Lewis in this case Ca Sa having been served
on defendant he returns, the following Schedule of his
property towit, one feather bed & bed clothes which he
claimes as exempt from Execution under the act of assembly,
              Robert Lewis

(P.120)
State   )
    Vs   )   Peace Warrant the attorney
John Fletcher)   General by leave of the court
                     enters a nole Prosequi and
the defendant came into court and assumes the costs.
It is therefore considered by the court that the State
recover of the Defendant the cost of this prosecution
according to his assumpsit and execution issued and
the defendant in mercy & &

State   )
 Vs   )   Peace Warrant the attorney General
William Have) by leave of the court enters a nole
        Prosequi and the defendant comes in-
to court and assumes the costs. It is therefore considered by the court that the state recover of the
defendant the costs of this prosecution according to
his assumpsit and the defendant in mercy & &.

Original Venire is releas'd from further attendance
at court.

Ordered by the court that Michael Lyon a juror of the
original pannel be released from any further attendance
at court.

Ordered by the court that Jul_ius A Dugger who was
ordered on yesterdy into the custody of the sheriff
be discharg'd from coustody.

State   )
 Vs   )   Indietmont Amos Gibson prosecutor
John Jones) The attorney General with leave of
        the court enters a nole prosequi
and the Defendant and Jas. W. Clawson Jr. came into
court and assumed the costs It is therefore considered by the court that the state recover of the defendand and James W. Clawson the costs of this prosecution according to thier assumption and the Defendant in mercy & &

(P.121)
Grand Jury, Samuel Montgomery foreman, Jacob Poland
Joseph Wilson William Banks George Cheffield William
Carrol Peter Have Bethuel Buck John Whitehead John
Ellis Samuel Montgomery John Fletcher Joseph Fletcher
Aaron Musgrave who were empanneled sworn and charged
Vincent Kelly aconstable sworn to attend the Grand
Jury Sci fa.

State   )
 Vs   ) The attorney General with leave of
John Jones) the court enters a nole Prosequi
        and the Defendant and James W. Claw-
son came into court and assume the costs. It is there-
foreconsidered by the court that the state recover of
the Defendant and Jas. W. Clawson the costs of this
prosecution according to their assumption an the defendant in mercy & &

State   )
   Vs   )   The attorney General with
Jas W. Clawson Jr)   leave of the court enters a
                    nole prosequi : the Defendant
comes into court and assumes the costs. It is therefore
considered by the court that the state recover of the
Defendant the costs of this prosecution and the Defendant in mercy & &.

(P.122)
State   )
   Vs   )   The attorney General with
James W. Clawson)   leave of the court enters
                    a nole prosequi and James
W. Clawson Jr came into court and assumes upon himself the costs. It is therefore considered by the
court *that James W. Clawson Jr the costs of said
prosecution and the Defendant in mercy & &.
*the state recover of the said

State   )
   Vs   )   The Defendant acknowledges
Arthur Sloan   )   himself indebeted to the
                    state in the sum of one hun-
dred dollars Aaron Finch & Alfred W. Taylor bail acknowledged themselves indebted to the state in the
sum of fifty Dollars each to be levied of thier goods
and chattles lands and Tennements to the use of the
state yet void on condition the said Sloan make his
personal appearance before the justice of our court
of please & & to be held for Carter county at the
court house in Elizabethton on the second Morlay in
February next towit, Tuesday second day of s'd
session then and there to answer to a plea of the
state and stand to and abide the judgement of the said
court and not depart the same without leave.

Ordered by the court that Abiel C. Parks be permitted
to keep an ordinary at Elizabethton for and during
the Term of one year on complying with the legal requisites of the law.

William Gott appointed to the commission of the peace
who came into open court and took the several oaths
required by law for a justice of the peace.

(P.123)   Smith, John   )
                Vs   )   Settled by award
            Even Heatherly &)   at equal costs.
            Thomas Heatherly)   It is therefore
                               considered by the
court that the Plaintiff Defendant recover of each
other thier & charges according to the award and that

the plaintiff and Defendants be in mercy to each other
& &.

Waugh & Finley)
   Vs   )   Covenant jury towit,
Isaac Tipton &)
James I. Tipton)

Samuel W. Williams Peter Wills William Allen Archibald
West Jacob Cammeron Peter Hunt Lewis Lewis Hugh McHenry
Samuel Howard John Koon Michael Hider Walter Blevins.
Good and lawful men chosen elected tried and sworn upon
thier oaths do find that the defendants have not kept
and preformed thier covenant as in their plea the alledged and assess the plaintiffs damage to one hundred
and fifty three dollars twenty four cents.
It is therefore considered by the court that the Plaintiff recover of the defendants the sum of one hundred
and fifty three dollars and twenty four cents by the
Jury aforesaid assessed and also there costs and charges in this behalf expended and the defendants in mercy
& &.

Lawson Goodwin)
   Vs   )   Case
Christopher Frick)   Jury towit.

Samuel W. Williams Peter Wills Archabald West William
Allen Jacob Cammeron Peter Hunt Lewis Lewis Hugh
McHenry Samuel Howard John Koon Michael Hider &
Walter Blevins, good and lawful men chosen elected &
Sworn upon thier oaths say they do find for the plaintiff (Plaintiff) (P.124) and assess his damage
to ten Dollars. It is therefore considered by the
court that the plaintiff recover of the Defendant the
sum of ten dollars assessed as aforesaid by the jury
aforesaid together with the costs which he hath about
his suit in this behalf expended an the defendant
in mercy & &. * tried

State)
   Vs   )   Continued on aft of Defend-
Robert Lewis)   ant comes into open court
                    and acknowledges himself in-
debted to the state in the sum of one hundred dollars
and Charles Lewis his Bail in the sum of fifty dollars
to be levied of their goods and chattles Lands an Tennements to the use of the state yet void on condition
the Defendant make his personal appearance at our
court of Please & &. to be held at the court house in
Elizabethton on the second Monday Febry next towit,

on Tuesday the second day of said Term and answer a
plea of the state and not depart the court without
leave first obtained.

Jacob Curtner for)
William Carter   )
        Vs   )   Covenant
Caleb Smith   )   The Defendant comes into
                           open court and confesses
judgement for the sum of one hundred and sixty two
Dollars Therefore it is considered by the court that
the Plaintiff recover against the Defendant the sum
of one hundred and sixty two dollars by him confessed
as aforesaid also his costs and charges in this behalf expended and that the Defendant be in mercy & &.
Stay execution three months.

(P.125)   George W. Greeway appointed to the commission of the peace came into court and took the
several oaths required by law for a justice of the
peace.

Lawson Goodwin   )
      Vs   )   Levellen Smithson summon-
Christopher Frick)   ed as a witness on behalf
                           the Deft being solemnly
called to come into court and give evidence on behalf
Christopher Frick came not but made default therefore
it is considered by the court that the sd. Levellen
Smithson forfeit agreeable to act of assembly and
that Sci Fa Issue & &.

Lawson Goodwin   )
      Vs   )   John Wilson and Lawson
Christopher Frick)   White prove there atten-
                           dance as witnesses in this
cause for three days each.

Court adjourned till tomorrow morning nine Oclock,
                              Jesse Cole,
                              John L Wilson,
                              G. Emmert
                              John Richardson.

(P.126)   November Session Wednesday 14th day of
the month court met according to adjournment present
the Worshipful,
              John Wilson
              George Emmert
              Jesse Cole &
              John Richardson.

Adam Rainbolt for)
Ezekiel Smith &)
Daniel Smith use)
    Vs) The defendants came
Hugh McHenry admr.) into court and con-
of Andrew McHenry &) fess judgment for
Hugh McHenry in his own right and) the sum of two hund-
Robert McHenry and Johnson Hampton) red and thirteen
    dollars.

It is therefore considered by the court that the plaintiff recover of the Defendants the sum of two hundred
and thirteen dollars the sum confessed by thedefendants
as aforesaid to be levied of the goods and chattles
of Andrew McHenry dec'd in the hands of Hugh McHenry
his administrator in the first instance and if nothing
is found then to be levied of the goods and chattles
lands & tenements of the defendant as also the costs
in this behalf expended.

State)
  Vs) Indictment.
Michael Slimp) The attorney General with leave of the
    court enters a nole Prosequi the De-
fendant comes into court and Joseph Slimp his Bail by
George W. Carter his attorney in fact comes into court
and assumes the costs. It is therefore considered by
the court that the state recover of the Defendant and
Joseph Slimp the cost of this prosecution and the defendant in mercy & &.

(P.127)
State)
  Vs) The attorney General with
Michael Slimp Sci Fa) leave of the court enters
    a nole prosequi and the
    Defendant assumes the costs
It is therefore considered by the court that the state
recover of the Defendant the costs about this prosecut-
ion expended and the Defendant in mercy & &.

State)
  Vs) Sci Fa.
Eli Rasor) The attorney General with leave of the
    court enters a nole Prosequi and the
Defendant assumes the cost. It is therefore considered
by the court that the state recover of the Defendant
the cost about this prosecution expended and the Defendant in mercy & &.

State   )
 Vs   ) Sci Fa The attorney General with leave
Jacob Slimp) of the court enters a nole prosequi
       and the defendant assumes the cost.
It is therefore considered by the court that the state
recover of the Defendant the costs of this Sci Fa and
the defend't in in mercy & &

Peter Parson)
 Vs   ) The plaintiff by his attorney comes
John Stuart &) into court and dismisses his suit and
Robert Stuart) and the Defendant came into court and
     assume the costs. It is therefore
considered by the court that the plaintiff recover of
the Defendant the cost which he hath about (about)
his suit in this behalf expended and the Defendants in
mercy & &.

(P.128)
Johnson Hampton)
 Vs   ) Case. In this cause came the
Jacob Mast) parties by their attorney
       and there upon a jury towit
Samuel Tinton Lewis Lewis Henry Grindstaff Samuel
Howard Joseph Cooper William Emmert Joseph Wilson
Abner McClude Hugh McHenry Greenberry Delashmit Jas.
Kerr and Benjamin Grindstaff good and lawful men
chosen tried and sworn the truth to speak upon the
issue joined between the parties thereupon the plain-
tiff by his attry. enters a non suit.
It is therefore considered by the court that the Defendant go hence without day and recover of the plaintiff
the costs which he hath about his defence in this behalf expended and the plaintiff for his false clames .

In the progress of the above cause of Hampton against
Most a Bill of exceptions was tendered and signed
and sealed and made a part of this record.

Gurtridge Garland   )
David Garland   )
Exmr. of Ezekiel Garland Dec'd)
   Vs   ) Debt. In this
Nathan Birchfield   ) cause came the
Wm Baker   ) Plaintiff by
            there attorney
and the Def't being Solemnly called come into court
and Defend this suit came not but made default.
It is therefore considered by the court that the
plaintiffs recover of the Defendants one hundred and

ninety four dollars and fifty cents the debt and
interest in the Plaintiffs declaration mentioned
together with the costs in this behalf expended.

(P.129)
John Smith)
   Vs)   This is continued as an affidavit
Lewis Lewis)   of the plaintiff.

Johnson Hampton)
   Vs)   Reuben Mast a witness proven
Jacob Mast)   7 days attendance in this
                      cause and also two hundred &
eighty miles traveling.

William Atkins)
   Vs)   By the agreement of the part-
Aaron Musgrave &)   ies time to next court is
Joseph Wilson)   given to declare plead & con-
                      tinued.

On motion It is ordered by the court that Wm Messick be
permitted to keep an ordinary in the Town of
Elizabethton for the space of one year from this date
he complying with the requisites of the law relating
thereto.

William Atkins)
   Vs)   For reason appearing to the
Aaron Musgrave)   satisfaction of the court
Joseph Wilson)   that a commission or commiss-
                      ions issue to any Justice of
the peace for Ash county state of North Carolina to
take the Depositions of Abner Smith and Thomas Suther-
land to be read as evidence on the trial of this cause
on giving ten days notice of the time and place of
taking the same to the defendant.

(P. 130)
James P. Taylor)
   Vs)   In this cause
The heirs of Andrew McHenry Dec'd.)   a scirei Facias
                      having been iss-
ued returnable to this court against Joseph Cooper
guardian of the minor heirs of said McHenry dec'd
and against Hugh McHenry Charles Hayes and Nancy his
wife formerly Nancy McHenry and Margaret McHenry the
other heirs of said McHenry dec'd and having now been
return'd made known to Joseph Cooper and not found
to be made known unto as the other it is ordered by
the court that as alias Sci Fa issue as to the last
mentioned heirs returnable to our next county court.

Tipton, Samuel)
    Vs   )
Jesse Jones)

In this cause Wm Carter by
James I. Tipton his deputy
sheriff having return'd an
execution that nothing of the defendants could be
found in his court of which to satisfy the same and
that he had summond Greenbury Delashmit as a gaurnis-
hee who being call'd appear'd in court and made the
following Disclosure towit, " That Jesse Jonespurches'd
of Samuel Tiptonhis interest in the Doe river forge
for a consideration payable in iron & grain his notes
& & and afterwards the garnishee & Lewis Anderson
purchas'd said Forge of Jones and held Jones bond for
the title and Jones (hald)   said Tipton bound for
title "the garnishee & said Anderson and bound to
pay the debt to Samuel Tipton & this debt upon which
Judgement in got by Tipton (P.131) an execution issued in one of the debts said garnishee and Anderson
"an bound to pay the next debt due by Jones to Tipton
became due 1st Janry next which an as aforesaid an
bound to pay and for two tons & a half of Iron as he
believes there are two other notes one for two and a
half tones and the other for three as he belives due
each January afterward For which we are bound as aforesaid garnishee has possession of the works since 28th
Feby last and has paid no rent but has*some iron on the
note which is matured into judgt and credited at the
rendition as he believes, *paid
    Said executier in predicated on a judgement render-
ed 15th August 1827 for one hundred and eighty eight
dollars & forty three cents and costs nine dollars and
thirty one and a half cents.
    It is therefore considered by the court that the
debt due by garnishee to Jones be condition'd his hands
for the use of plff & that the garnishee surrender to
the sheriff of Carter county so much bar iron as will
be sufficient according to the price put upon the iron
in the recovery against Jones as will be sufficient to
pay and satisfy the Plaintiffs debt cost & charges and
the costs of this garnishment & that the sheriff sell
the same accordingly and that execution issue favoring the Plaintiff against the said Delashmit for the
said sum of one hundred and eighty dollars & forty
three cents with the interest and the further sum of
nine Dollars & thirty one and a half cents costs with
the costs of this suit discharable by the said
Delashmit surrendering to the Sheriff the Iron as afore
said and that the defendant in mercy & &. * eight

Monday Nov. 14th 1827

(P.132)   Continuation of the garnishment of James
Hughs Towit "James Hughs being examined further states
that the tools were sold as the property of John Sturt
as he understood that the said   executions "against
John & Robert Sturt and whether they were sold as Roberts
or not he does not know or how the office will apply
the money I "answer myself bound to deliver the note
or the Iron to who ever delivers my reciept on my get-
ting my money I took upon my reciept the same as my
note He does not consider himself inlebted to John
Sturt not does he know of any body else owing him but
Obrian got and Obrian as aforesaid - nobody got me to
buy the tools I bought them of my own accord- It was
not my éntention to defraud Sturts creditors "in the
purchase In these several causes executions having
been issued by the clerk of the court of Pleas & for
Carter county returnable to the present sessions of
the county court with the following ballance due there
on towit John Sanders as John Sturt.
One hundred dollars sixty six cents price & interest
Godfrey & Christian Carriger Exrs. Vs John Sturt
fifty six dollars & fifty cents princ'l & Interest
John Carriger Vs John Sturt one hundred and twenty
dollars & fifty four cents princ'l & interest.
and that he could find nothing of the defendants on
which to levy said executions but that he had sum-
mon'd James Hughs as a garnishee (P.133) in said
cases who appear'd in court and being sworn according
to law made the forgoing disclosures and the court
now here having heard said examinations and heard argument thence and fully understood the same do consider order and adjudge that the note held by the
said Hughes on Obrian got & Obrian for Twelve hundred and fifty dollars in bar iron at one hundred
and fifty Dollars per ton payable at thier Forge on
Doe river due the first day of January 1828 be given
up by the said Hughes to the sheriff of Carter county
and that he sell the same or so much thereof as will
be of value sufficient to satisfy the said John Sanders
the said sum of one hundred Dollars sixty six cents
and the said Godfrey and Christian Carriger Exrs. the
said sum of fifty six dollars and fifty cents and the
said John Carriger the said sum of one hundred and
twenty dollars and fifty four cents principle & interest with all costs and charges and the costs of this
garnishment subject to the ballance due said Hughs on
his executions being first paid and satisfied and
that execution issue accordingly-

From which judgement of the court the said James Hughs pray'd an appeal in the motion of a writ of error to our next circuit court to be held at Elizabethton on the third Monday of March next which is granted & enters into bond and security accordingly.

(P.134)   John Sanders Vs John Sturt Godfrey & Christian Carriger Exrs. John Sturt, John Carriger Vs John Sturt. for as much as it appears from the garnishment of James Hughes taken in these causes that the fine of Obrian Tot Obrian as indebted to the said John Sturt by note in iron twelve hundred and fifty Dollars at one hundred and fifty per Ton payable the first of January sixt at thier Forge on Doe River & that they have not been summond on motion of the Plaintiff it is ordered by the court that a judicial attachment issue at the suit of each of said Plffs to be levied in the hands of Obrian Tot & Obrian and who shall appear and answer a garnishee &c &c.

(P.135)   Ordered by the court that William Peoples Esqr. take in a list of the taxable property and polls in Capt McInturff District for the year 1828. John S. Williams Esquire Capt Pattons District George W. Greenway Esqr. Capt Courley District George Emmert Esqr. Capt Drakes old District. John Richardson Esqr. Capt   Haves District Jeremiah Campbell Esqr. Capt Grindstaff District Lawson White Esqr. Capt Clawsons District Richard Donally Esqr. Capt Arnolds District and Jesse Cole Esqr. Capt Jacksons District.

A deed of conveyance from Charles N. George, Peter Hunt & Nancy Hunt to Jesse Cole for one hundred and twenty five acres was acknowledged in open court by the maker thereof and the said Nancy Hunt wife of Peter Hunt being examined by the court seperate and apart from her husband touching her freedom in execution the said deed said she executed the same freely voluntarily of her own free choice without the persuasion or any other undue influence of her husband or any other was as to the said obligors admitted to record let it be registered.

(P.136)
John Kennedy &)
Thomas D. Greer)
John Kennedy &)
Thomas Emmerson)
& Isaac Wilson)
        Vs   )   In this cause William Carter
Henry D. Johnson) sheriff by his Deputy James
John Stuart   Garnishee) I Tipton having returned the
                           following Execution towit.
Kennedy and Greer againt Henry D. Johnston Kennedy and
Emmerson against said Johnston and Isaac Wilson against
the said Henry D. Johnston, indorsed thereon no proper-
ty found of said Johnston out of which to satisfy said
Execution and also having sum moved John Stuart as a
garnishee who being called came into court and being
first duly sworn according to law made the following
statement and disclosure I sold to Henry D. Johnston
the house and lot I formerly owned in Elizabeth on
which Jesse Adams now lives which he paid me for every
cent but I have never Executed to said Johnston a deed
for said property and the title is still in ned
I do not know that, I ever gave hima bound for a title
but am certain I never made him a deed , I do not owe
Henry D. Johnston anything and except the aforesaid
house and lot I have none of the Effects of said Johnston in my hands nor do I know of any in the hands
of any other person the aforesaid Executions are predi-
cated on judgements abtained in this county court
against the said Henry D. Johnston as follows towit.
Kennedy & Greer against Henry D. Johnston for thirty
nine Dollars forty five cents debt five dollars &ten
cents cost Kennedy &Emmerson against said Johnston
for sixty nine Dollars thirty seven & half cents Debt
& ten dollars seventeen & half cost and Isaac Wilson
against said Henry D. Johnston for Eighty dollars debt
ten dollars & fifty seven & half cents costs.
    It is therefore considered by the court that the
plaintiffs recover of the said John Stuart garnishee
as aforesaid the said sumes of money towit.
Kennedy & Greer the sum of forty four (P.137)
Dollars fifty nine cents and Kennedy and Emmerson the
sum of seventy nine Dollars fifty five cents and Isaac
Wilson the sum of ninety dollars fifty seven & half
cents together with the costs of this garnishment
subject nevertheless to be satisfied by the sale of the
said house and lot in Elizabethton and that Execution
issue accordingly.

Vincent Kelly constable proves two days on the Grand
Jury at the November sessions of this court 1827.

John Nave Jr   )
    Vs   )   Vincent Kelly
Riland Murray &   )   constable re-
Jabez Murray his security)   turned to court
                                        a Ca Sa Issued
                                        by a justice of
the peace favoring John Nave Jr against Riland Murray
for the sum of six dollars eighteen cents debt and one
Dollar cost together with a bond with Jabez Murray
his security to appear at the court of please and
quarter sessions towit, at the court house in Elizabeth
ton on the second Monday of November 1827 then and there
to pay the aforesaid sum of money on surrender his property or take the bendfit of the insolvent debtors oath
and the said Riland Murray failing to appear to pay the
sd. money or surrender his property or take the insolvent debtors Oath on motion of the sd. John Nave by
his attoy. Wm K. Blain it is considered by the court
that the sd. John Nave Jr.

(P.138)recover of the said Riland Murray and the said
Jabez Murry   his security
the said sum of six Dollars and eighteen cents and also
the costs and charges and also the costs of this motion
and the Defendant in mercy & &.

Pharoh Cobb for the use of W. Massengale & C. W. Rutledge adr. of D. Sturt dec'd -Vs- John Sturt.
Now filed time allow'd deft to plead so not to delay
the trial.

Wm F. Harris assignce & &)
    Vs   )   Now filed a time
John Sturt   )   allowd. the deft.
                          to plead so as not
to delay the trial at next court.

Isaac Taylor Jur. assignce)
    Vs   )   Covenant In this
Charles Berry   )   cause the deft
                          being solemnly
call'd to defend his suit came not but made default
and for as much as Plffs damages or uncertain it is
order'd that a jury come at our next court and inquire of the damages the plff has sustain'd & &.

Wm P. Cherts   )
        Vs   )   Time to plead so as not to
John Hampton   )   delay.

(P.139)
W. B. Carter   )
      .Vs   )   Continued.
A & S Fulton   )

David Wade   )
        Vs   )   Continued.
Wm Carter   )
)
J. Keys   )
J. Hampton &   )
J. Campbell   )

H. D. Johnson for)
E. Carters use   )
        Vs   )   Continued
James B. Morley   )

Jacob Curtner   )
        Vs   )   Continued.
Vaut   (Vaught) Heaton)

John Smith   )
        Vs   )   Continued.
Lewis Lewis   )

Samuel Bailey &   )
Pleasant Profit   )   On motion of the plaintiffs
        Vs   )   counsel a rule is granted to
Jacob Slimp   )   shew cause why the certionari
                           should be dismissed and it is
considered by the court on hearing the causes assigned
that the rule be made absolute and that this cause be
dismissed and the plaintiff recover of the Defendant
& security John Jones the amount of the judgement before the justice (P.140) being twenty eight dollars
fifty seven & half cents debt and one dollar costs
with twelve and half per cent per annum interest
thereon together with the costs accrued on the certionari and the defendant in mercy &c.

George W. Rutledge)
   Vs   )   Continued
Joseph C. West)

Abiel C. Parks prays the court that his mark may be
recorded which is granted which mark is as follows
towit two under Keels one each ear.

Court adjourn'd untill tomorrow nine oclock,

                  Jesse Cole,
                  John Richardson
                  Geo. Emmert.

      Thursday Novr. 1827

Court met according to adjournment, Geo. Emmert John
Richardson and Jesse Cole Esqrs.

For reasons appearing to the court It is ordered by
the court that Charles Bassendine be released from
the tax on two hundred and fifty acres of land for
the year 1823 & 1824.
Court adjourned until court in course,
                  Jesse Cole,
                  Geo. Emmert
                  J. Richardson.

(P.141)
State of Tennessee)
Carter county   )   At a meeting of court of
                  please & quarter sessions
opened and held for Carter county at the court house
in Elizabethton on the second Monday of February in
the year of our Lord 1828 and the fifty second of
American Independance present the Worshipful,
           Jeremiah Campbell
           George Emmert
           John L. Wilson
           William Peoples
           George Greenway
           John Richardson
           James Hays
           Richard Donally
           John Hampton
           J. White.
Five Justice present, Reuben Carver produced in open
court the scalp of a wolf adjudged over six months
old.

James Chambers produced in open court the scalp of a
wolf adjudged over six months, old (nd to Tipton)

Eppy Woodby produced in open court the scalp of a
wolf adjudged to be over six months old-
And the said Reuben Carver James Chambers and Eppy
Woodby being sworn, upon their oaths say that thay
killed the wolves in the county aforesaid since
the 1st day of January 1811 and it appearing to the
satisfaction of the court that the said Reuben
Carver, James Chambers and Eppy Woodby killed the
wolves in the county aforesaid it is therefore
ordered that the said Reuben Carver, James Chambers
& Eppy Woodby be allowed the sum of three dollars
each to be paid out of the state Treasury for killing
said wolves.

Ordered by the court that A. C. Parks and C. Smith
be appointed commissioner to settle with the collectors of the county rivenue for 1828 agreeable
to act of assembly of 1827.

(F.142) Green Moor appointed to the commission
of the Peace came into open court and took the several
oaths required by law for a justice of the peace.

Ordered by the court that Thomas McInturf overseer
of the Mill road from said McInturfs to David Waines's
mill & house the following hands to work on said road
(towit) Isaac Carroll, Abram Miller and Jacob Miller

Ordered by that Robert Maclin be appointed a commissioner to settle with the Entry taker of the county
aforesaid.   Isd

Ordered by the court that Lawson White and Johnson
Hampton Esquires Be appointed a committie to settle
with Hugh McHenry administrator of Andrew McHenry
Deceased and report to next court.

John Richardson Esqr. returned a list of the taxable
property & poles in Capt Haves District for 1828.

Ordered by the court that Tho. McInturf John Wright
Saml. Bogart Israel McInturf Jesse Maddox, David
Haines Caldwell Brown, Ephraim Buck, George Haines,
Jacob Miller & (F.143) Wm McNabb, be appointed a
jury to view Mark and lay off a road from John
Wilsones to David Waines Mill & report to next court.

Ordered by the court that, Lawson Goodwin, be appoint-
ed overseer of the road from the Mrs. Mary Smiths to L.
Whites to intersect the road on Bones creek at David
Brummets.

Ordered by the court Wm Obrein be appointed overseer
of the public road in the room of Jacob Simmerly and
have the same hands and bounds that Simmerly had.

Ordered by the court that Leonard Morgan be appointed
overseer of the public road in the room of John I
Ingram and that he have the same hands and bounds
that Ingram had.

Ordered by the court that Joseph Howel be appointed
overseer of the public road in the room of John Brit
and have the same hands & Bounds that Brit had.

(P.144)   Ordered by the court that John Loyed be
appointed overseer of the public road in the room of
Jeremiah Whaley from Julius Buggers to Vanhooses
and have the same hands and bounds.

Ordered by the court that the hands living on Caldwell
Browns farm and David Dichs farm be attached to the
Hands of Adam McInturf hands overseer of the public
road from the fork of the road on Nathl. McNabbs
land to the county line towards Jonesborough.

Ordered by the court that Edward Pondry be appointed
overseer of the public road from the mile post in
Wm Greens lane to the road that leads from Elizabethton
to Reeves Iron works and that the hands living on the
farms of Saml. Lucks farm on the McNabb branch Saml.
Pattons farm Tho. Rows' farm John Havns farm George
Havns farm and George Williams's farm be the hands to
work on said road.

Ordered by the court that a certificate Issue to
Elizabeth Humphreys for her allowance from Feby.
session 1827 up to Feby. session 1828 for ten Dollars.

(P.145)   Ordered by the court that 1 David Nave
2 Joseph Glimn, 3 James Hampton 4 Jacob Simmerly,
5 Abram. Drak, 6 Danel Stover 7 Isaac Fite Senr.
8 Jacob Koon 9 Lazarus C. Inman 10 Jas. Clark, 11
John Keener, 12 Israel McInturf, 13 William Baker
14 Isaac Shoun 15 Abrm Low, 16 John Thell, 17 John
Dugger Jr, 18 Casper Cable 19 Joseph Renfro 20
John Fletcher 21 Wm Nave, 22 Caleb Smith 23 Daniel
Neel, 24 Joseph Vaught, 25 Abrm Nave &26 Lewis Wills
be jurors to May session 1828.

The assignment of a plat & certificate of Survay from
David Gwinn to William Jones for fifty acres of land
acknowledged in open court by the said David Gwinn

and amited to record let it be certified to the register of the land office & &.

Exhibited and acknowledged in open court a deed of
conveyance from Valentine Bowers to Eli Wave for one
hundred acres of land and admited to record let it be
registered.

(P.146) Exhibited and acknowledged in open court
a deed of conveyance from Alfred W. Carter to Henry
Wave for one hundred and twenty five acres of Land
and admited to record let it be registered.

Ordered by the court that a contingent tax be laid
levied and collected for the year 1828.
On each 100 acres of land   12½
On each town lot ----------------- 25
On each free poll---------------- 12½
On each Slave-------------------- 25
On each Stud or Jack the season
of one mare on each Merchant---500
On each Hawker or pedlar ------2-50

That an addition tax be laid levied and collected for
the year 1828 on each 100 acres of land---12½
On each town lot------- -----------------25
On each free poll-----------------------12½
On each slave---------------------------25
On each Stud or Jack--------------------25
On each Merchant------------------------250
On each Hawker or pedlor----------------1-25

A deed of conveyance Joseph Heaton & others to Saml.
Howard & George Brown for three acres of land ack-'d
in open court by the said Jos. Heaton and admited
to record let it be registered ack'd & recorded on
the part of the others heretofore May session 1827.

(P.147) Ordered by the court that a county poor
tax be laid levied and collected for the year 1828.
On each 100 acres land-----------------19¾/4
On each town lot-- -------------------37½
On each free poll-------- -------------19¾/4
On each slave --------------------------37½

    A majority of the justices present the court pros-
ceded to the Selection of five Justices for the hold-
ing court for the year 1828 towit Wm E. Carter,
Green Moore, George Emmert, James Keyes & William Gott
Esquires.
Court adjournd untill tomorrow nine oclock,
                              Geo. Emmert
                              J. Keyes
                              W. B Carter
                              William Gott
                              G. Moore.

(P.148)   Tuesday February the 12th 1828

Court met according to adjournment.
Present the Worshipful,
                    William B. Carter,
                    Green Moore
                    George Emert
                    James Keys and
                    William Cott   Esquires.

On motion ordered by the court that James P. Rhea Esqr.
be appointed solicter protorm.

State   )
  Vs   )   By leave of the court the
Johnathan M. Drummet)   atto Genl. enters an Nole-
                               prosequi & that the county
pay the costs and that the clerk issue certificate
for the same.

Ordered by the court that Wm Doran & Samuel E. Patton
be released from attending as jurors at this session.

William Carter Shff. returned the Venirci Facias
Executed from which the following persons was drawn
gran' Jurors and the court appointed, George Lacy
Foreman, Larkin Thompson, Solomon Cross Wm Jones
Joseph Robinson Andrew Chown Wilson Paddox Lewis
Morgan Abraham Nave Abraham Miller Tho. Buck, John
Hatcher and Bailss Miller.
    Impaneled sworn and charged & withdrew.

Vincent Holly constable sworn to attend the grand
jury.

(P.149)   Five Justices present, Uriah Banks, produced in open court the scalp of a wolf adjudged by the
court over six months months old, & the said Uriah
Banks Being sworn upon his oath saith that he killed
sd. wolf in Carter county since the First day of January 1811, and it appearing to the satisfaction of the
court that said Uriah Banks killed said wolf in the
county aforesaid it is therefore ordered by the court
that said Uriah Banks be allowed three dollars for killing said wolf to be paid out of the state Treasuer.

State   )
  Vs   )   And the Defendant being
Arthur Sloan   )   charged upon the bill of
                              Indietment and for plea
there to saith that he is not guilty thereof and
puts himself on his country and James P. Taylor atto.

Genl. who prosecutes on behalf the state do the same
whereupon came a jury & the Jurors of that Jury towit,
Samuel Erwin William Cross Aaron Owins Joseph Roe
Nickolas Grindstaff Manuel Jenkins Caleb Cox John Cook
William Obrien Abraham Whaley John Haun &Daniel Odonel
Chosen Elected tried & sworn upon thier oaths, say do
find the Defendant Guilty in manner & form as charged
in the bill of Indictment, it is therefore ordered by
the court that said Arthur Sloan be fined twenty five
cents pay the costs of this prosecution and be in
mercy & &.

(T.150)
David McNabb)
       Vs)   Plaintiff Dismisses his suit
Samuel Lusk)   .   & Defendant assumes costs
                     therefore it is considered
by the court that the plff. recover of the defendant
his costs and charges put to and about his suit in
that behalf Expended and that the defendant may be in
mercy & &.
    14th Feby 1828 Rec'd the fees Geo Williars.

Archibald Williams &)
George D. Williams)
       Vs)   And now at this day came the
George W. Carter)   parties by their attornies
                     and thereupon came a Jury and
the Jurors of that Jury towit,
Benjamin Ryder Wm Allen Tho. Nave Abner McLeod Nickolas
Fayn James Heatherly Samuel Howard David Powers Samuel
Drake John Matheway and George Blevins, chosen Elected
tried and sworn upon thier oaths, say do find that the
Defendant hath not paid the debt in plffs declaration
mentioned and by reason of the Detention thereof assess
the plaintiffs damage to Eighteen dollars and sixty
nine cents therefore it is considered by the court
that the plaintiff recover over against the deft their
debt of one hundred & seventy eight Dollars & forty
cents costs aforesaid and Damage aforesaid.
By the Jury aforesaid in manner aforesaid and form
aforesaid assessed and also thier costs and charges
put to and about thier suit in that behalf Expended
and that the Defendant may be in Mercy & &.

(P.151)
Samuel Cranford)
       Vs)   And now at this day came the
David Odel)   parties aforesaid by thier
                     attorneys and there upon
came a Jury and that Jury towit,

Benjamin Hyder William Allen Thos. Nave Abner McLeod
Nich Payne James Heatherly Samuel Howard David Bowers
Samuel Drake John Hatheway and George Blevins Chosen
Elected, tried and sworn upon thier oaths say do find
that the defendant hath not paid the Debt in the plff
declaration mentioned and by reason of the detention
thereof assess the plaintiff Damage to thirty seven
Dollars therefore it is considered by the court that
the plaintiff recover of the Defendant the Debt in
the Declaration mentioned of four hundred & forty five
dollars 18cents and also his damages costs & charges
put to and about his suit in that behalf expended and
that the Defendant may be in mercy & &.

John Richardson Esqr returned a list of the taxable
property & polls in Capt. Haves District for the year
1828 and,

Jesse Cole Esqr. in Capt. Jacksons District for the
year 1828.

(F.152)   George W. Rutledge)
               Vs   )   In this case an
            Joseph C. West   )   attachment Having
                                        been Issued at the
suit of the plaintiff against the Defendant, and come
to the hands of William Carter sheriff of Carter county
& he having relieved said attachment to our August
court of please and quarter session of the county
court of Carter that he had attach'd one negroe boy
named Isaac the property of Joseph C. West the 30th
May 1827 also one Negroe named Billey 30th May 1827
and the said Joseph C. West having failed to replevy
(the)   the same agreeable to act of assembly all furt
her   proceedings on said attachment were staid by order
of the said court six months and the defendant nowbe-
ing solemly call'd came not but make default it is there
fore considered by the court that the plaintiff, recover of the Defendant five hundred and twelve dollars
the debt in the Declaration mentioned and thirty two
dollars twenty eight cents   thereon from the due
of said Debt together with his costs about his suit
in this behalf Expended and that the Defendant in
mercy & &

(153)   Jesse Cole Esqr. returned a list of the
taxable property & polls in Capt. Jackson District
for the 1828.

State) Charged plea not Guilty
Vs) Jury towit, Benjamin Tyder
Robert Lewis) Wm Allen Tho Nave Abner
McLeod Nich Payne Mecajah Brumit Samuel Howard
David Bowers Samuel Drake John Hatheway George Blevins
John Smith, chosen elected tried & sworn upon thier
oaths say do find the Defendant Guilty in manner ':
form as charged in the bill of Indietment it is therefore ordered by the court that the Defendant be fined
five dollars and in custody of the sheriff untill fine
& costs of this prosecution be paid & &

A deed of conveyance from John Nave to Christian
Carriger for one hundred and forty five acres of land
acknowledged in open court and admited to record let
it be registered.

A deed of conveyance from John Nave and Christian to
Thomas Foster for one Hundred and fifty acres of land
acknowledged in open court and admited to record let
it be registered.

(P.154) A deed of conveyance from John Nave senr.
to William Stover for ninety four acres of land acknowledged in open court and admited to record let it
be registered.

A deed of conveyance from Alfred M. Carter to Solomon
Ward for three hundred acres of land acknowledged in
open court and admited to record let it be registered.

A deed of conveyance from Alfred M. Carter to John
Nave for one hundred acres of land acknowledged in
open court and admited to record let it be registered.

A deed of conveyance from Alfred M. Carter to John
Nave for ninety four and a half acres of land acknowledged in open court and admited to record let it
be registered.

A deed of conveyance from Christian Carriger to
John Nave for one hundred and ninety acres of land
acknowledged in open court and admited to record
let it be registered.

A deed of conveyance from George Wilson to Thomas
Boar for one hundred and twelve and one half acres
of land lying and being in the county of Lincoln in
the state of Tennessee was acknowledged in open
court by the said Geo. Williams the maker thereof

and admited to record and ordered to be certified for
registration in the county Where the said land lies.

(P.155)   A bond from Nicholas Carriger to Godfrey &
C. Carriger.
Exhibited an proven in open court by John Stover and
Thomas Foster subscribing witnesses proven in open
court which is in the following Words towit know all
men by these present that I. Nicholas Carriger of
Lincoln county and State of Tennessee did on the eight
day of October 1813 purches a certain tract of land
containing five hundred acres lying & being in the
county and state aforesaid of Nathaniel Taylor of Carter county which land I Bought for Godfrey Carriger Senr.
for the sum of twenty five hundred Dollars which sum
was paid by the said Godfrey Carriger unto the said
Nathaniel Taylor in full payment for the land aforesaid
as will appear by the deed of conveyance bearing date
the 8th day of October 1813 now now therefore in consideration of the payment being made by the said
Godfrey Carriger Senr. now deceased I promise covenant
and agree to convey the before described tract of land
unto Godfrey Carriger and Christian Carriger Executers
of Godfrey Carriger deceased or thier assignees in as
full and ample a manner as it was conveyed to me by
said Nathaniel Taylor for the true and faithful perfor-
mance I do hereby bind Myself & my heirs in witness
whereof I have hereunto set my hand and seal this 24th
day of March 1826,

Nicholas Carriger.
(Seal)

Attest
John Stover
    His
Isaac W Arrowood
    Mark
Thomas Foster.

(P.156)   Court adjourned untill tomorrow nine oclock,

Geo. Ermert,
William Cott,
George W. Greenway.

Wednesday Morning Feby 13th 1828

Court met according to adjournment, present,
George Emmert
George W. Greenway
& William Gott.
Esquirs.

The minutes of yesterday procedings were read an signed.
James P. Taylor Atty Genl.calld. upon the clerk in the
presence of the court to produce the proper reciepts
from Treasure & & for the year 1827 which was severally
produced & read according and ordered to be recorded
towit, "The clerk of the county court has filed with
"the Treasurer of East Tennessee "a statement of the
state tax chargeable to the sheriff of "Carter county
for the the year 1827 and also the bond of Wm Carter
Shff & collector for said county Decr. 1st 1827,
Miller Francis
Treasurrer of
East Tennessee
By Wm Swan.

15th Decr. 1827 reciev'd of George Williams nineteen
Dollars eleven & a fourth cents being" The amount of
the fines assessments by him "collected from Novr.
session 1826 up to 22nd Nov " 1827 or pre statement
by him rendered,
Ezl Smith.
Trustee for Carter C.

(P.157) Rec'd from the clerk of the county court
of Carter the "Statement of tax collected by him for
the use of the state " from the first of Oct. 1826 to
the first of October " 1827 certified as the law Diricts also one hundred "and thirty three Dollars fifty
five cents & seven mills "The amount with which he is
chargeable as appears "by said return after deducting
his commissioners " $123.45

Miller Francis,
Treasurer of East Tennessee
by Wm Swan.

Ordered by the court that J. P. Taylor be assign'd as
counsel for John Bradburn a pauper who sues in the
court and by agreement of counsel it stands to make
up the pleadings so as to try at August court next.

George Emmert Esqr. return'd a list of the Taxable
property and polls in Capt Drakes Company for 1828.

George Greenway return'd a list like wise.

Wm A. Harris assignee   )
    Vs   )   This day came
John Stuart   )   the parties by
                                      thier attornies
and thereupon came a jury towit, George Lacy Larkin
Tompson So. Cross Wm Jones Joseph Robertson Andrew
Shown Wilson Maddox Lewis Morgan Abrm Nave Abrm
Miller Thos. Buck & John Hatcher, who being elected
tried and sworn the truth to speak upon the Issue join'd
do say they find that the defendant has paid the debt
& interest in the declaration mentioned except the sum
of three hundred and fifty one dollars and eight cents
It is therefore considered by the court that the Plaintiff recovered of the defendant the said sum of three
hundred and fifty one dollars and eight cents the sum
so found by the Jury and thecosts of this suit and the
defendant in mercy.

(P.158)
Wm P. Chester   )
    Vs   )   For reasons appearing to the
John Hampton   )   court it is ordered that a
                             commission issue to any one
justice of thepeace of Jefferson county Tennessee and
to any one justice of the Peace of Montgomery county
Virginia to take the testimony of Thomas Ireland in
Jefferson county & John Bayor of Montgomery county
on giving the Plaintiff ten days notice to Jefferson
and twenty Days to Montgomery county This testimoney
on behalf of Defendant.

Isaac Taylor   )
    Vs   )   Covenant
Charles Berry   )   In this cause came the parties by thier attorney and thereupon came a jury towit
Samuel Ervin Joseph Row Manuel Jinkins Nicholas Cribe-
staff Wm Cross Jas. Heatherly Jno. T. Bowen John Smith
Hugh Wilson Hugh McHenry & Thomas Nave who being elected tried and sworn the truth to speak upon the writ of
inquiry awarded in this case upon thier oaths do say
that deft has not kept & perform'd his covenant and
assesses Plff damage to ninety four Dollars it is therefore considered by the court that the Plff recover of
the deft the damages so assess'd by the Jury and the
costs of this suit and that execution issue'd.

State   )
   Vs   )   For satisfaction reasons
Wilson Maddox   )   shwn to the court a nol-
                          lprosequi is enter'd in
this case or the Defendants paying the costs and
thereupon came the defendant & William McInturf and
assumed upon there selves the payment of the costs.
It is therefore considered by the court that the
state recover of said Maddox & McInturf the costs of
this suit according to assumpsit and that execution
issue.

(P.159)
James P. Taylor
   Vs
Joseph Cooper guradin pendents lits Lydia Cullen-
berger, Archibald Lipp, Lea Sheets, Andrew Sheets
Polly Sheets, Hugh Sheets & Betsy Sheets children
of Mary Sheets formerly Mary McHenry dec'd and Hugh
McHenry Charles Hays & Nancy his wife formely
Nancy McHenry and Margaret McHenry the other heirs
of Andrew McHenry Decas'd.

        The Plaintiff having at the August session of this
court in 1826 recover'd a judgement against Hugh
McHenry administrator of Andrew McHenry dec'd John L.
Williams David McNabb & William McNabb for eighty
four Dollars and eighteen cents and five mills for his
debt and costs and execution having issued against
the goods and chattles rights & credits of Andrew
McHenry which were in the hands of the said administrator & the sheriff return'd that he could find
nothing and the plea of fully administerd having
been found for said administrator a Scici Facias
on motion of said J. P. Taylor issued against the
said Joseph Cooper gaurdian pendent lite of the
miniors heirs of Mary Sheets formerly Mary McHenry
& Hugh McHenry Charles Hays & Nancy his wife formely Nancy McHenry & Margaret McHenry the other heirs
of said Andrew returnable to our November court 1827
to show cause if any they have why Plff should not
having executions of the land of the said Andrew which
decended to them which Sci Fa was return'd to our said
court by William Carter Sheriff of Carter county"
made known to Joseph Cooper 1st Oct 1827 not made
lnown to the other heirs they not found in my county
7th Nov 1827 and thereupon an alias Sci Fa issued returnable to our February court 1828 & was return'd
by William Carter Sheriff as aforesaid madelnown to
Hugh "McHenry 26th January 1828 also on Theodosia
Roberts formerly Theodosia Heaton 27th Jany 1828 the
other "heirs not found 1st day of February 1828

And the said defendant to whome said Sci Fas. had been made known being call'd to come & shew cause why plff should not have execution of the lands of the deceas'd in thier hands come not (P.160) and two Nihiles having been return'd as to the balance of said heirs.

It is considered by the court now here that the Plaintiff James P. Taylor have execution against the lands and tenements of the said Andrew McHenry deceas'd which deceasded to the said named heirs on the death of the said Andrew for his Judgement for debt and costs of suit together with the costs of this suit and that execution issued.

John Sturt   )
   Vs   )   In this case on motion of Wm
Henry Massengale)   K. Blair atty & came a jury
                   towit, Saml Irvin Jos. Row
Manl Jinkins Nicholas Grindstaff Wm Cross Jas. Weatherly
Jno T. Bowen Jno. Smith Hugh Wilson Hugh McHenry Thos.
Nave & Hardin Brown, who being elected tried and sworn
to inquire whether John Sturt against whom Judgement
was this day rendered was the security of Henry
Massengale and the said Jury do say that the said Sturt
executor said not to Godfrey Carriger as the security
of Henry Massengale and it appearing to the court that
the said John Sturt was sued by Wm A Harris assignee
of Christian Carriger & & And that Judgement was rendered against him for the sum of three hundred and fifty
one dollars and eight cents the ballance of the debt,
together with eight dollars & fifty cents the costs of
said suit.

It is therefore considered by the court now here on
motion of Wm K Blair that the said John Sturt recover
of the Defendant the said sum of three hundred and
fifty one Dollars and eight cents with the further
sume of eight Dollars & fifty cents the costs of said
suit together with the costs of (P.161) thismotion
and the defendant in mercy.

State   )
  Vs   )   The defendant in this cause
Jesse Adames)   being charged by the atty
               Genl on the bill of Indictment plead guilty. It is therefore considered by the
court for such his offence that he be fined five dollars. It is therefore considered by the court that the
state recover of the deft the fine and the costs of
this suit and he is ordered in custody of the sheriff
until fine & costs are paid.

Ordered that Wm Peoples Esqr. take a list of the taxable property in Capt McInturfs company.

George Riddle)
    Vs) A rule is allowed the Plff
Elishia Williams) to shew cause why the certionari should be dismiss'd
and an argument of the same it is considered by the
court that said rule be discharged.

Wm Adkins)
    Vs) The Plff by his atty Aaron
Aaron Musgrave &) Finch Dismisses his suit.
Jos Wilson) It is therefore considered
by the court that the defendants recover of the Plff thier costs about thier suit
in this behalf expended and the Plff in mercy.

George Brown)
    Vs) In this case an attachment
H.D. Johnson) having been issued &levied
upon the land of said Dept
and he being solemly call'd to come into court and
replevy the property attach'd came not but made default. It is therefore considered by the court that
the Plff recover of the left eighteen dollars the
debt in attachment mentiond with the costs of said
attachment together with the costs of this suit &
that execution issue.

(P.162) A. M. Carter for)
         E. Hatheways use) Plaintiff by atto
         Isaac McNabb) Dismisses his suit
and Elijah Hatheway
assumes costs, therefore it is considered by the court
that Isaac McNabb Recover against the said Elijah
Hatheway his costs & charges put to and about his suit
in that behalf Expended and the Elijah may be in mercy
& &.

Vincent Kelly constable proved his attendance for two
days at this session for which he is allowed agreeable to law

Court adjourn'd untill tomorrowmorning 9 oclock.

William Gott,
George W. Greenway,
Geo. Emmert,

Thursday morning court met according to adjournment, present the Worshipful,

Wm Gott,
George Greenway &
George Emmert .

The minutes of yesterday was read & signd this day.

A bill of sale from Nathan Webb to Henry I. Carter for a negroe woman named Hasty acknowledged in open court and admited to record let it be registered.

(P.163)
Abm. Lewis   )
Elisha Lewis   )
John R. Howard &   )
Stephen M. Jackson assignees)
     Vs   )   In this cause
James I. Tipton   )   came James I.

Tipton and confessed a judgement for one hundred and twenty dollars and seventy six cents. It is therefore considered by the court that the plffs recover of the deft the said sum confessed with the costs of this suit & be in mercy. Plff atty stay execution three months.

Wm B. Carter   )
    Vs   )   In this cause an attachment
H. D. Johnston)   having issued favoring the
                       Plff against the goods and
chattles lands & tenements of the deft and the same having been levied on four hundred acres of land of the defts in Carter county on waters of little Doe adjoining the lands of George Cross White and others and now here return'd to court and the said deft being call'd to come into court and replevy the land attached came not but made default.

It is therefore considered that the plff recover of the deft one hundred and eight dollars and thirty two cents the debt in the attachment & declaration mention'd with the further sum of seventeen Dollars & seventy four cents interest the same making in the whole one hundred and twenty six dollars and fifty nine cents together with the costs of this suit and the defendant in mercy.

(P.164)
A. C. Parks)
   Vs   )   Covenant.
John Scott)   This day came the Plff by his atty and
the Deft being sollemly calld. to defend the suit came
not but made default . It is therefore considered by
the court that the Plaintiff recover of the Deft one
hundred and sixty six dollars and forty five cents but
because it is uncertain what damage Plff has sustaind
it is considered by the court that the Jury come at
next court and inquire of said damages & &.

Isaac Taylor)
Assessr)
   Vs   )   The Deft in this cause was
Stephen Jackson)   solemly calld to come in and
defend the suit and came not but made default and because it is uncertain what damage the Plff has sustaind it is ordered that a jury come at next court to
inquire of the damages & &.

A. C. Parks who was appointed deputy Entry taken
on this county by A. W. Taylor came into court and
took the oath presented by law.

Reuben Miller proved his attendance as a constable for
three Days for which he is allowed agreeable to law.

(P.165)   Ordered by the court that Abial C Parks
be appointed a constible for the Law for the next two
years who thereupon entered into bond in one thousand
dollars with J. P. Taylor & A. W. Taylor his securities
for the same & thereupon took the several oaths prescribed by Law & turnd forth as such.

John ? Smith)
   Vs   )   Vincent Kelly constable returnd an
Lion Pierce)   Execution Issued by a Justice In fav-
             our of the plff for the sum of three
dollars debt & fifty cents costs agt the Deft search
made no goods & chattles found in my county whereon to
levy this Execution, then levied on twenty nine acres
of land on Stoney on the North side of said creek with
a mill thereon, where the Widow Pearce now lives
December 5th 1827 Vincent Kelly constable For which
return appearing to the court it is therefore ordered
that the shff sell said land or so much thereof as shall
be of value sufficient to satisfy said Execution & costs
of this motion.

Wm Parsons)
   Vs   )   Vincent Kelly constable returnd an
Lion Pierce)   Execution Issued by a Justice of the

peace in favour of the plff agt the Deft for the sum
of six dollars & twelve cents Debt & fifty cents costs
Search made no goods & chattles found whereon to levy
Execution, then levied on twenty nine acres of land
lying on the north side of Stoney creek whereon the
widow Pearce now lives including a mill. Decr 5th 1827
Vincent Kelly constable, for which return appearing
to the court it is therefore ordered by the court
that the shff sell sd land or so much thereof as shall
be of value sufficient to satisfy said Execution &
costs of this motion.

Court adjournd_ until Court in cause,

William Gott,
George W. Greenway
Geo. Emmert.

(P.166)
State of Tennessee   )
Carter County   )   At a meeting of the court
                             of Pleas and quarter sessions
for Carter county at the court house in Elizabethton
on the second Monday in May in the year of our Lord
1828.
Present the Worshipfull,

George Emmert
Jesse Cole
John Richardson
John L. Williams
John I. Wilson
Ezekiel Smith
Johnson Hampton
William B. Carter
Julius Dugger
William Gott
Green Moore and
Jeremiah Campbell   Esqrs.

Five Justice present, Peter Snider and Christian
Snider produced in open court the scalp of a wolf
each adjudged by the court over four months old and
the said Peter & Christian having sworn upon their
oaths, say they killed the wolves which the scalps
came off in the county aforesaid since the first day
of January 1811 and it appearing to the satisfaction
of the court that the said Peter & Christian killed
the sd wolves in the county aforesaid it is therefore
ordered by the court that the sd Peter & Christian be
allowed three Dollars each for killing said wolves to
be paid out of the State Treasury.

For reasons appearing to the court it is ordered
that John Dugger be released from attending as a
Juror at this Session.

(P.167)
    Peter Brown & John Guthrid   Serveuing partners of
Morgan Brown & Guthrid.
                        Vs
Mark Reeve Casper W. Reeve Robert Reeve Jobe W. Reeve
and Nathan Burchfield and the defendants came into open
court and confessed Judgement for six hundred and seventeen Dollars and thirty five cents therefore it is considered by the court that the said Peter Brown & Guthrid
Serveuing partners of Morgan Brown & Guthrid recover
over against the aforesaid defendants the aforesaid
sum of six hundred seventeen Dollars thirty five cents
for there debt and also thier costs and charges put
to and about thier suit in that behalf expended and
that the defendants may be in mercy &c.
Stay execution six months.

For reasons appearing to the court it is therefore
ordered by the court that Isaac Fite be released from
attending as a Juror at this session.

Hampton Hyder appointed to the commissioner of the
Peace came into open court and took an oath to support the constitutions of the United States of
America and of the state of Tennessee also the several oaths required by law to be taken by justice
of the Peace.

(P.168)   Ordered by the court that William Simmerly
be appointed overseer of the Public road leading up
Gap creek from the mouth of Boyds lane to the divide-
ing ridge and that the following hands on Joseph
Hyders farm Michael Hyders farm John Inman the
Maguhans and John Boyds farms.

Ordered by the court that Nathan Burchfield work on
the main road from the end of his road wherein he is
overseer to the Main road that leads to George Wains's
and that all the hands on the lands of Mark Reeve
& sons John Britt William Britt James Orton Nathan
Burchfield Jnr Benjamin Mosely William Ingram Nicholas
Finy William Gourly and Jabez Murray be his hands.

Ordered by the court that Jesse Jinkins be appointed
overseer of the public road from Obrien Gott & Obriens
forge to the ford of the River Watauga Just below
Leonard Bowers in place of William Gott and that John
Edwards be added to the hands that work on said Road.

Ordered by the court that Leonard Shown be appointed
overseer of the public road from Chowns X roads to the
fork of the road at John Wagners land & have all the
hands worked in the bounds by Isaac Musgrave down Roans
creek from John Wagoners land.

(P.169)   Ordered by the court that part of the road
running by the forge of O Brien Gott & O Brien be attend so as to run as follows after crossing at the usual place for a below the house where Joseph O Brien
now lives then to run between the house and the river
and so on the best way to intersect the old way.

Ordered by the court that the following hands be
attached to Samuel Drake overseer of the public road
leading from Carters ford to the head of Indian creek
towit the hands on John Lyons farm Samuel Irvines
and George Hydivers farm.

Ordered by the court that Thomas L. Snodgrass be
appointed overseer of the public road in the room
of Ezekiel Lyons & have the same bounds and the same
hands that Lyons had.

Ordered by the court that George Blevins be appointed overseer of the public road leaving the Stony
Creek road a small distance below the Baptist meeting
house leading first between Brooks & Carrigers farms
to Bowers ford on Watauga River and work the follow-
,ing towit the hands on the farm formerly occupied by
Henry Nave the hands on Reuben Brooks,s farm and the
hands on Carrigers farms.

Ordered by the court that William Taylor be appointed overseer of the public road from James Gouelys to
Richard Greers and that the hands living on the branch
above Gourlys be the hands to open an work said road.

(P.170)   Ordered by the court that Johnson
Hampton William Jones John Ingram Elijah Smith
Jacob Snider John Shields Larkin L. Wilson William
Snider and John Wilson or any five of whom shall
or may make any changes in the public road leading
from the Doe River Cove to the widow Smiths that
can be made advantageously to the public & make
report to next court.

Ordered by the court that   John Hatcher Emanuel
Jinkins John Glover William Stover Isaac Tipton Snr.
Henry Nave on J. Tipton farm, Baless Miller John Carriger
William R. Blevins Garland Wilson Joseph Hyder John

Inman Jonathan Taylor John Lowdermilk Alexander M.
Wilson Christian Snider Peter Snider Adam Mast Samuel
E. Patton Thomas Rowe James Gourley John Dunlap James
L. Bradly Barnabas Oaks George W. Carter and William
Dugger Jnr be Jurors to the circourt (Circuit court)
at September Term 1828.

Ordered by the court that John Wagner be appointed
overseer of the stage road from the fork of the road
at the mouth of his lane to the top of the divideing
Ridge between Garland Wilsons and Andrew Wilsons and
have the hands at Jacob Hamptons on John Wagners
land Samuel Cross's William & Thomas McQueens Garland
Wilson & Reuben Millers farms.

(P.171) Ordered by the court that Ewins Heatherly
Arthur Pierce Moses Estep Nathaniel Taylor Nicholas
Pain John Rowe Isaac Dunlap Daniel Stout Andrew Shown
Enoch Duncan Nathaniel Taylor Samuel Gourley David
Moody Jacob Wagner Benjamin Wilson Jacob Smith
Hezekiah Smith James Bradly Joseph Wagner Valentine
Vanhuss William Bunton James Bunton Teter Wave Abrm
McLeod Robert Morris Moses Huffman Samuel Tipton Junr
& John Hathaway be Jurors to August session 1829.

Ordered by the court that in future in all elect-
ions the Sheriff shall open and hold precinct elect-
ions at Showns A roads and at Johnson Hamptons
agreeable to act of Assembly in such case made and
provided.

Ordered by the court that Jonathan Lugh be appointed
overseer of the public road leading from Archibald
Williams's to the county line near John Tiptons and
that the hands on John Dunlaps & Henson Hunts farms
John L. Williams's two lowour farms David Hains's
where E. Hendry lives Edmond Williams's John Ellis's*
farms be the hands to work on said road* & William Ellis's

Ordered by the court that Thomas D. Love Moses Banks
William Garland Uriah Banks Epphen Wilson William Baker
Sammuel McKenny Nathan Burchfield Jabez Murray be appointed a jury to view and mark a road from the state
line on the top of the Iron Mountain intersecting
the road laid off by a Jury in N. Carolina by the nearest practicable rout to the fork of the road near
William Bakers in the Limestone cove and report to
next court.

(P.172)   Ordered by the court that Andrew Arrendell
be appointed overseer to open a road of thesecond class
from the stage Road at Andrew Wilsons on little Doe to
intersect the Laurel Road at the divideing ridge between Thomas Johnsons & the widow Dorans and have all
the hands in the said bounds between the two old roads
not attached to the main Stage road and all the hands
north of where the new road is to run untill the said
road is opened.

Ordered by the court that Samuel Courly be appointed
overseer of the public road in the room of Nathaniel
T. Edens and have the same hands and bounds that Edens
had.

Ordered by the court that John Shown be appointed overseer of the stageroad from William Shown Lane to the
top of the divideing ridge between Andrew Wilson &
Garland Wilsons & have all the hands worked by Stephen
Jackson west of the said Ridge

    Ordered by the court that the report of a jury of
View this day made from Wilcoxes to David Haines's
mill be rejected and that John Wright Samuel Pogart
Thomas McInturff Jesse Matocks David Haines Calwell
Brown Ephraim Duck George Hains and William McNabb
bea Jury of View to examine all the routs from
Wilcoxes to Hains's mill and Select such pass to sd
mill as will suit best takeing into View the public
and individual good and so as not to subject the
county to damages for going through cleared land.

(P.173)   Stephen Tilson appointed constable came
into open court and took the several Oaths required
by law for a constable and entered into bond with
John Wilcox Ephraim Fuck and William McNabb his securities in the final sum of one Thousand Dollars with
condition Sec. bond.

    On motion to allow Julius Dugger twenty Dollars
for the support and maintainace of an orphan child
called Alfred Ward for the last six months that being the last allowance that he is entitled to Jesse
Cole Yea William Gott Yea John Richardson Yea
John L. Williams Yea G. Moore Yea J. Hampton Yea
G. Emmert Nay J. Wilson Nay Hampton Hyder Yea.
    It is therefore ordered that the said Julius be
allowed twenty Dollars for the support an maintainace of said orphan child.

On motion for an allowance of one hundred Dollars
to Sidny Smith for the maintainance of Mary Smith
one of the poor for two years & nine months up to
this time yeas G. Moore J. Hampton J. Cole G. Emmert
J. Dugger J. Richardson J. Wilson J.L. Williams H.
Hyder. It is therefore ordered that the s id Sidney
be allowed the sum of one hundred Dollars for the support and maintairance of sd Mary for the time aforesaid.

On motion to allow William Carter shff fifty dollars,
for his exofficio services for this year 1828 yeas J.
Dugger J. Cole J. Richardson G. Moore J. Wilson J.
Hampton G. Emmert W. Gott Nay J. L. Williams. **H. Hyder**
It is therefore ordered by the court that William Carter
Shff be allowed fifty Dollars for his exofficio services
from May session 1827 up to May session 1828

(P.174) On motion to allow George Williams clerk
fifty Dollars for his exofficio serveces for the year
1828 yeas J. Dugger J. Cole J.L.Williams J. Richardson
G. Moore J. Wilson H. Hyder W. Gott G. Emmert & J.
Hampton It is therefore ordered that the sd George
Williams be allowed the sum of fifty Dollars for his
exofficio service from May session 1827 up to May session 1828.

On motion to allow George Williams Clerk fifteen dollars for making out the tax list for the year 1828
yeas W. Gott J. Duggar J. Campbell J. Cole G. Emmert
G. Moore J. Wilson H. Hyder and J. Hampton.
It is therefore ordered that the sd George Williams
be allowed the sum of fifteen Dollars for making out
the tax list for the year 1828 .

State)
Vs) In this cause by leave of the court
Alfred Samms) the attorney General enters a nols ro-
siqul on the defendants paying costs
and thereupon Edmond Sarms appeared in open court and
agreed to be the said Alfreds Security for the costs.
It is therefore considered by the court that the state
recover of the said Alfred and Edmund Sams the costs
of this prosecution as will in this court as before
the Justice of the Peace and that the defendants in
mercy &c &.

A deed of conveyance from John Blevins Armstead Blevins
Bonapart Blevins and William Blevins to William R.
Blevins for one hundred acres of land proven in open
court by George W. Scott and James Lovelace two of the
subscribing witnesses thereto and admited to record
let it be registered.

(P.175)
State   )
  Vs   )   In this case by leve of the court the
James Adams)   attorny General enters a noliprosequi
and Jesse Adams agrees to be security for the costs.
       It is therefore considered by the court that the
state.recover of the said James and Jesse Adams the
costs of this prosecution as will in this court as before the justice of the Peace and that the defendants
be in mercy & &.

State   )
  Vs   )   And the defendant being charged upon
Benjamin Clark   )   the bill of Indictment and he for plea
                          thereto saith that he is guilty there-
of therefore it is considered by the court that the defendant be fined six and one fourth cents and that the
state recover against the defendant the fine and costs
of this prosecution and that the defendnt in mercy & &.

       A deed of conveyance from Joseph Wilson and Anna
Wilson his wife to Thomas Duggar for thirty four acres
of land proven in open court By Michael Pierce one
of the Subscribing witnesses thereto and continued
for the probate of the other witness Benjamin Burns.

       A deed of conveyance from David Garland to Nathan
Burchfield for sixty acres of land acknowledged in
open court by the said David Garland the maker thereof
and admited to record let it be registered.

       The assignment of a plat and certificate of survey
from William Asher to John Baker for fifty acres of
land proven in open court by John Duggar one the subscribing witnesses thereto.

(P.176)   A deed of conveyance from John Asher to
William Duggar for eighty acres of land proven in
open court by John Duggar Senr and John Dugger Jun-
ior two of the subscribing witnesses thereto and admited to record let it be registered.

       A deed of conveyance from Jacob Cable Adam Mast
Coonrod Cable John Cable Benjamin Cable Joseph Cable
Sarah Doman Peter Cable Samuel Cable John Jones Daniel
Cable and Elizabeth Cable to Casper Cable for fifty
acres of land proven in open court by John Duggar and
William Duggar two of the subscribing witnesses there-
to and admited to record let it be registered.

A deed of conveyance from Charles N. George Peter
Hunt Nancy Hunt Clark B. Haywood Eliza George Daniel
ODell and Francess ODell to Jesse Cole for one hundred acres of land acknowledged in open court by Clark
B. Haywood Eliza George Danul ODell and Francess
ODell his wife and the said Eliza George and Francess
ODell wife of Danel ODell being examined by the court
seperately and apart from thier said husbonds saith
that they executed the same freely and voluntarily
and of thier own accord without persuasions fear or
threats and admited to record let it be registered.

(P.177)   Ezekiel Smith Trustee made the following
report towit a report to the county court of Pleas &
quarter sessions agreeable to an act of assembly &
to show the state of the state public money for the
procceding year 1827 money recieved by me Ezekiel
Smith Trustee for Catere county as follows towit
of the sheriff William Carter in money 215 dollars
in claimes indorsed to the Sheriff from No 63
to No 82 $116.18/4
                                             361.69
in do do from No82 to No103 which claims is filed
to his conduct in the settlement of his account.
Rec'd of George Williams Clerk in cash   19.11½

                                      ─911.98

Money disbursed from the Trustees office of
Carter county and to who paid as follows towit
To Matthias Keen one of the poor $55.00
To A.C. Parks for the county services 59.25
To A. W, Willians do do   5.00
To David Wald constable claims   2.00
To James Campbell do   8.00
To C. M. D. Gourly do   3.00
To George Williams for his services353.62½

                           493.62½ ─────

I do certify that the above is correct according
to the accounts filed* 12th day of May 1828,
  *in my office & C this   Ezekiel Smith,
Trustee for Carter Cty.

(P.178) Court adjourned untill to morrow morning
nine oclock,
                        Geo. Emmert
                        William Gott
                        G. Moore
                        Jesse Cole.

Tuesday May 13th 1828 court met according to adjournment Present the Worshipfull,

George Emmert,
Esqrs. Green Moore and
William Gott.

John and Alexander Ritter)
        Vs   )   William B. Carter
William B. Carter   )   in his proper person came into open
court and confessed Judgement for four hundred twenty
seven Dollars & fifty five cents.
Therefore it is considered by the court that the Plaintiff recover over against the defendant the aforesaid
sum of four hundred and twenty seven Dollars fifty five
cents and also thier costs and Charges put to and
above there suit in that behalf expended and that the
defendant may be in mercy &c.

Isaac Taylor assignee)
        Vs   )   Stephen Jackson
Stephen Jackson   )   in his proper person came into open
court and confessed judgement for seventy Dollars forty
cents.
    Therefore it is considered by the court that the
Plaintiff recover against the defendant the aforesaid
sum of seventy Dollars fortycents and also his costs
and charges put to and about his suit in that behalf
expended and that the defendant may be in mercy &c.

(P.179) For reasons appearing to the court it is
therefore ordered that John Kenn be released from
service as a Juror at this session.

John C. Taylor   )
        Vs   )   Plaintiff by his
Richard Arrendell   )   attorney dismisses
                          his suit and the
defendant assumes costs.
        Therefore it is considered by the court that
the Plaintiff recover over against the defendant his
costs and charges put to and about his suit in that
behalf expended and that the defendant be in mercy &c.

William Carter Esqr. Sheriff returned the Venirei Facias
executed from which the following good and lawfull
men were drawn in due form of law towit and the court
appointed Caleb Smith Foreman, Joseph Climp David
Nave Lewis Wills William Nave Daniel Stover Daniel Neel
Christopher McInturff Samuel Drake Abraham Nave John
Fletcher Jacob Keeln & Abraham Lowe.
Impaneled sworn charged and with drew to enquire of
thier presentments.

Vincent Kelly constable sworn to attend the Grand Jury.

William Borin appointed constable and entered into bond
with Abraham Tipton Joseph Slimp and David Waide his
securities in the sum of one thousand Dollars with condition Sec bond- and the sd William appeared before W.
B. Carter Esqr. and took the several Oaths required by
law to be taken by a constable.

(P.180)   State   )   And the defendent being
                  Vs   )   charged upon the bill of
            Joseph Renfro)   indietment and he for plea
)   thereto saith that he is
guilty thereof. Therefore it is considered by the court
that the defendant be fined six one fourth cents and that
the state recover the aforesaid fine of six & one fourth
cents and the costs and charges put to and about that
behalf expended* and that the defendent be in mercy & &.
 *over against the defendant
James Estep)   For reasons appearing to the court on
      Vs   )   motion of the plaintiff by his attorn-
Isaac Estep)   ey a rule and commissioner to take the
deposition of George Wilson Nancy Wilson Bedant Beard
and Isaac Guinn Ashe county North Carolina twenty days
notice to the defendant whereupon the proceedings aforesaid were continued.

(P.181)   Josiah Clawson)   The Defendant being ar-
                  Vs   )   rested on a Ca Sa Issued
            George Oliver)   by a justice of the peace
and the defendent came into open court and took the insolvent debtors oaths and in this case

Reuben H. Harrison)   A ca sa having been issued by a
        Vs   )   justice of the peace and the de-
George Oliver   )   fendent being arrested thereon
and having taken insolvent debtors oath in each case
and returnd the following schedule towit one half of
one canoe one pot- one tub one table Peter Lewis owes
me twenty pounds Iron James Lewis owes me ten pounds
iron Pleasant Williams twenty five pounds & Charles
Lovelace fifty cents. The abouve is all the estate &
debts oweing & due to me & &.   May 13th 1828.
                                       his
                              George X Oliver
                                       mark
Which property and debts assigned by the sd Oliver to
the sheriff for the benefit of the sd Josiah Clawson
& Reuben H. Harrispn. Therefore it is considered by
the court that the said George be discharged from the
custody of the sheriff & &.

John Bradburn)
  Vs)   Refered to the arbrtration
Matthis Salts)   of William Jones Jacob Simmerly
                  Benjamin Ryder and John Shields
and if they cannot agree they to choose a fift man and
award to be the judgement of this court **.there returnàble
to next court**
(P.182)
William P. Chester)
  Vs)   For reasons appearing to the
John Hampton)   court the above cause is con-
                tinued on affd of deft on
rule & commission to take the deposition of Thomas
Irland of Sevier County and Thomas Hampton of Monroe
county on Defendants giving Plaintiff ten days notice
of time and plead before some justice of said county.

J. W. Renfro)
  Vs)   In this case the defendant
Robert Blevins)   Blevins returned the follow-
              ing schedule of his property
except what by law he is allowed to retain a twenty
dollar bill passed to me by A.W. Head an insolvent man
on bank he has one bed and furniture one cow & calf
six knives & forks & some Delph Plats & a half sett
cups & Saucers which by law he claimes as exempt from
execution,
             Robt J. Blevins.
It is therefore considered by the court that the sd
Robert Blevins go hence without day and that the said
Robert Blevins recover of the said James his costs and
charges put to and about his defence have execution
therefore.

Isaac Wilson)
  Vs.)   And the bonds be-
Jacob Slimp)   ing taken to the
)   sheriff in each
S. Baily & F. Proffit) of these cases the
  Vs)   Ca Sa in each of
Jacob Slimp & the state) these cases is squa-
  Vs)   shed
Jacob Slimp)

(P.183)

John Carriger)
  Vs)   The defendent in
William R. Blevins) his proper person

comes into open court and confesses Judgement for
sixty eight Dollars and all legal costs.
    Therefore it is considered by the court that the
said John Recover of the sd William the aforesaid
sum of sixty eight Dollars and his costs and charges
of suit in that behalf expended and that the defendent
in mercy &c.
    Stay execution one & half months

George W. Rutledge
        Vs
Joseph C. West

Jesse Cobb   )
        Vs   )   John Stuart a Garnishee sum-
Jos. C. West   )   ond in this case being sworn
                               he Deporth   as follows to-
wit he executed a note to Joseph C. West the deft for a
quantity of bar Iron due in the last fall that Alferd
W. Taylor he believes has the note & claimed payment
of it from this   deponist he told me he was a ting for
West the note is for upwards of Fifty Dollars it is
all the debt or property of his in my hands he left
some waggon gears in my cellar I have seen some of the
gears since on Jos. Renfro horse & James W. Renfroes
horses Alfred W. Taylor also told me West owed him con-
siderable. I also understood A. W. Taylor had a note
on Robt Stuart and James Renfro the amount he does not
know . I bought two negroes of est for $750.
I paid him in cash & horses for the negroes & I do not
owe one cent on that account.

(P.184)
Wm A. Harris Assignee   )
        Vs   )   Robert Stuat
John Stuart   )   summoned as a
                                    Garnishee and
sworn upon his oath deposeth that he does not owe
John Stuart any thing and has none of his property
in his hands.
    I bought the Stills of John Stuart and paid him
for them one hundred Dollars in debts. I paid for
him the stills were sold at execution sale and bought
by James Renfro & by him sold to David Stuart and by
David to my father the Reeves owe my father the
amount I do not know My Father had a note on James
Hughes for seventy five Dollars and my father lost it
and it is found now in William Carter Sheffs hands
James Hughes being sumoned as a Garnishee in the case
of Harris assignee & & Vs John Stuart deposeth .
    I do not owe him a cent I bought a negro Girl

named Hannah of John Stuart for one hundred and fifty
Dollars I executed my due bill for seventy five Dollars to Stuart, I was to pay seventy five Dollars to
James H. Fyffe I gave My word to John Stuart to pay
the debt to Fyffe say $75 I gave my note for seventy
five Dollars I recieved five tons of Iron I bought of
John Stuart I agreed to settle their Judgement against
John Stuart one favoring John anders one other favoring John Carriger and one other favoring Christian
Carriger those then amounted to two hundred and eighty
seven Dollars or upwards Stuart owed me one hundred
and sixty in Judgments Stuart gave me one obigation
on OBriens & Cott for $ 1250 in Iron on that note
I have recieved five tons of Iron at one hundred and
fifty Dollars per ton I bought the whole note it is
as I please whether I pay one other cent or not.
I told Stuart if you see proper (P.185) to risk me
in this way I would if I had good luck to sell the
Iron give you what I see proper when I come back I
would not bind myself to pay anything more if there
is any thing over and above my advances and expences
on the sale of the Iron I will pay him if I Please
John Stuat the ballance I want nothing of Stuart but
my money and expences said Carnishee further stated
that it was my intention when I bought the note to
pay John Stuart whatever the Iron sold for over and
above my advances trouble and expences when I returned after sale and it was my intention to do so in
addition to the sum before stated .

I have assumed twenty Dollars I am responsible for
that sum which I have paid and agree to pay for Stuart
that execution on the judgements I hold against Stuart
were Issued and levied by one Weatherly a constable
on the property of John Stuart Jno. Stuat told me he
wanted the execution rend I told him The note I held
on Cott & Obrins he might run if he pleased the execution I have them levied on his property the executions
were issued and levied on two setts of Blacksmiths
tools and were sold and I bought the tools at $40.41
I never got prossession of the tools Stuart has sold
the tools since one sett to Michael Hyder for one
thousand two hundred pounds Iron the other set and
gone down the river in Capt Jones Boat in which
Robt Stuart went. I have given John Stuart credit my
contract binds me to do it at the time I bought the
tools I had Cott & Obrins note in possession the note
mortgaged to my Judgement after the sale of the tools
by (P.186) Weatherly Stuart acknowledged the honesty
of my debt and sold me the OBrien note for the satisfat-
ion of my debt and the other advances before mentioned

and after I had made a discloseure in my former Garnishment to Sanders mentioned in this Garnishment.
James W. Renfro sumoned as a garnishee and sworn
upon his oath in the before mentioned suit deposeth
I promised to pay the fourth part of the interest at
six per cent on the Decree in chancery of Alfred M.
Carter against John Stuart for two years for the Rent
of part of the land I lived on which was about $1300.
I cannot tell whether I have paid it till Stuart and r
me Settle Stuart has sued me for it before Esqr. Emmert
but whether there is a judgement or not before Emmert
I cannot tell I bought a couple of Stills & ten still
tubs under Hughes Judgt_ I left them in the still
house I never sold them to David Stuart I understood
Robert Stuart took the stills off but where to I do
not know I bought three head of horses sold under Hughs
executions for one Dollar and seventy five cents two
of the horses are at Stuarts I executed my note to the
officer for and not paid yet - I got possession of
ninety one Dollars of a boy that was bringing it to
Stuart and it was Stuarts money John Stuart got of
me fifty Dollars the ballance I have accounted with him
for in a settlement I sued John & Robert Stuart and recovered Judgt against Stuart for upward of ninety dollars William Messeck had $200. in Srices of
(P.187) Stuarts I garnished Messeck and got sixty
are sixty one Dollars on this Judgement and one of
my fathers for the ballance Stuart and his sons property was levied on and I bought some stacks of rye
and father bought his John Stuarts household furniture six executions were levied on the property four
of Hughes's my fathers and mine my father held a note
on John Stuart which I took for my father my father
did not tell me to take the note I executed the note
in Stuarts name it is all nothing the property was let
left in Stuarts hands and he has deposed of it or it
remaines there I gave fifteen Dollars to William Smith
for a judgement on John Stuart- Stuart had paid all th
the judgement but fifteen Dollars the Judgement was
about thirty five Dollars I got all the money for the
whole Judgement the Judgement My father got against
Stuart was without consideration the Judgement against
John and Robert Stuart in my name I obtained for
upwards of ninety Dollars was without consideration
as to John Stuart I settled with Robert Stuart for
it and he Robert signed his name as security for his
father to it his fathers name got there without his
knowledge but I executed my note to Robert Stuart &
John Stuart or Robert alone for the same amount or
there abouts which was the consideration for the

note I got on them I have got back since from Robert
Stuart said note without paying any (P.188) thing
for it John Stuart and me settled with you this Smith
Debt and the money I got of the Boy and credited a note
with the amount of $125 which note I held for two
horses I sold him which last note was given on a
bonafide sale I never took any of the property I
bought under the other execution me nor my father
I beleive that is under mine and my fathers executions.
Court adjourned untill'tomorrow morning nine oclock,

Geo. Emmert,
Jesse Cole
William Gott.

(P.189)   Wednesday May 14th 1828 court met according to adjournment present the Worshipful,

George Emmert,
William Gott,
Jesse Cole &
John Richardson.

State)
 Vs) In this case with leave of
Radford Ellis) the court the attorney General enters a noleprosequi
and the defendent assumes costs.
    Therefore it is considered by the court that the
state recover of the said Radford the costs & charges
of this prosecution and that the defendant may be in
mercy & &.

State)
 Vs) In this case with leave of
John Ellis) the court the attorney General enters a noleprosequi
on the defendents assuming all costs.
Therefore it is considered by the court that the state
recover of the defendant the costs and charges of this
prosecution and that the defendant may be in mercy & &.

P. Cobb for G. W. Rutledge & Michael Massengills use
Vs John Stuart

Demurrer on argument of counsel and all and singular
those persons being sworn and fully understood it is
considered by the court that the Demurrer be sustained on to the first plea and overruled as to the second
and that the Deft have leave to plead to Issue.

(P.190)   Ordered by the court that the Sheriff bring
to our next court two orphan children a son & Daughter of Nancy Morris towit Lucritia and Jonah that said
children may be provided for as the law directs.

State   )
Vs   )   And the defendent being charg-
William R. Blevins   )   ed upon the bill of Indiet-e
                                ment and thereto saith that
he is guilty thereof. Therefore it is considered by the
court that the defendant be fined fifty cents and that
the state recover of the aforesaid William R. the afore
said sum fifty cents, and the costs and charges of this
prosecution and that deft may be in mercy & &.

John Smith   )
Vs   )   In this case a rule is allow-
Lewis Lewis   )   ed to shew cause why the Ca
                                Sa Issued by the otherssaid
John should be aquashed an argument of counsel and for
reasons appearing to the court the rule is made absolute It is therefore considered by the court that the
said Lewis Lewis go hence without day and that the
said Lewis recover of the said John his costs and
charges put to and about his defence in that behalf
expended and that the said John may be in mercy & &

A deed of conveyance from Jacob Lowe to Abraham Lowe
for eight acres of land proven in open court by A. W.
Taylor and Joseph Cooper two of the subscribing witnesses thereto and admitd to record let it be registered.

    A deed of conveyance from Jacob Lowe to Abraham
Lowe for one hundred acres of land proven in open
court by A. W. Taylor and Joseph Cooper two of the
subscribing witnesses thereto and admited to record
let it be registered.

(P.191)   State   )   And the defend-
             Vs   )   ent being charg-
             Alfred   Rockhold)   ed upon the bill
                                        of Indietment and
for plea thereto saith that he is not guilty thereof
and puts himself upon his country and James P. Taylor
attorney General who prosecuts on behalf of the state
doth the like and thereupon came a Jury towit,
Jacob Sinnerly Joseph Vaught Lazarus C. Inman Isaac
Shown John Shell Charles Lovelace Ewins Heatherly
John Adams Elisha Williams Stephen Lewis Thomas Ellet

& William Garland Good and lawful men chosen elected
tried and sworn on thier oaths do say they find the
deft not Guilty It is therefore considered by the
court that the costs of this prosecution on behalf
of the state alone be taxd to the county of Carter
leaving the costs on behalf of defendant not taxed to
the county

(P.192) State   )   The defendant being charg-
           Vs   )   ed upon the bill of Indiet-
           James Lovelace)   ment and he for plea there-
                              to saith that he is not
guilty thereof and puts himself on his county and James
P. Taylor attorney General who prosecutes for the state
does the same whereupon came a Jury towit,
James W. Renfro Thomas Nichols John T. Borin Abner
McLeod Matthias Broiles Stephen Parsons Jacob Poland
John Smith Matthw Salts Moses Huffman Ansel Carden
Samuel A. Irvin good and lawful men chosen elected
tried and sworn upon thier oaths do find the defendant not guilty It is therefore considered by the
court that the county be taxed with the costs of this
prosecution on the part of the state only that the
county Trustee pay the same out of any monies not
other wise appointed leaving the defendants costs
not taxed to the county.

State   )   Jacob Poland a witness in this
    Vs   )   case proven his attendance for
Alfred Rockhold)   two days.

A deed of conveyance from John Wilson to Johnson
Hampton for one acre of land acknowledged in open
court by the maker thereof and admited to record
let it be registered.

(P.193)   Court adjourned to meet at 9 oclock
on tomarrow,

                              Geo. Emmert
                              William Gott
                              John Richardson.

     Thursday May 15th 1828 Court met according to
adjournment Present the Worshepfull,

                              W. B. Carter,
                 Esqrs   Wm Gott
                              George Emmert
                              John Richardson

Jerry Ornduff) In this case a Ca Sa having been issu-
    Vs   ) ed by George Emmert Esqr on a Judgement
Moses Huffman) rendered by him against the deft and
             he having been taken in execution on
said Ca Sa and now he appeared in pursuance of a bond
taken in pursuance to an act of assembly and claimed
the benefit of the Insolvent debtors laws the said
Huffman returnd into court a schedule of his property
and effects in the words following (Viz) "In this case
the said Moses Huffman says It is entirely insolvent
and does "not posess as much property as by court he is
entitle to law "he has an unsettled account with Messrs
Gott & Obriens.

(P.194)   And if any thing is due he assigns it to Wm
Carter shff for the use and benefit of Plff also if
"Any thing is due him from the Revd M. Ward "he done
some work for him but at the time he "done it did not
contemplate charging him as he done it by way of paying him for his ministerial duties, Moses Huffman.

And thereupon he took the oath of insolvency in pursuance to act of assembly and was discharged accordingly.

Isaac Wilson) In these several causes
    Vs   ) Ca Sas having been issued
Jacob Slimp) and the body of said Slimp
Saml. Bayles & P. Proffit) taken in execution on
    Vs   ) each Ca Sa and bonds
Jacob Slimp) taken for his appearance
   and   ) at this court in each case
State Vs Jacob Slimp) and now has return'd to
       this court on motion of
Aaron Finch atty for Slimp rule allowd him to shew
cause whey the bonds taken should be quashed each case
and said rules now comission'd for argument and argument being heard and fully understood it is considered
by the court that said rules be made absolute and
that said Slimp in the two civil cases recover his
costs of the plff and they be in mercy.

(P.195) State)
    Vs) In this cause the de-
John Smith) fendant having been
  &) taken in execution
Ewens Heatherly) on Ca Sas issued in
   Vs) said cause and bond
John Smith) being taken for his
     appearance at this

court according to act of assembly and said bonds being now here return'd to court the said Smith return'd a schedule of his property which is in the words following (Viz) "one cow & calf three head of sheep one sow & two pigs one Gum two ovens two pots one bead containing 15lb feathers & some bead clothing one half dozen plats two half doz forks one Tot tea cups eightt tea cups four tea spoons two loomes one wheel one pr cards one ox one hoe one handsaw ten or adozen planes eight or ten chisels one oregan one table two beadsteads one note on George Overbay for thirty five cents one on Jacob Taylor eight pounds iron one Judgt on Benjamon Peters for five Dollars or there abouts Jonathan lips one Dollar, one GrindStone, one Judgment on John Berry for twenty eight Dollars and I am oweing him about the same & I think on settlement there would not be much differance, John Smith.

This is all the property or debts that I have that I recollect at this time I do asign over to the shff of Carter cty all the property in the within schedule for to satisfy a Judgement that the stats recover against me given under my hand & seal this 14th day of May 1828 seal

his
John X Smith
mark

And thereupon the oath of insolvent Debtors undertaken by him & he accordingly discharged.

(P.196) Wm.Shown) In this case Plff dismiss-
              Vs   ) es his suit and assumes
     Joseph Cooper) the costs before the Magistrate and Joseph Cooper
assumd the court cost It is therefore considered by the court that they respectively recover of each other the costs according to thier assumpset an in mercy

Francis Mcfall)
       Vs   ) In this cause came the parties
Caleb Smith) by their attornies and thereup-
                    on came a jury"Viz"
Jacob Simmerly Joseph Vaught Lazarus Inman Isaac Shown John Shell Stephen Parsons Wm R. Blevins Gatewood Blevins John Smith Ewin Heatherly Elisha Williams & Thomas Lovelace who being elected tried & sworn the truth to speak upon the issue joind do say defendant has not kept and preformed his covenant as in pleading he has alledged and assesses the plaintiffs damage to

one hundred and eight Dollars and seventy five cents
It is therefore considered by the court that the Plff
recover of the defendant his damages by the jury assesse'd with his costs about his suit in this behalf
expended and the deft in mercy & &.

(P. 197) State) In this cause the defend-
Vs) ant Wm R. Blevins been
Wm R. Blevins) charged on the bill of
indietment and plead
guilty It is therefore considered by the court that
the said defendant for suit his offence be fined fifty
cents thereupon it is considered by the court that the
state recover of the defendant the fine aforesaid together with the costs of this prosecution against him
and Armstead & John Blevins his securities who came
into court and with said defendant as sumed the fine
& costs - and defendant in mercy.

State) The defendant in this cause being
Vs) charged plead guilty & is fined by
Wm Perry) the court twenty five cents It is therefore considered by the court that the state recoverₑ
of the deft the fine aforesaid with the costs of this
prosecution and the defendant in Mercy.

State)
Vs) The defendant being charged on the
John Blevins) bill of Indietment pleads guilty
and is fined by the court for such
his offence fifty cents and thereupon Armstead
Blevins and Willian R. Blevins as the security of the
said John Blevins assumed the payment of the costs &
fine It is therefore considered by the court that the
state recover of the said John Blevins and the said
Armstead & William R. Blevins the fine and costs aforesaid and the defendants in mercy

(P. 198)
State)
Vs) In this case the defendant be-
Gatewood Blevins) ing charged pleads guilty and
is fined by the court for such
his offence fiftycents and the costs and thereupon
Wm R. Blevins John Blevins & Armstead Blevins for
and on behalf of said defe ndant assumed the fine
and costs It is therefore considered by the court
that the state recover of the said defendants the fine
and cost aforesaid and that execution issued.

State)
  Vs) In this cause the defendant
Armstead Blevins) being charged pleads guilty
and for such his offence is
fined fifty cents and thereupon Wm R. Blevins & John
Blevins for and in behalf of said Armstead assumed
upon themselves the payment fo the fine and costs of
this case it is therefore considered by the court
that the State recover of the defendant the fine and
costs aforesaid and that execution issued.

State)
  Vs) In this case the deftnby J.
Mathew Blevins) Kennedy his attorney pleads
guilty and for such his af-
fence is fined by the court fifty cents and thereupon
Wm R. Blevins John Blevins & Armstead Blevins for and
in behalf of said motion assumed the fine and costs
of this case It is therefore considered by the court
that the state recover of the said Mathew Wm R. Armstead & John Blevins the fine and costs of this prosecution and that execution issued.

(P.199)
State)
  Vs) In this case the defendant
Daniel Blevins) being charged pleads guilty
and is fined by the court
for such his offence fifty cents and David Bushong
for and in behalf of said
Defendant assumd the costs & fine It is therefore
considered by the court that the state recover of
the defendant and said Burshong the fine and costs
of this prosecution and that execution issued.

State)
  Vs) In this case the defendant
John Blevins son of) being charged pleads guilty
Mathew) and is fined by the court
for his offence fifty cents
Wm R. Blevins John Blevins & Armstead Blevins for and
in behalf of said John the fine and costs.
It is therefore considered by the court that the state
recover of the defendant and the said Wm R. Armstead
& John Blevins the fine and costs of this prosecution
and that execution issued.

State)
  Vs)   Defendant being charged pleads guilty
John Right)   and is fined by the court for such
         his offence fifty cents and thereupon
Wm R. Blevins Armstead Blevins and John Blevins assumed for and on behalf of said defendant the fine aforesaid ·with the costs of this prosecution It is therefore
considered by the court that the state recover of the
defendant and his securities the fine and cost of this
prosecution and that execution issued.

(P.200)
State)
  Vs)   The defendant being charged
Wm Ward alias Right) pleads guilty and is fined
         by the court for such his
offence fifty cents and thereupon Jacob Bushong is
behalf of said Defendant assumed the fine and cost
of this prosecution It is therefore considered by the
court that the state recover of the defendant & his
security said Burshong the fine and the costs of this
prosecution and that execution issue.

State)
  Vs)   Peace Warrant In this cases with
Wm R. Blevins) leave of the court a noleprosequi
         is entered & thereupon the defend-
ant assums the costs It is therefore considered by the
court that the state recover of the defendant the
costs of this prosecution according to his assumpsit
and that execution issued.

State)
  Vs)   Peace Warrant In this cause
Armstead Blevins) with leave of the court a
         noliprosequi isentered and
the defendant assumes the costs it is therefore considered by the court that the state recover of the
Defendant the costs of this prosecution according to
his assumpsit and that execution issue.

(P.201)
State)
  Vs)   Peace Wt In this cause with leave
John Blevins) of the court a noleprosequi is en-
         tered and the Defendant assumes
the costs It is therefore considered by the court
that the state recover of the Defendant the costs
of this prosecution according to his assumpset
and that execution issue.

State   )
   Vs   )   Peace Wt In this cause with
Gatewood Blevins)   leave of the court a nolepro-
                     sequi is entered and the de-
fendant with Wm. R. Blevins his security assumes the
costs It is therefore considered by the court that the
state recover of the defendant and the said W. R.
Blevins the cost of this prosecution according to there
assumpset and that execution issue.

State   )
   Vs   )   Peace Wt In this case with
James Blevins)   leave of the court a nole-
                     prosequi is entered and the
deft by Wm R. Blevins assumes the costs.
It is therefore considered that the State recover of
the defendant and Wm R. Blevins his security the costs
of this prosecution and that execution issued.

State   )
   Vs   )   Peace Wt In this cause a nol-
Wm Blevins   )   eprosequi with leave of the
                     court is entered and the de-
fendant By Wm R. Blevins his security assumes the costs
It is therefore considered by the court that the state
recover of the defendant and the said Wm R. Blevins
the costs of this prosecution the defendants in mercy.

(P.202)
State   )
   Vs   )   In this case with leave of
Gatewood Blevins)   the court a noleprosequi is
& Caty Hughs   )   entered and the defendants
assume the costs and John Blevins for and in behalf
defendants assumes the costs.
It is therefore considered by the court that the state
recover of the defendant and the said John Blevins the
costs of this prosecution according to thier assumpset
and the defendants in mercy

A.C. Parks   )
   Vs   )   Time to make up pleadings so
John Allison   )   as not to delay trial.

Owen Edwards)
   Vs) In this cause came these par-
Charles Bassendine &) ties by thier attornies and
P. W. Markland) thereupon came a jury (Viz)
                  Jacob Simmerly Joseph Vaught
Lazarus C. Inman Isaac Shown John Shell Stephen Parsons
Wm R. Blevins Gatewood Blevins John Smith Ewins Heatherly
Elisha Williams Thomas Lovelace who being chosen elec-
ted tried and sworn the truth tospeak upon the issue
Joined do say defendant has not kept and performed his
covenant as in pleading he has alledged and assess the
Plaintiffs damage to one hundred and twenty five dollars seventy cents It is therefore considered by the
court that (P.203) the Plaintiff recover of the defendant his damages by the Jury assessed with the costs
& & charges about his suit in this behalf expended
and that the deft may be in mercy.

A. M. Carter)
   Vs) In this cause came the par-
Henry Grindstaff) ties by thier attornies and
thereupon came a Jury (Viz) John ^Right Russel Royston
Allen Royston Robert Stuart Taylor McNabb Wm Alles
Jacob Cameron Armstead Blevins John Adams Joseph Cooper
Daniel Blevins and Jonathan Clark who being chosen elected tried and sworn the truth to speak upon the issue Joined do say do find that the deft hath not paid
the debt in the Plaintiffs declaration mentioned and
for reason of the detention thereof assess the plff
damage to three Dollars therefore it is considered by
the court that the Plff recover of the deft the sum
of one hundred Dollars the debt in plffs declaration
mentioned and also his damages costs and charges put
to and about his suit in that behalf expended and
that the defendant be in mercy & &.

(P.204)
A. M. Carter)
   Vs) And now at this day comes the
Henry Grindstaff) partis aforesaid by there
                  attornies and thereupon came
a Jury (Viz) John Right Russel Royston Allen Royston
Robert Stuart Taylor McNabb Wm Allen Jacob Cameron
Armstead Blevins John Adams Joseph Cooper Daniel Blevins
and Jonathan Clark chosen elected tried and sworn upon thier oaths say do find that the defendant has not
paid the debt in the Plffs declaration mentioned and
by reason of the detention thereof assess the Plaintiffs
damage to six Dollars therefore it is considered by

the court that the Plffs recover against the deft in
the Plffs declaration mentioned and also his damages
by the Jury in manner aforesaid and form aforesaid
assessed and also his costs and charges put to and
about his suit in that behalf expended and that the
defendant may be in mercy.

Abial C. Parks)
   Vs)   And now at this day came
John Scott)   the parties by thier atto-
          rneys and thereupon came
a Jury (Viz) John Right Russel Royston Allen
Royston Robert Stuart Taylor McNabb William Allen
Jacob Cameron Armstead Blevins John Adams Joseph
Cooper Daniel Blevins and Jonathan Clark chosen elected tried and sworn upon thier oaths do find that the
defendant hath not kept and performed his covenant as
in pleadings he hath alledged and assesses the Plaintiffs damage to one hundred and seventy nine Dollars
and (P.205) seventy three cents therefore it is considered by the court the Plaintiff recover against the
defendant the aforesaid sum of one hundred seventy
nine Dollars seventy three cents by the Jury aforesaid in manner and form aforesaid assessed and his
costs and charges put to and about his suit in that
behalf expended and that the defendant be in mercy & &

David Garland)
   Vs)   And now at this day came
Nathan Burchfield)   the parties by thier attor-
         nies and thereupon came a
Jury (Viz) John Right Russel Royston Allen Royston
Robert Stuart Taylor McNabb William Allen Jacob
Cameron Armstead Blevins John Adams Joseph Cooper
Daniel Blevins and Jonathan Clark chosen elected
tried and sworn upon thier oaths say find that the
deft hath not paid the debt in the Plffs declaration
mentioned except the sum of one hundred and seventy
two dollars seventy four cents.
It is therefore considered by the court that Plff
recover of the defendant the said sum of one hundred
and seventy two Dollars and seventy four cents the
ballance due as by the Jury assess'd together with
the costs of this suit and the deft in mercy Exn
Staid by order of Plff three months.

(P.206)
O. B. Ross)
   Vs)   William Carter Esqr. shff
Jacob Slimp)   returned an execution issued

by a Justice of the peace in favor of the plff for
the sum of nineteen Dollars ninety four cents with
Interest from the 22nd June 1827 till paid with Legal costs levied on all the household furniture in
Jacob Slimps house of every description also a
quantity of Rys and wheat in the Sheaf to be sold
at said Slimps house on the 1st day of September
next also levied on a four acre entry of said Slimps
lying at the mouth of Mill Creek adjoining or near
the saw mill tract levied on the 4th day of July 1827
for which return appearing to the court.
It is therefore Ordered that the sheriff sell said
entry or so much thereof as shall be of Value sufficia-
nt to satisfy said execution and costs of this motion.

Geo W. Carter)
        Vs   )   William Carter Shff returned
Jacob Slimp   )   an execution Issued by a Jus-
                          tice of the peace in favor ?
of the plff for fifteen Dollars twenty seven cents
debt & fifty cents costs with Interest from the 22
June 1827 Levied on a quantity of household furniture
and small grain to be sold at the house of said Slimp
on the first day of September next also levied on a
four acre entry at the mouth of Mill creek adjoining
or near the saw mill tract the property of Jacob Slimp
levied the 4th day of July 1827 for which return appearing to the court it is therefore ordered that the shff
sell entry or so much therof as shall be of value sufficient to satisfy said execution and costs of this
motion.

(P.207)
J.P. Taylor for   )
G. W. Carters use)
        Vs   )   William Carter shff returned
Jacob Slimp   )   an execution Issued by a
                             justice of the peace infavor
of the Plff for the sum of Ten Dollars thirty three
cents debt with Interest from the 22nd June 1827
Levied on all the household furniture in Jacob Slimps
house also a quantity of wheat and Rye to be sold at
the house of said Slimp on the first day of September
next also levied on a four acre entry of Jacob Slimp
lying at the mouth of Mill creek adjoining or near
the saw mill tract levied on the fourth day of July
1827 for which return appearing to the court it is
ordered that the shff sell said entry or so much
thereof as shall be of value sufficient to satisfy
said execution and costs of this motion.

Geo. W. Carter   )
     Vs   )   William Carter Shff returned
Jacob Slimp   )   an execution issued by a jus-
                             tice of the peace in favor
of the Plff for the sum of twenty Dollars & twenty five
cents and fifty cents costs with interest from the 22nd
June 1827 levied on all the household furniture in
Jacob Slimps house a quantity of wheat and Rye in the
sheal to be sold at said Slimps house on the forst day
of September next also levied on a four acre entry of
said Slimps lying at the mouth of Mill creek at adjoining or near the saw mill tract levied the fourth day of
July 1827 for which return appearing to the court it
is therefore Ordered that the sheriff sell said entry
or so much thereof as shall be of value sufficient to
satisfy said execution the costs of this motion.

(P.208)
Geo W. Carter   )
     Vs   )   William Carter Shff returned
Jacob Slimp   )   and execution issued by a
                             justice of the peace favor-
ing the Plff for the sum of twenty seven Dollars twenty five cents debt and fifty cents cost with int erest
from the 22nd June 1827 levied on all the household
furniture of every description in Jacob Slimps house
and aquantity of wheat and Rye in the sheaf to be
sold at sd Slimps house on the 1st day of September
next also levied on a four acre entry of Jacob Slimps
lying at the mouth of Mill creek adjoining or near
the saw mill tract levied the fourth day of July 1827
for which return appearing to the court it is therefore
ordered that the shff sell said entry or so much thereof as shall be of value sufficient to satisfy execution
and the costs of this motion.

Geo. W. Carter   )
     Vs   )   William Carter shff return'd
Jacob Slimp   )   an execution issued by a Jus-
                             tice of the peace favoring
the Plff for the sum of twelve Dollars four cents debt
and fifty cents costs with interest from the 22nd June
1827 levied on all the house hold furniture of Jacob
Slimp also a quantity of Rye and Wheat in the sheaf to
be sold at the house of said Slimp on the first day of
September next also levied on a four acre entry of Said
Slimp lying at the mouth of Mill creek adjoining or
near the saw mill tract levied on this fourth day of
July 1827 for which return appearing to the court it
is therefore ordered that the shff sell said Entry

or so much thereof as shall be of value sufficient
to satisfy said execution and costs of this motion.

(P.209)

John L. Lusk assignee)	
Vs)	Vincent Kelly constable
Micajah Brummit)	returned an execution
	issued by a justice of

the Peace for the sum of forty two Dollars seventy
one cents debt and fifty cents costs favoring of
the Plff with interest from the 16th February1828
search made no goods and chattles found in my
county whereon to levy this execution then levied
on a certain tract of land Lying in the limestone
cove it being the place whereon Brummit now lives
adjoining the landsof Banks and others number of
acres not known for which return appearing to the
court It is therefore ordered that the shff sell
said tract of land or so much thereof as shall be
of value Sufficient to satisfy said execution and
the costs of this motion.

Alban McNabb)	
Vs .)	Vincent Kelly constable
Moses Morris)	returned an execution
	Issued by a justice of the

peace favoring the Plff for the sum of twenty five
Dollars eighty eight cents debt and fifty cents
costs with interest from the 10th March 1827 search
made in my county no goods and chattles found whereon to levy this execution then levied on fifty acres
of land on the waters of Roans creek whereon Moses
Morris now lives for which return appearing to the
court it is therefore ordered that the sheriff sell
said tract of land or so much thereof as shall be
of value sufficient to satisfy said execution and
the costs of this motion.

(P.210)

Henry Molton Assignee)	
Vs)	And now at this day come
William Daniels)	the parties aforesaid by
	thier attornies and thereup

on came a jury (Viz) John Right Russel Royston
Allen Royston Robert Stuart Taylor McNabb William
Allen Jacob Cameron Armstead Blevins John Adams
Joseph Cooper Danl. Blevins &Johathan Clark- elected tried and sworn upon thier oaths say do find
that the deft hath not kept and performed his covenant as in pleading he hath alledged and assess
the Plffs damage to ninety one Dollars and twenty
one cents therefore it is considered by the court
that the Plff recover of the deft his damages

aforesaid by the Jury in manner aforesaid and form
aforesaid assessed and also his costs and charges
put to and about his suit in that behalf expended
and that the defendant may be in mercy & &.

George Lacy)
    Vs)   Compromised suit dismiss-
Alexander Lacy)   ed & the defendant assum-
                           es costs It is therefore
considered by the court that the Plff recover of the
defendant his costs and charges put to and about his
suit in that behalf expended and that the deft may
be in mercy & &.

(P.211)
George Riddle)
    Vs)   Plff Riddle suffers a none
Elisha Williams)   suit therefore it is con-
                           sidered by the court that
the deft Williams may go hence without day and it is
further considered by the court that the said Elisha
Williams recover over against the said George Riddle
his costs and charges put to and about his defence in
that behalf expended and that the said George be in
mercy & &.

State)
    Vs)   John T. Borin proves his
Alfred Rockhold)   attendance as a witness in
                           this case for two days and
Thomas Nichols for three days.

State)
    Vs)   Squire Estep proven his at-
W. R. Blevins & others) tendance as a witness in this
                           case for two days David Bush-
ong for three days Daniel Blevins for three days William
Right for three days Jacob Bushong for three days
Jonathan Clark for three days John Richardson for three
days Thomas Livelace three days an Felty Rosenbalm for
three days.

John Smith)
    Vs)   Ewins Heatherly proves his
Ewins Heatherly)   attendance as a witness in
                           this case for three days and
Russel Royston for two days and Allen Royston for two
days.

(P.212)
P. Cobb for G. W. Rutledge &)
Michael Massengills use)
executors of D. Stuart Decd)
      Vs)   And now at this
John Stuart)   came the parties
                           by thier attornies
and thereupon came a Jury Viz. Caleb Smith Joseph
Slimp David Nave Lewis Wills William Nave Da niel Niel
Daniel Stoyer Christian McInturff Samuel Drake Abraham
Nave John Fletcher Jacob Kuhn good and lawful men chos-
en elected tried and sworn upon thier oaths say do find
that the defendant is entitled to the sett off pleaded
except the sum of thirty two Dollars and twenty eight
cents which sum of Plff Debt remaines due It is therefore considered by the court that the plff recover of
the deft the sum of thirty two Dollars and seventy
eight cents the balance of Plffs Debt due after allow-
ing so much of his set off as he is intitle to together with the costs of this suit and defendant in
Mercy.

(P.213)
William Calvert)
      Vs)   Thomas Finch by his atty in
Thomas Finch)   fact John Kennedy appeared
                   in open court and confesses
Judgement to the Plff for the sum of eight hundred
thirty four dollars, being the amount of a bill single
other interest thereon up to this date wherefore it is
considered by the court that the shff recover of the
said Deft the said sum of Eight hundred & thirty four
Dollars and his costs about his suit in this behalf
expended for which plff may have execution.

Joseph C. West)
      Vs)   In this case the Defendant
John Stuart)   having faild to make any
                 Defence it is considered
by the court that Plff have Judgement by default and
that a jury came at next court to enquire of plffs
damages.

George W. Rutledge) In this case John Stuartbeen
      Vs)   summ'd as a garnishee and at-
J. C. West)   tended and at a former day
     &)   of this term made his disclos-
Jesse Cobb)   ure and for as much as there
      Vs)   is nothing in his hands of
Joseph C. West)   Defts it is considered by the
                 court that said garnishee be

discharged and that Plff pay the cost of garnishment.

John Stuart proved two days attendance in this suit as a garnishee.

Wm A. Harris   assignee)   Robert Sturt summond as a
      Vs   )   garnishee appeared at a
John Stuart   )   former day of this court
                         and made his disclosure
and for as much as he has nothing of Defendants it is considered that he be discharged and that Plff pay the costs of this garnishment Robert Sturt proved one days attendance as a garnishee in this case.

(P.214)
Wm A Harris Assignee) James Hughs and James W.
      Vs   )   Renfro who were summon'd
John Sturt   )   as garnishee in this case
                        appear'd at a former day
of this court and made thier Disclosures and for as much as there is nothing in there hands of defendants It is considered by the court that said garnishee be discharged and that Defendant recover of Plff the costs of said garnshements.

Court adjourn'd untill court in causes,
                                 W. B. Carter,
                                 Geo. Emmert
                                 William Gott.

(P.215)

State of Tennessee)   At a meeting of a court of plea-
Carter County   )   se and quarter sessions held
for Carter county at the court House in Elizabethton
on the second Monday in August the year of our Lord 1828
Present the Worshipful,

                    John Wilson
                    George Greenway
                    William D. Carter
                    Wm Peoples
                    Jesse Cole
                    Wm Gott
                    James Keys
                    George Emmert
                    John Richardson   Esquires.

Alfred M. Carter Clerk of the circuit court of Carter
county applyed for a appropreation for the payment of
costs in criminal cases which has accrued in said court
and which is chargeable to the county (towit)
State Vs Wm. Scot & Sarah Scot and others and the state
against James J. Tipton amounting to the sum of the
thirteen Dollars and fifty cents a megority of the said
Justice of said county being present towit John Wilson
George Greenway William D. Carter William Peoples Jesse
Cole William Gott James Keys & George Emmert and John
Ritision and apearing to the satisfaction of the court
that the said account has been refered to James P.
Taylor Esqir. eternal Generial who after Examining
said accompt, has sertified to the ackret and justices and Clerk of this cort having cal'd there names of
each of the justices of aforesaid and there vots I
trid others John Wilson Yea George Greenway Yea
William B. Carter Nea William Peoples Yea Jesse
Cole Yea William Gott yea James Keys yea George
Emmert yea and John Ritision Yea and there appearing
a megority for the appropreation said clame .

(P.216)   It is therefore ordered by the court that
said clame be read according to the provision of the a
act of the assembly in such cases made & provided and
be sertified no other county Trust Tee for payment
for which said sum of thirteen Dollars and fifty cents
beand the same is hereby approperiated out of any
County money not otherwise approperiated

The assignment of a plat and sertificate of servay
from Jacob Slimp to Mikel Slimp for twenty five
accare of land proving in open court by Joseph
Slimp Eli Razor two subscribing witnesses there to

The assignment of a plat and sertificate of Servay
from Jacob Slimp to Mikle Slimp for twenty five acres
of land proven in open cort by Joseph Slimp and Eli
Rasor two subscribing witnesses there to

The assignment of a plat and certificate of Servay
from Jacob Slimp to Mikle Slimp for one hundred acres
of land proven in open court by Joseph Slimp and Eli
Rasor two Subscribing witnesses thereto

The assignemt of a plat and certificate of a servay
from Jacob Slimp to Mikle Slimp for fore acres of
land proven in open cort by Joseph Slimp and Eli j
Rasor two subscribing witnesses thereto

The assignemt of a plat and certificate of servay
from Daniel Shelly to John L Wilson for fifty acres
of land proving in open court by Isaace Snider and
Mikel Snider two subscribing witnesses there to

(P.217)   The ass ignemt of a plat and certificate
from John Morgan to John Shields for two hundred acres
of land acknowledge in open court there maker there of
John Morgan and admitted to record

Exhibited and acknowledged in open clurt a deed of conveyance from Vaught Heaton to James P. Taylor &
Alfred W. Taylor for fifty acres of land proven in op-
en court by William Bridges & Peter R asor two subscribing Witnesses thereto and admited to record let
it be registered

Ordered by the court that part of the public road
by Jesse Jenkins be so attend or changed and run a
new way that Jesse Jenkins has opened round a new
field he has cleared about the old road

Ordered by the court that Jas. J Tipton John Williams
David Nelson Lazarus C. Inman Tho. Nichols & Jesse
West be a jury to view marks & lay off a road Round
the base of the hill on which his J.F. Taylors house
stands on to take out at or near the Inmans shop or
old saw mill and intersects the old road below Bucks
old house & report to next court

(P.218)   Ordered by the court that Larkin Wilson
be appointed overseer of the public road in the room
of Wm Miller and have the same hands & bounds that
Miller had & Daniel Cables hands untill the alteration is done

Ordered by the court that Smith Campbell be appointed overseer of the Public road in the room of Daniel Smith and have the same hands & Pound that Smith had and all living in that bounds

Ordered by the court that Hugh Wilson be appointed overseer of the public Road in the room of Wm Brumet and have the same hands & bounds that Brumer had

Ordered by the court that John H Vaught be appointed overseer of that part of the road that Adam Snyder had and have the same hands & bounds that Snider had

Ordered by the court that Jacob C. Smith be appointed overseer of the Public road in the Room of Daniel Cable and have the same hands & bounds that Cable had

(P.219)   The assignment of a plat &Certificate of Survay from Pleasant Bowman to Elisha Rainbolt for fifty acres of land Proven in open court by Johnson Hampton and Reuben Miller two subscribing Witnesses thereto

Ordered by the court that a road leading from the head of Lick creek to the Sullivan county line be made Void & that John Mottorn & Wm Smith be attatched to the Indian creek road

Reuben Miller appointed constable who came into open clurt and Entered into bond with Johnson Hamton and William Carter his securities in the sum of one thousands Dollars and took the several Oaths required by law for a constable (see bond)

Benjamin Grindstaff appointed a constable who came in To open clurt and Entered in To bond with Henry Grindstaff John Justice and Harden Brown his securitie in a bond of the sum of one thousand Dollars with several Oaths required by law for a constable (see bond)

(P.220)   Where as it is represented to this court upon Oath That The Three youngist Childern of Henry Ritchie (towit) two little girls and a boy are in Extreem suffring condition it is there fore ordered by the court that the sheriff provide instantly and take custody of the said Children and bring them before thiscourt and that the clerk essue to the sheriff in entanter to the above Effect

Ordered by the court that John L. Lusk be appointed overseer of the public road in the room of Isaac Taylor Jr. from the mouth of Sirmerlys lane to James Gourleys branch and that the hands living on the farms of Mary Taylor Michael Hyder Hannah Overholse Samuel Lusks James Gourley Caswell Taylor Isaac Taylor Sr Charles Lisenby Thomas Hatcher be the hands to work on the road under said overseer

Ordered by the court that Green Moore have liberty to change the road on his own land along the way he has now opened Begining where the New Way leaves the old road across a small point and along the foot of the hill and extending along the old road about fifty yards about the ford on Bicks creek not varying from the old way not varying more than one hundred yards

(P.221)   Ordered by the court that Russell Royston be appointed overseer of the public road in the room of John Taylor and have the same hands and bounds towit from George Hinkles to Daniel Chances and that all the Hands living on Stoney creek from Burrows Forge as low as George Hinkles and Permeanas Lovelace be the hands to work said road

Ordered by the court that Baldin Howard be appointed overseer of the public road in the room of Michael Smithpeter and have the same hands & bounds

Ordered by the court that John Howard be appointed overseer of the Public road in the room of Daniel Shell from the forks of the road above Daniel Baker to James Bradleys and work the same hands that Shell worked

Ordered by the court that, James Blevins Frederick Shoun, Jonathan Range Tobias Hendrix John Williams Saml Montgomery Elijah Harden John Berry Jesse Jenkins John Lyons Wm Greer Joseph Brown Silas Helton James Shields William Mullins John Ward David Warner Casper Cable Charles Justice David Brument John Insor Anderson Kite Abraham Haun John Grindstaff Tho Elliott & Reuben Brooks be Jurors to next session 1828

(P.222)   Ordered by the court that William Gott William B. Carter & David Nelson be appointed agent for the county of Carter to contract with some punctual workman to finish the court house in the town of Elizabethton towit make sash when needed put in glass in all windows make shutters hang them with suitable

hin-es repair door & Window sils put suitable Locks on
the doors & in short do all the work that may be in
thier openion necessary to close in said house in a de-
cent strong suitable manner & imploy a painter & &
furthermore said men are empowered to purshase the
glass putty, oil & paints on the cr·dit of the county
for the purpose of finishing off said house in a re-
spectable manner, They will make report to the next
court how they have executed the trust,

J. Hampton   William Peoples
J. H. Hyder   George Emmert
J.   Keys   Geo. Greenway
Jesse Cole   William Cott
Ezekiel Smith   W. B. Carter.

(P.223) A Deed of conveyance from Isaace P. Tipton
for four hundred & twenty three acres of land in said
county was proven in open court by John Tipton & John
Jobe the subscribing witnesses there to and ordered
to be recorded let it be registered Isaac Tipton Senr

State   )   In this case the attorney
     Vs   )   General by leave of the
Elizabeth Lacy &   )   court enters a noleprosequi
Catharene Lacy   )   & the defendants in proper
person with Samuel Lacy thier security assessed u--
on themselves the costs It is therefore considered by
the court that the state do recover of said defendant
& the said Samuel Lacy security as aforesaid the costs
so by them assumed for which execution shall issue

Abiel C. Parks
Bail of Christopher Frick.
At the suit of Lawson Goodin against said Frick sur-
renders the sd Frick in discharge of himself as bail
aforesaid & was ordered in custoday of the sheriff

(P.224)   John McKinney produced in open court the
scalps of two wolves adjudged by the court to be
over six months old & the said John being sworn
upon his oath saith that he killed the wolves in
the county aforesaid since the 1st day of January
1811 & it appearing to the satisfaction of the court
that sd John did kill sd wolves in the sd county of
Carter it is therefore considered by the court that sd
John Mckinney be allowed three dollars for each of
said scalps so allowed by the court & to be paid by
the state Treasurer

Rheuben Miller appointed constable who came into open
court & entered into bond with Johnston Hampton &
William Carter his securites in the sum of one thousand
dollars and took the several oaths directed by law and
was qualified to act as constable

The mark of Hezekiah Smith of his stock a cross out
of the under part of the left ear

(P.225)   Ordered by the court that Lawson White & E
Ezekiel Smith Esqs be appointed a committie to settle
with John J. Wilson Executor of Samuel Wilson dec'd make
report to the next court

Gutherage Garland produced in open court the scalp of
two wolves adjudged by the court to be over six months
old & the said Gutherage being sworn upon his oath stated that he killed said wolves in the county of Carter
since the 1st day of January 1811 and it appearing to
the satisfaction of the court that the said Gutherage
killed the said wolves in the county aforsaid
It is therefore ordered by the court that said Gutherage
be allowed three dollars for each wolf to be paid by
the state Treasuer

Samuel E. McQueen appointed constable who came into op-
en court & entered into bond with William R. Blevins &
William Arnold in the sum of one thousand dollars took
the several oaths & qualified to act as constable for
said county

(P.226)
George Helms   )   The plaintiff in this cause dismisses
      Vs   )   his suit & the defendant assumes open
Abel Duggar   )   himself the costs It is therefore or-
                     dered by the court that the plaintiff
do recover of   the defendant his costs so assumed by
the defendant & the defendant in mercy & &

Elijah Hathawy &
John Scott bail of Mathew Salts constable surrendered
in open court the body of said Mathew in discharged
of themselves as bail and the said Mathew having failed
ed to give other & sufficient security it was therefore ordered by the court that said Mathew be removed
from office

Benjamen Grindstaff was appointed constable and entered into bond with Henry Grindstaff John Justice &
Harden Brown in the sum of one thousand dollars took
the oath prescribed by law & was qualified as constable

(P.227) George Williams Clerk of this court presented to the court a list of cases in criminal prosecut-
ion chargeable to the county of Carter & applied to the
court for an appropration fix the payment thereof towit State Vs John Smith same Vs John Royston same Vs
Michael Slimp same Vs John Jones same Vs John Jones &
James W Clawson Sr. same Vs James W Clawson Sr same Vs
James W. Clawson Jr. same Vs Eli Basor same Vs Jacob
Slimp same Vs John Royston same Vs obert Rolling
same Vs John Moorefield Jr same VsJohn Moorfield Jr.
State Vs Thomas Paxton & the State against Michael
Slimp amounting in the whole to the sum of one hundred
fifty eight dollars & eighty five cents and a majority
of the acting justices of the county being present to-
wit John J. Wilson George Creenway William B. Carter
William Peoples Jesse Cole William Cott James Keys
George Emmert & John Richardson Esqr. & it appearing
to the satisfaction of the court that said account has
been referred to James P. Taylor attorney General
for the 1st solecetial District

(P.228) Who after examining said account has certified the same to be accurate & Just and the clerk of
this court haveing called the name of each of the mag-
estrate aforesaid & haveing recieved his vote by yea &
nay the vote stood thus for the appropration John Wilson
Yea George Greenway Yea William B. Carter yea William
Peoples Yea Jesse Cole Yea William Cott Yea James Feyes
yea George Emmert Yea & John Richardson yea and there
being an unanimous vote in favour of said appropration
for the satisfaction of said it is therefore ordered
that claim be recorded according to the provision of
the act of assembly in such case made & provided & be
certified to the county Trustee for payment for which
purpose the said sum of one hundred fifty seven dollars forty seven cents & five mills be and the same is
hereby approprated out of any county money not otherwise approprcated court adjourn'd untill tomorrow
Morning 9 oclock,

      W. B. Carter
      William Cott
      Geo. Emmert.

(P.229)   Tusday August the 12 1828

Court met according to adjournment present the,
                William B. Carter
                George Emmert
                William Gott
                James Keys and
                Jesse Coal Esqr.

William Carter Esqr Sheriff returned the Vinira Facis
executed from which following persons was drawn grand
Jour and the court appointed Benjomon Wilson Foreman
Abner McLeod William Benton Ewins Heatherly Enoch Dunkin
Hezkiah Smith Moses Estep Nich Fain Arthur Pierce Joseph
Wagoner Andrew Shown Daniel Stout & Valentine Vanhuss
Empaneled sworn & charged and withdrew to enquire of
thier present ments Vincent Felly constable sworn to
attend the Grand Jury

State Grant to Johathan Lips 100 acres Rec'd tax G.
William

(P.230)
State   ) The defendent came into open court and
  Vs   ) confessed himself indebted to the state
Jonathan Hyder) in the sum of one hundred Dollars to
                 be levied of his goods & chattles land
and tenements and void on condition that he appear before the Justice of our court of please and quarter
sessions now in session from day to day to answer to
a charge of the state and not depart said court without leave

State   ) Samuel W. Williams Bail of the deft
  Vs   ) came into open court &acknowledged
Jonathan Hyder) himself indebted to the state in
                 the sum of one hundred Dollars to
be levied of his goods & chattles lands and tenements
and void on condition that Jonathan Hyder appear before the justice of our court of Please & quarter sessions now in session from day to day to answer to a
plea of the state and depart the same without leave

(P.231)
State.   ) The defendent come into open court
  Vs   ) & acknowledged himself indebted to
William Estep) the state in the sum of one hundred
                 Dollars and Enoch Duncan Bail acknow-
ledged himself indebt to the state in the sum of one
hundred Dollars to be levied of thier goods & chattles
lands & tenements and void on condition that said Estep
appear from day to day before the Justice of our court
of please and quarter session now in session and not

depart the same without leave

Ann Gifford)   The defendent being arrested on a
   Vs   )   case issued by a justice of the peace
James Kerr)   came into open court and took the in-
                solvent debtors oath and returned a
schedule of his property in the following words towit
one Pot one Skillet six plats six knives & forks three
chairs and one straw bed and three quilts a small
patch of Potatoes a small patch of cabbages a small
account on William OBrien
    The amount not known $4 in Iron this 12th August
1828 James Kerr
It is therefore ordered that the shff sell said property towards the satisfaction of the debt of the plaintiff and that the deft be discharged from the custody
of the sheriff

(P.232)
James Guinn   )   The defendant being arrested on a
   Vs   )   Ca Sa Issued by a Justice of the
John Rasor Jr.)   peace came into open court and
                took the insolvent debtors Oath and
returned a shedule of his property in the following
words towit anote on John Wooldridge executed to himself
for two hundred pounds of coffee which note is in the
hands of H.B. Hampton D shoff one Do on Turner Proffitt
for one hundred and thirty Pounds of Iron one forty
cord Pit of coal one horse and three head of cattle
thirteen head of hogs a one horse waggon five sheep &
some household furniture and interest in some stand-
ing corn returned this 12th August 1828 JohnX (his
mark) Rasor It is therefore ordered by the court
that the Sheriff sell said Property towards the satisfaction of said debt and that the defendent be discharged from the custody of the Sheriff

Isaac Taylor   )   The defendants in thier proper
   Vs   )   person came into court open court
John C. Helms &)   and confessed Judgement for the
Owen Edwards   )   sum of ninety three Dollars and
                seventy five cents Debt and costs
Therefore it is considered by the court that the
plaintiff recover over against the Deft the sum of
ninety three dollars & seventy five cents for his
debt and also his costs & charges put to & about his
suit in that behalf expended & that the Defts in
mercy

(P.233)

State) The defendant by Wm Carter pleads
Vs) Guilty an' Wm Carter assumes cost
Dory Wallace) & fine therefore it is considered
by the court that Deft be fined
fifty cents & that the state recover against the
said Dory Wallace & William Carter the fine and
costs & costs of this prosecution and that the defendants be n mercy & &

State) The defendant being charged on the
Vs) bill of Indictment and he for plea
William Boren) thereto saith that he is Guilty
thereof therefore it is considered by
the court that the deft be fined two dollars and fifty
cents and that the state recover against the Defendant
the fine and costs of this prosecution and that the
defendant be in mercy & &

State) The attorney General by leave of the
Vs) court Enters a Noleprosequi and the
Thomas Lovelace) Deft & James Lovelace assumes costs
therefore it is considered by the
court that the state Recover over against the defendants
the costs of this prosecution and that the defts may
be in mercy & &.

A deed of conveyance from Joseph Wilson to Tapley
Wilson & Wm Arnold for one hundred & four acres of
land acknowledged in open court and admitted to record
let it be registered

(P.234)

State) The attorney General by leave of the
Vs) court Enters a noleprosequi and
Polly Parker) Thomas Lovelace and James Lovelace
assumes the costs therefore it is
considered by the court that the state recover over
against the said Thomas & James the costs of this prosecution and that the said Thomas & James be in
mercy & &

State) The defendant being charged
Vs) upon the bill of Indictment
Moses Hickenbottom) and He for plea thereto saith
that he is note Guilty thereof
and puts himself on his country and James P. Taylor
attorney General who prosecutes on behalf of the state
doth the same whereupon came a jury and the Jurors

towit Isaac Dunlap Nathaniel Taylor Robert Morris
James Bradley James Dunton Jacob Smith Jacob Wagner
Moses Huffman James Hughs Pleasant Proffit Emanuel
Jenkins &Ephraim Lewis chosen Elected tried & sworn
upon thier oaths say do find the defendant not Guilty in mannor & form as charged in the bill fo Indietment it is therefore considered by the court that
the said Moses Hickenbottom be fined ten Dollars and
in custody of the sheriff thirty (TP.235) days and
that the state recover of the defendant the fine &
costs of this prosecution and that the defendant pay
the same or give security beofre he be liberated out
of the custody of the sheff

State	)	The defendant being charged
Vs	)	upon the Bill of Indictment
Charles M.D. Gourley	)	and he for plea thereto saith
		that he is guilty thereof

Therefore it is considered by the court that the defendant be fined two dollars and fifty cents pay the costs
of this prosecution & be in mercy & &.

State	)	The defendant being charged
Vs	)	upon the bill of Indictment
Barnabas Oaks	)	and he for plea thereto saith
		that he is guilty thereof

thereof it is considered by the court that the defendant
be fined fift cents pay the costs of this prosecution
and be in mercy

A deed of conveyance from John Baker to Hight Moorland
for one hundred and thirty acres of land proven in op-
en court by Daniel Stout & George P. Stout two subscribing witnesses thereto & admited to record let it be
registered

(P.236)

State	)	The defendant being charged upon the
Vs	)	bill of Indictment and he for plea
Elisha Smith	)	thereto saith that he is not Guilty
		thereof & puts himself on his country

and thereupon came a jury towit Isaac Dunlap Nath
TaylorRobert Morris James Bradley James Dunton Moses
Huffman Elisha Williams Philimon Lacy Emanuel Jenkins
George Blevins Ephraim Lewis & Jacob Wagner sworn upon
thier oath say do find the defendant not guilty on motion and for reasons appearing to the court it is considered by the court that Barnabas Oaks the prosecutor

be taxed with the costs of this prosecution and that
the state recover against the said Barnabas the costs
of this prosecution & that the defendant may be in
mercy & &.

State	)	John Wilson Elisha Smith Jacob Smith
Vs	)	and Hezekiah Smith proved one days
Bes. Oaks	)	attendance as witnesses in the above
		case

Thomas Heatherly appointed constable came into open
court and entered into bond in the sum of one thous-
and dollars with John Glover Solomon Ellis Ewings
Heatherly John C. Helms & Lewis Lewis his securitys
(see bond)

(P.237)   A deed of conveyance from Isaac Taylor Jr.
to Alferd W. Taylor for one hundred & seventy five and
one half acres of land acknowledged in open court by
the said Isaac & admitted to record let it be registered

A deed of conveyance from William Ellis to Samuel
Williams & George P. Williams acknowledged in open
court by the said William Ellis & admitted to record
let it be registered

Ordered by the court that Henry Have be appointed
overseer of the public road in the room of Wm Stover
& have the same hands & bounds

Ordered by the court that the overseer of the public
road from Bradleys to Vanhoose to James Bradleys on
Roan creek work through or keep up the public way
of Elisha Rainbolts lane in stead of the old way

A deed of conveyance from Samuel E. Patton to Thomas
Roe for thirteen acres of land was acknowledged in
court by the said Elisha & admitted to record let
it be registered

(P.238)   A deed of conveyance from James Hughes
to William Ellis for two hundred & sixty two acres
of land was acknowledged in open court by the said
James Hughs & admitted to record Let it be registered

Ordered by the court that Jacob Range be overseer
of the road leading by Harts to Duncins ford and
that his bounds commence at the point on south side
of watauga There said road leaves Stage road &

work to Dongin Ford & have the same hands that Reubin
Lacy had the former overseer

Court adjourned untill tomorrow morning 9 oclock.
                                        Geo. Emmert
                                        William Gott
                                        Jesse Cole

                    Wednesday Augt. 13th 1828

Court met according to adjournment Present the Worshipful
                    Wm. Gott
                    George Emmert
                    & Jesse Cole   Esqrs

State   ) Charged plea Guilty court fine twenty
  Vs   ) five cents therefore it is considered
Jonathan Hyder   ) by the court that the state recover
                    of the Deft the fine & costs of this
prosecution & that Deft in mercy & &.

(I.239)   Wednesday August the 13th 1828 court met
according to adjournment Present the Worshipful

                    William Gott   )
                    George Emmert &)   Esquires
                    Jesse Cole   )

Jerret Arnold   )
     Vs   ) On motion of plff by atto a rule to
Joseph Cooper   ) show cause Why the certionari be dis-
                    missed rule to quash the proceeding
had before the Justice of the peace

Adam Bryles   )   On motion for a judgment
     Vs   )   ag't Wm Carter shff for an
Moses Humphreys   )   Escape continued untill
Elisha Humphreys &)   tomorrow
John Scott   )

Thomas Gourley appointed constable came into open court
and entered into bond with Charles M.D. Gourley and
William Gott his securitys in the sum of one thousand
Dollars & &.

State   ) And the defendant being charged upon
  Vs   ) the bill of Indictment and he for plea
Thos Nichols   ) thereto saith that he is not Guilty
                   thereof and puts himself on his count-
ry and thereupon came a jury towit

Isaac Dunlap Nathaniel Taylor Robert Morris James
Bradley Jacob Smith James Bunton Jacob Waggoner
Teter Nave John Roe Thomas Gourley Owen Edwards
Emanuel Jenkins (P.240) Josen   elected & tried
upon thier oaths do say that they find the Defendant
guilty in manner and form as charged in the Bill of
Indictment   Therefore it is considered by the court
that the Deft be fined twenty five cents and that the
state recover against the Defendant the fine and and
costs of this prosecution and that the Defendant may
be in mercy " &

State   ) The Defendant being Charged on the
   Vs   ) bill of Indietment and he for plea
William Estep) thereto saith he is guilty thereof
                      therefore it is considered by the
court that the defendant be fined six & a fourth cents and in custody of the sheriff until fine and costs
be paid or give security
Enoch Duncan assumes fine and costs It is therefore
considered by the court that the state recover against
the said Estep & Enoch Duncan the fine and costs of
this prosecution and that the said William May be in
mercy & &

James Estep) Ordered by the court that a commiss-
   Vs   ) ion issue to any Justice of the peace
Isaac Estep   ) for Ash County North Carolina to take
                      the deposition of James Swift Enos
Isaacs John Estep & Joel Dyer that said Deposition may
be read on the trial of (P.241) the above cause and
that the plaintiff give Defendant five days notice of
the time and place of taking the same

John Smith) Now at this day came the parties afore-
   Vs   ) said by thier attorneys and thereupon
Lewis Lewis) came a Jury towit Isaac Dunlap Nathaniel
                     Taylor Robert Morris James Bradley
Jacob Smith James Bunton Jacob Wagoner Teter Nave John
Roe Thomas Gourley Owen Edwards & Emanuel Jenkins chosen
elected tried and sworn upon thier oaths say they do
find for the Plaintiff and assess his damage to six cents
and the fourth of a cent therefore It is considered by
the court that the plaintiff recover of the Deft the
damage assessed as aforesaid by the Jury aforesaid together with the costs in this behalf expended and that
the Defendant be in mercy

Andreson Hutchens)   Now at this day came the
       Vs   )   parties aforesaid by thier
David Hanes   )   attorneys and thereupon came
                    a Jury towit Isaac Dunlap
Nathaniel Taylor Robert Morris James Bradley Jacob
Smith James Bunton Jacob Wagner Peter Nave John Roe
Thomas Gourley Owen Edwards and Samuel Jenkins
Chosen elected tried and sworn (P.242) upon thier
oaths s ay do fine for the Plaintiff and assesses his
damage to one hundred and fifty Dollars and twelve cents
Therefore it is considered by the court that the plaintiff recover against the Defendant his damage aforesaid
assessed and also his costs and charges put to about
suit in that behalf expended and that the Defendant be
in mercy &c &c

Joseph C. West)   Now at this day came the parties afore-
       Vs   )   said by thier attorneys and thereupon
John Stuart   )   came a jury towit.   Isaac Dunlap
                    Nathaniel Taylor Robert Morris James
Bradley Jacob Smith James Bunton Jacob Wagner Peter Nave
John Roe Thomas Gourley Owen Edwards Samuel Jenkins
Chosen elected tried & sworn upon thier oaths do say
they find for the plaintiff and assess his damage to
one hundred and eleven dollars fifteen cents
Therefore it is considered by the court that the plaintiff recover against the Defendant the aforesaid sum of
one hundred and eleven Dollars fifteen cents by the
Jury in manner & form aforesaid assessed and also his
costs and charges put to about his suit in this behalf
expended & the left in mercy &c &c

(P.243)
D & J Bacon for   )   Now at this day came the
D. J. Shavers use   )   parties aforesaid by thier
       Vs   )   attornies and thereupon came
Marke Reeve   )   a jury towit Isaac Dunlap
Casper.W. Reeve   )   Nathaniel Taylor Robert
Robert Reeve   )   Morris James Bradley Jacob
Jobe W. Reeve   )   Smith James Bunton Jacob Wag-
                    ner Peter Nave John Rowe
Thomas Gourley Owen Edwards & Emanuel Jenkins chosen
Elected tried & sworn upon thier oaths say do find
for the plaintiff and assess his damage to seventy
three dollars and eighty five cents
therefore it is considered by the court that the plain-
tiff recover against the Defendants the aforesaid sum
of seventy three dollars and eighty five cents by the
Jury aforesaid assessed and also his costs and charges

put to and about His suit in that behalf Expended and
that the defendants may be in mercy & &.

D. Bacon for	)	Now at this day came the the
D. Shavers use	)	parties aforesaid by thier
Vs	)	attorneys & thereupon came a
Mark Reeve	)	Jury towit Isaac Dunlap Nathaniel
Casper W. Reeve	)	Taylor Robert Morris James Bradley
J.W. Reeve	)	Jacob Smith James Bunton Jacob
Robert Reeve	)	Wagner Teter Nave John Roe Thomas
		Cowrley Owen Edwards & Manuel

Jenkins Chosen Elected tried & sworn upon thier oaths
say do find for the plaintiff and assess his damage to
seventy four dollars fifty five cents ($.244)
Therefore it is considered by the court that the plaintiff recover against the Defendants the aforesaid sum
of seventy four dollars and fifty five cents by the
Jury aforesaid assessed and also his costs and Charges
put to about his suit in that behalfexpended

Luster Waily	)	Now at this day came the parties
Vs	)	aforesaid by thier attorneys and
Casper Reeve	)	thereupon came a Jury towit
Mark Reeve	)	Isaac Dunlap Nathaniel Taylor
Robert Reeve	)	Robert Morris James Bradley Jacob
J.W. Reeve	)	Smith James Bunton Jacob Wagner
Clayton Reeve	)	Teter Nave John Roe Thomas Cowrley
		Owen Edwards Manuel Jenkin

Chosen elected tried and sworn upon thier oaths say do
find for the plaintiff and assess his damage to fifty
five dollars and ninety cents Therefore it is considered by the court that the plaintiff recover against the
defendants the damage aforesaid assessed by the Jury
aforesaid and also his costs and Charges put to about
his suit in this behalf expended and the Defendants
in mercy & &

E. M. Carter for	)	Now at this day came the part-
J. F. Deaderick	)	ies aforesaid by thier attor-
Vs	)	neys and thereupon came a jury
Casper W. Reeve	)	towit ($.245) Isaac Dunlap
Mark Reeve	)	Nathaniel Taylor Robert Morris
Robt Reeve	)	James Bradley Jacob Smith "
J.W. Reeve	)	James Bunton Jacob Wagner
Elijah Embree	)	Teter Nave John Roe Thomas
		Cowrley Owen Edwards &

Manuel Jenkins Chosen elected tried and sworn say do
find for the plaintiff and assess the damage to one
thousand thirty seven dollars & fifty cents

Therefore it is considered by the court that the plaintiff recover against the defendants the damage afore-i
saidassessed by the Jury aforesaid and also the costs
and charges put to about his suit in this behalf expended and the defendants in mercy & &

A. C. Parks	)	Now at this day came the parties
Vs	)	aforesaid by thier attorneys and
John Allison	)	thereupon came a jury towit

Benjam Wilson Abner McLeod
William Bunton Hezekiah Smith Moses Estep Nichs Pain
Arthur Pierce Joseph Wagnor Andrew Chown Daniel Stout
&Ewins Heatherly Valuntine Vanhuse Chosen elected tried
and sworn upon thier oaths say do find for the plaintiff
and assess his damage to five dollars
Therefore it is considered by the court that the plaintiff recover against the defendant the damage aforesaid assessed by the Jury afrresaid and also his costs
and charges put to about his suit in this behalf expended and that the defendant be in mercy && from which
Judgement the defendant prays an appeal to our next
circuit court of law to be held for Carter county at
the court house in Elizabethton on the (p.246)
third Monday of September next and entered into Bond
of the sum of one hundred dollars with Alfred W. Taylor
his security

John Crumley	)	Vincent Kelly constable returned &
Vs	)	Execution Issued by a justice of the
Demsey Richey	)	peace in favour of the plff for the

sum of nineteen dollars & eighty
two cents Debts & fifty cents costs. Search made in
my county no goods and chattles found in my county
Whereon to levy this Execution then levied on 40 Acres
of land lying on the north side of Stoney creek adjoining John Grindstaff & others also on Entry one
hun'red acres on the south side of said creek whereon said Richie now lives 13th Augt 1'29 for which return appearing to the court it therefore ordered by
the court that the shff sell said land or so much
thereof as shall be of Value to satisfy said Execution
& costs of this order

William Evans	)	Vincent Kelly constable returnd
Vs	)	& Execution Issued by a Justice
Dempsey Ritchey	)	of the peace in favour of the plff
		for the sum of forty two dollars

and forty two cents & one Debt & fifty cents costs half
Search made in my county no goods & chattles found
whereon to levy this Execution. Levied on forty acres
of land lying on the north side of Stoney Creek adjoining John Grindstaff and others also an entry one
Hundred acres whereon said Ritchie now lives

11th Augt 1828 for which return appearing to the
court it is therefore ordered by the court that the
sheriff sell said land or so much thereof as will
be of Value to satisfy said Execution & costs of
this order

(P.247)
Acklin Woods & Isaac Allison witnesses in the foregoing case proved thier attendance two days each travaeling to and from twenty six miles each

State   )   Ordered by the court that
  Vs   )   the Defendant be released
Moses Hickenbottom)   of the Imprisonment and that
                       the fine be mitigatedto five
dollars. Jesse Cole assumes fine and costs therefore
it is considered by the court that the state recovers
against the Defendant and Jesse Cole the fine aforesaid and also the costs of this prosecution and the defendant in mercy

State   )   William Jones a Witness proves his
  Vs   )   attendance for three days
C. M.DGourley   )

Daniel Chance   )   Vincent Kelly constable return'd
  Vs   )   an Execution Issued by a justice
Demsey Ritchie   )   of the Peace in favor of the plff
                       for the sum of Eleven Dollars &
seventeen cents & fifty cents costs search made in my
county no goods and chattles found whereon to levy
this Execution then levied on forty acres of land
lying on the north side of Stoney Creek adjoining
John Grindstaff and others, also an entry one hundred acres on the south side Stoney creek whereon said
Richie now lives for which Return appearing to the
court it is therefore ordered that the sheriff sell
said land or so much thereof as will be of Value to
satisfy said Execution & this order

(P.248)   Ordered by that David Nelson William
Messeck Joseph Taylor Jesse Adams & Jacob Camron be
a jury of review & Examine the Main Road from the
east end of A. M. Carters house in Elizabethton eastward-
ly & report to this court what alteration be made thereon so as not to injure the public & report to this
court what alteration can be made thereon so as not
to injure the public said alteration and that the
sheriff of Carter county fourth with execute this order

Who made the following report towit we the under
named Jurirs being sworn agreeable to law hath examined the road set fourth in the petition do report that we are of openion that (that) no injury
will result to the public in the change of the public road we have marked out the road to run down the
street by A. M.Carters house then with the street
as to continue the old Road and cross the race and
cross the Race at the old ford above the tan yard
Road & shut up or dosanul the old Road, from A. M
Carters, house leading by his Machancly untill it intersect the present described road on the east side
of the race

(P.249) A deed of conveyance from Lenard Shoun
to Frederick Shoun for two hundred acres land proven
in open court by W. B. Carter & Wm Carter two subscribing witnesses thereto & addmitied to record let
it be registered

(. ') A deed of conveyance from Lenard Shown to
Andrew Shown for one hundred & Eighty three acres
land proven in (in) open court by W. B. Carter & Wm.
Carter two subscribing Witnesses thereto & addmited
to record let it be registered

A deed of conveyance from Johnston Hampton to Lenard
Shown for two hundred & trenty four & a half acres
land proven in open court by W. B. Carter one of the
subscribing witnesses thereto & contianued for futher
probate

A deed of conveyance from Lenard Chown to Isaac Shown
for two hundred & trenty four & a half acres land prov-
en in open court by W. B. Carter & William Carter two
subscribing witnesses thereto and addmited to record
let it be registered

A deed of conveyance from Lenard Chown to John Shoun
for one hundred acres land proven in open court by W.
B. Carter & Wm Carter two subscribing Witnesses thereto and addmited to record let it be registered

A deed of conveyance from Lenard Shoun to William
Shoun & Joseph Shoun for three hundred & forty acres
of land proven in open court by W.B. (P.250)
Carter & William Carter two subscribing witnesses
thereto addmited to record let it be registered

and the court then adjourned till tomorrow nine oclock

W. B. Carter
William Gott
J. Hampton
Geo. Emmert
John J. Wilson

Thursday 14th August 1828 court met according to adjournment Present Wm Gott W. B. Carter Johnson Hampton George
Emmert & John J. Wilson Esqr.

Adam Broyles Vs
William Carter Sheff)   It appearing to the satisfaction of
of Carter county   )   the court that on the 16th May
                            1828 then issued from the court of
pleace and quarter session of Carter county awrit of Capias
ad satisfaciendum at the suit of said Adam Broyles against
Moses Humphreys Elisha Humphries & John Scott which writ
came to the hands of Abiel C. Parks Deputy sheriff of said
Wm Carter sheriff of Carter county on the 15th August 1826
for the sum of one hundred & thirty one Dollars fifty five
cents Damages & the further sum sixteen dollars fifty five
cents costs and the said A. C. Parkes Deputy sheriff as
aforesaid having Executed said writ of Ca Sa on the bodies
of Moses & Elisha Humpheys and committed them to the jail of
said county on the (P.251) 29 July 1828 and they escaped
and on the 4th August 1828 the said A. C. Parks Deputy
sheriff as aforesaid executed said writ on John Scott and
the jail having been broken suffered the said John Scott to
go at large whether so ever he would whereupon motion of
the said Adam Broyles by his atty it is considered and adjudged by the court that judgement be entered up against the
said William Carter Sheriff as aforesaid for the said sum of
one hundred & thirty one dollars fifty five cents the debt
in said writ of Ca Sa mentioned with interest thereon at
the rate of six per cent from said 15th August 1826 amounting to the sum of fifteen Dollarsseventy Eight cents amounting in all together sum of one hundred & forty seven Dollars
thirty three cents and also the further sum of sixteen dollars fifty four cents the costs of said suit and also costs
of this suit for which execution may Issue

A deed of conveyance from Henry H. Nave &Polly"his wife to
James P. Taylor for seventy acres of land was acknowledged
in open court by Henry H. Nave and the said Polly Nave wife
of said Henry H. Nave by being examined by the court separately and apart from her said Husband acknowledged that she exe-
ecuted the same freely Voluntarily and of her own free will
and accord without the threats, persuasion or other undue
influeance of her husband, whereupon said deed was admitted b
to record let it be registered

(P.252) A deed of conveyance from Samuel Tipton senr.
to George Lacey for seventy acres of land was proven in
open court by Isaac Tipton & Abraham Tipton and ordered
to be recorded let it be registered

James F. Taylor) Vincent Kelly constable returned an
    Vs   ) execution issued by a justice of peace
Thomas Wetherly) in favor of the pliff for the sum of $15.
77 Debt and fifty cents costs, levied
on one hundred & fifty acres of land Lying on the south side
of Stoney creek adjoining Ewin Weatherly Moses Estep Wm
Garland 14th Augt. 1828 from which return it appeared no
goods & chattles were to be found it is therefore it is
ordered by the court that said sheriff of Carter county sell
said land or so much thereof as shall be sufficient to
satisfy Debt & costs and the costs of this order

James J. Tipton) Vincent Kelly constable returned an
    Vs   ) execution issued by a justice of the
Thomas Wetherly) Peace against the Deft for the sum of
seventy nine Dollars twenty seven
cents Debt and fifty cents costs, search made in my county
no goods & chattles found whereon to levy this Execution
then levied on one hundred & fifty acres of land adjoining
Evans Wetherly Moses Estep Wm Garland lying on the south
side of Stoney creek Augt 14th 1828 it appearing to the satisfaction of the court that there were no goods & chattles
of the Defendant were found therefore it is considered by
the court that (P. 253) the shff of Carter county sell
so much of said land to levied on as will be of value sufficient to pay said debt & costs & the costs of this judgment

Samuel Maxwell.) Judgment by default and writ of en-
    Vs   ) quiry of damage awarded
Elijah Hathaway)

Johnson Hampton) The sheriff having returned upon the
    Vs   ) writ in this cause that the defendant
Thomas Carver) cannot be found in this county on application of the plaintiff by his at-
torney it is ordered that a Judicial attachment issue returnable to next court.

John Smith   ) In this cause the plaintiff by his at-
    Vs   ) torney moved the court for Judgment
Lewis Lewis &) against the defendants for and on ac-
Stephen Lewis) count of the said Lewis's failing to appear in compliance with a Bond taken by Abial C. Tarks Dy
Shff by virtue of a Casa served on said Lewis at the suit
of said Jno. Smith an argument of which motion the court re-
fused to grant the Judgment It is therefore considered by
the court that the defts recover of the plaintiff the costs
about this notion in this behalf expended and that Execution Issue accordingly.

(P.254)

State	)	On motion of James D. Taylor for errors
Vs	)	shown to the court it is ordered by the
Wm R. Blevins	)	court that the taxation of costs be corr-
		ected by rejecting the attendance of the

witnesses to the amount of thirteen Dollars and fifty cents
and the costs of constable Heatherly to amount of one dollar and seventy five cents

State	)	For reasons appearing to the satisfaction
Vs	)	of the court It is ordered that twenty five
Wm R. Blevins	)	cents in the attendance of each witness be
A. Blevins	)	rejected that much being erroneous
J. Blevins	)	

J. Arnold	)	In this case it appearing to the satisfact-
Vs	)	ion of the court that a part of the papers
Joseph Cooper	)	in this cause were not returned towit the
		dilivery bond It is ordered that an alias *

certiorari issue to Thomas Johnson Magr and Thomas Heatherly
them or either of them to send up said Bond to next court
requiring
(P.255)

Saml. W. William and Abraham Tipton commissioners appointed
by the court made thier report in the following words towit
   We the commissioners appointed by the court of Carter to
make settlement with the former Trustee of this county having proceeded to discharge our duty as commissioners fined
on due examination the following ballances due the county
for the years here after named Viz

for the year 1819	---- --- ------------	187.06
For the year 1820	------------------------	16.63½
Do the year 1821	------------------------	0.30¼
Do the year 1822	------------------------	98.56
Do the year 1823	------------------------	67.09½
Do the year 1824	------------------------	531.26½

Therefore report the aggregate amount due the county as appears
from the books of the commissioners to be nine hundred and
two Dollars ninety one & one half cents August 14th 1828

                                        Saml. W. Williams cones,
                                        Abrm Tipton cones.

Ordered by the court that Saml. W. Williams be allowed Six
Dollars and Abraham Tipton six dollars for service rendered
as commissioners up to this 15th Augt. 1828 and that certificates issued to each therefore

P.256)

m Carter)   It appearing to the satisfaction of
Vs)   the court that William Carter Shff
lisha Humphreys)   of Carter county has this had judge-
oses Humphreys))   ment rendered against him as sheriff
ohn Scott)   for one hundred and thirty one Dollars
                 & fifty five cents damages and the fur-
her sum of fifteen Dollars and seventy eight cents with the
um of sixteen dollars & fifty five cents costs being the
mount of Judgement & costs Adam Broyls recovered in our said
ourt against the said defendants amounting to the sum of
ne hundred and sixty three Dollars & eighty eight cents
ith the sum of three Dollars and ninety cents the costs of
he motion against him amounting in the whole to one hundred
nd sixtyseven Dollars & seventy eight cents on motion of J.
. Taylor it is ordered & adjudged that the said William
arter had judgement against the said Defendant for the sum
f one hundred and sixty seven Dollars &twenty eight cents
ith the costs of this motion It is therefore considered by
he court that the Plff recover of the Defendants the said
um of one hundred and sixty seven Dollars and seventy eight
ents with the costs of this motion & that execution issued & &.

P.257)   Vincent Kelly constable proved his attendance as
constable two days at this court & Reubin Miller constable
our days at this court

. F. Taylor assignee)   The Plff dismisses his suit and de-
Vs)   fendant assumes costs it is there-
oseph Wilson)   fore considered by the court that
                 the plff recover of left the costs
f this suit & he be in mercy

ourt adjournd until court in cause,

                              Geo. Emmert
                              J. Hampton
                              John J. Wilson
                              W. B. Carter
                              William Cott.

P.258)   State of Tennessee Carter county at a meeting
f court of Pleas and quarter session holden for Carter
ounty at the court house in Elizabethton on the second
onday & November in the year of our Lord one Thousand eight
undred and twenty eight Present the Worshipful.
                              George Emmert
                              John J. Wilson
                              Jesse Cole
                              William B. Carter
                 Esquires.   James Keys
                              William Cott
                              Ezekiel Smith
                              George Greenway
                              William Peoples.

Mary Haun Exhibeted in open court the last will and Testament of Matthias Haun deceased it was proven by George Williams and Adam Haun two subscribing witnesses thereto and ordered to be admitted to record

Mary Haun wife & relect of Matthias Haun decd. comes into open court and enters into bond with George Haun and Adam Haun securities in the penal sum of five hundred dollars see bond and was quallified as Executrex

(P.259)   Ordered by the court that John Forrister be appointed administrator of Margarett Forrister decd. and the said John entered into bond with James Keys and William Arnold his securities in the sum of two hundred Dollars with condition (see bond) and was qualified as the law directs

Ordered by the court that James P. Taylor attorney General be allowed fifty dollars for his ex officio servivies for the year eighteen hundred and twenty eight.
     George Williams clerk calling each justice name present those who voted for the above appropriation George Emmert Aye John J. Wilson Aye Jesse Cole Aye William B. Carter Aye James Keys Aye William Gott Aye Ezekiel Smith Aye George Greenway Aye and William Peoples Aye and there appearing a majority in favor of the appropriation. It is therefore ordered by the court that the aforesaid sum of fifty Dollars be appropriated out of any county moneys not otherwise appropriated

A deed of conveyance from Isaac Campbell to George Smith for seven and one half acres of land was acknowledged in open court by the maker thereof Isaac Campbell and admitted to record let it be registered

(P.260)   On motion of William B. Carter for an appropriation of fifteen Dollars for the support and maintainance of Thomas Doherty and wife two of the poor of this county and George Williams Clerk of this court calling the Justices present by name those voting for the appropreation are the following towit George Emmert Aye John J. Wilson Aye Jesse Cole Aye William B. Carter Aye James Keys Aye William Gott Aye Ezekiel Smith Aye George Greenway Aye and William Peoples Aye and there appearing a majority of the acting Justices of the peace for said county in favor of the appropriation It is therefore ordered by the court that William B. Carter be allowed the sum of fifteen dollars to be paid out of the poor tax

Ordered by the court that Lazarus C. Inman be appointed
Guardian of Martha Bayles Infant of Daniel Bayles decd.
aged eight years and enters into bond with James Clark
his security in the sum of five hundred dollars (sec.
bond)

Ordered by the court that the Indenture entered into by
David McNabb security of Thomas Carver to whom Levi Vaun
an Infant boy was bound be released and that the Executor
of the sd. McNabb be discharged from all liability on said
endenture or bond

(P.261)   Ordered by the court that the report of the
Jury of View as to the change in the road on James P.
Taylor place as follows be affirmed and that the overseer
work the same whereon said Taylors shall have opened and
cleared out the new road

Ordered by the court that Ezekiel Smith Esqr. take in a
list of the taxable property and polls in Captain Grindstaffs
company for the year 1829 Jesse Cole Esquire in Captain
Howards old district Green Moor Esquire in Captain Wilson
district Lawson White in Captain Burns district John
Richerson Esquire in Captain Haves district William Cobb
Esquere in Captain Courleys district William B. Carter in
Captain Drakes district John L. Williams in Captain Greens
district and William Peoples Captain McInturffs district

A deed of conveyance from Edward Austin Sr to Absolom
Loved for twenty three acres of Land was proven in open
court by Andrew Arnold and James Keys the two subscribing
witnesses thereto and admitted to record let it be registered

A deed of conveyance from Felex Brown to Joseph Smith for
seventy acres of land proven in open court by Caleb Smith
and James Keys two subscribing witnesses there to admitted
to record let it be registered

(P.262)   A deed of conveyance from Nicholas Kelso to
Daniel Foust for fifty acres of land was proven in open court
by James Hughs and Joel Cooper two subscribing witnesses ten
thereto & admitted to record let it be registered

A power of Attorney from Joseph Wilson to Ezekiel Smith in
the following words to it know all men by these present
that I Joseph Wilson of the county of Carter and state of
Tennessee do make constitute and appoint Ezekiel Smith of
the county and state aforesaid my lawful agent and attorney, to do and get for me so far as to transfer and assign
over to Thomas Dugger four Platts and certificates of survey two of fifty acres and two of twenty five acres all in

Carter county on the north side of Watauga river on the
Bovers Dam branches and in witness I have hereunto set
my hand and seal this 11th day of November 1825

Hardy Pierce) Test.   Joseph Wilson (seal)
John Ward   )

Was proven in open court by Hardy Pierce one of the subscribing witnesses thereto and also by John Ward the other subscribing witness thereto and admitted to record let it be registered

(P.263)   A deed of conveyance from Thomas Jones to Elisha
Rainbolt for one hundred acres of land was proven in open
court by Ezekiel Smith and Hardy Pierce two subscribing witnesses thereto was admitted to record let it be registered

A deed of conveyance from Right Mourland to Henry Stout for
one hundred and thirty acres of land was proven in open
court by William B. Carter and James B. Mourley two subscribing witnesses thereto was admitted to record, let it be registered

A deed of conveyance from Ezekiel Smith to George Smith for
fifty acres of land was acknowledged in open court by the
maker thereof, Ezekiel Smith was admitted to record let it
be registered

A plat and certificate of survey from John White Head to
John Grindstaff for one hundred acres of land was acknowledged in open court by John White Head admitted to record

A deed of conveyance from Thomas Jones to Elisha Rainbolt
for forty acres of land was proven in open court by Ezekiel
Smith and Hardy Pierce two subscribing witnesses thereto
and admitted to record let it be registered

(P.264)   Ordered by the court that Elijah Smith be overseer of the public road in the room of Larkin L. Wilson
from the ford of the river below David Holleys to the new
road opened by Isaac T. Avery and have the same hands subject to work under Larkin L. Wilson

Ordered by the court that John Baun Abraham Baun John Greer
William Greer, George Williams John Taylor John Britt &
William Britt or any five of whom may be a Jury to view,
mark and lay off a road from the fork of Dry creek, to the
road passing Reeves Iron works, over the Iron Mountain and
report to next court

Ordered by the court that Isaac Campbell be releas'd of the tax on ninety acres of land for the year 1828

For reasons appearing to the court It is therefore ordered that Smith Campbell be released of a poll tax for the year 1828

The assignment of a plat and certificate of survey from James W. Clawson ot Elisha Rainbolt for one hundred acres of land was proven in open court by Thomas Duggar and Able Duggar two subscribing witnesses thereto

Ordered by the court that Elisha Rainbolt be appointed overseer of the public road in the room of James Bradleys from James Bradleys to Van Hooses and have the same Hands that the former overseer had

(P.265)   Ordered by the court that Moses Price be appointed overseer of the public road in the room of David Price and have the bounds and hands that David Price had

Ordered by the court that Isaac Tipton be appointed overseer of the public road in the room of George Lacy and have the same hands & bounds that George Lacy had

Ordered by the court that Michael Hyder Junr. be appointed overseer on the public road at the forks of the roadbetween James Gourleys and Jonathan Hyder and to intersect the Jones Bourgh road near Mrs. Taylors on the Watauwa River and work the same hands that Benjamine Hyder worked

Ordered by the court that Adam Post be appointed overseer of the public road in the room of Matthias Baker and have the same bounds and hands that said Baker had

Ordered by the court that Alexander Woods be appointed overseer of the public road in the room of Jonathan Poland and have the same bounds and hands that Poland had

Ordered by the court that William B. Carter George Emmert and Ezekiel Smith Esquires be appointed a committe to settle with Reuben Miller and William Carter adminestrator with the will annexed of Jeremiah Miller dec'd make report of thier settlement to next court.

(P.266)   Elisha Smith constable returne'd and ecuection Issued by a justice of the peace in favor of John J. Wilson against William Brummet and Hugh Wilson for the sum of Eighteen Dollars and thirty seven cents search made no goods nor chattles found in my county but levied on a tract of land supposed to be fifty acres the property of William Brummit known by the name of the sink hole place willed by his father in law to said Brummit September 28th 1828

from which return it appearing to the satisfaction of the
court that there are no goods and chattles found It is there
fore ordered by the court that the sheriff sell said land
or so much thereof as will be sufficient to satisfy said execution together with the costs

Ordered by the court that Lawson Goodwin overseer of the
road from Mrs. Smiths to Lawson Goodwins have the following hands towit Lawson Whites hands Joshua Perkins, John
Perkins, Lawson Goodwin & hands, John Jestice Charles
Jestice Joseph Vaun and hands on Charles Mourland farm &
William Lewis farm
Ordered by the court that Benjamin Foster Jr be appointed
overseer of the public road in the room of Henry Nave and
have the same hands & bounds that Henry Nave had

(P.267)   Ordered by the court that Wm Mullens, John Ingram
Jacob Miller, Abram Drake, John K. Insor,Geo, Lacy Brien
Obrien Tho. Buck John Mathorn, Michl Hyder, Jas. B. Moorley
John Shown, Wm. Baker, John Britt, Jas Orton, Tho. Johnson
on the Laurel Leo Shown John Richardson, Arthur Pearce
Christian Carriner, Reuben Brooks, Lawson White Johnson
Hampton Senr. Wm Harden, Danl Stout,
Be Jurors to our next circuit court of law to be held for
Carter county at the court house in Elizabethton on the
third Monday of March next.

Ordered by the court that Valentine Bowers, Robt. Maclins
Jesse Adams Saml. Drake Wm Stover, John Nave, Geo. Smith
Wm OBrient Benja. Hyder Wm Perry Jas. W. Renfroe G. M.D.
Gourley Jona. Foland, Andw. Wilson, Benja. Gentry, Isaac
Carrol, Saml Smith, Benjam Moseley, Huse Harden, Manley
Wilson, Philip Shell Jas. Gilliland, Jas. Bradley, Joseph
Warner Thos. Crow &Godfrey Nave be Jurors to Feby. session
1829

    (P.268)   Alfred M. Carter clerk of the circuit court
of Carter county presented a list of cases in criminal Pros-
ecutions chargable to the county of Carter and applied to
this court for an appropreation for the payment thereof towit state Vs James Atcheson Bill of cost
Justice James Keys------------------------------   0.50
Const. William Donally Serving warrant------   50
Entering final determination of suit---------   1.60
Expences accured in conveying Deft to Jail Coudty2.75

State   )   Justice Hampton for recognizance0.75
Vs   )   M Smithpeter serving warrant----0.50
Peter Rasor)   Sheriff Carter summoning 8 witnes
                     ses-------------------------------2.00

Clerk 4 continuances ------------------------------------1.60
Do 4 afts.-- 0.80
Do 8 subpr.-- 1.60
Do Indietment-- 1.00
Do charging prisoner and entering plea----------- 0.60
Do Recognizance------------------------------------ 0.50
Do Entering final Judgement---------------------- 1.60
Do Taxing costs--------------------------------------- 0.50
Attorney General------------------------------------ 2.50

State	)	J. Hampton Justice taking bond	0.75
Vs	)	M. Smithpeter serving Warrant--	0.50
Vant Heaton	)	Clefk 4 continuances------------	1.60
		Do 4 Afts---------------------	0.80

Do 9 subpss.-- 1.80
Do Indietment-- 1.00
Do charging prisoner entering plea-------------- 0.60
Entering final Judgement------------------------- 1.60
Recognizance--------------------------------------- 0.50

(P.269) Taxing costs---------------------------$0.50
Attorney General--------------------------------2.50

| State of Tennessee |) | First Judicial circuit Carter |
| Carter County |) | county Septr. Term 1828 |

State Vs Peter Rasor, In this cause the defendant being charged upon the bill of Indietment pleads not guilty
and puts himself upon the country and the atto. Genl.
doth the like and thereupon came a Jury of good and lawful men (Viz) John L. Allen, John Lyon, Radford Ellis,
Thomas Rowe, Robert Sanders, Reuben Landsdown, William
Nave, Samuel Lacy, Richard Kelly, James Morgan, Samuel
Gourley & Samuel Tipton who being elected tried and sworn
the truth to speak upon the issue of travers and thereupon
the Jury aforesaid were respited from rendering thier verdict
untill tomorrow Friday the 19th Septr. 1828

State Vs Peter Rasor The Jury who were respited from rendering thier verdict on yesterday came into court and upon thier
oaths do say the Deft is not Guilty as charged in the bill
of Indietment whereupon it is considered by the court that
the Deft be Discharged and that the county of Carter pay the
costs of this prosecution that accured on behalf of the state
Clerk for Indietment--------------------------------------100
Do Capias--1-
Do intering Defts plea----------------------------------- 60
Do final Judgment---1-60
Do taxing costs--- 50
Do 8 subps--160
Shff Carter Execut capias--------------------------------100
Do 8 witnesses---200

```
Writ on behalf the state Geo Bradly---------------- 1-
J. Hampton Senr.-------------- --------------------- 1-5
T. Ward--------------------------------------------- 1-
J. Wagner------------------------------------------- 1-
J. Stout-------------------------------------------- 1-
S. Stout-------------------------------------------- 1-
D. Stout-------------------------------------------- 1-
Do Atto Genl.--------------------------------------- 2-50
```

And it appearing to the satisfaction of the court that the
abovecases having been refferred to the attorney General
and he having reported thereon that he has examined the
said claims and find them legal and Just and George Williams
Clerk of this court having called each Justice name and those
voting for the approperation George Emmert Yea John J. Wilson
Yea Jesse Cole Yea William A. Carter Yea James Keys yea
William Gott yea Ezekiel Smith yea George Greenway yea and
William Peoples yea and there appearing a majority of the
acting justices of the peace for said county in favor of
the approperation It is therefore ordered by the court that
the sum of _____ be approrreated for the payment
of said claims out of any county moneys not other wise appropreated

(P.270)   And the court adjourned till tomorrow nine
oclock,

                              W. B. Carter,
                              William Gott,
                              J. Keys,
                              G. W. Greenway,
                              Ezl. Smith.

Tuesday November 11th 1828 court met according to adjournment, Present the Worshipful,

                    William P. Carter,
                    William Gott,
                    Ezekiel Smith &
                    James Keys   Esqrs.

For reasons appearing to the court It is therefore ordered
that Charles Justice & Frederick Shown be released from
attending as Jurors at this session

Ordered by the court that Lewis Kade be fined five Dollars
for swearing in contempt of the court and be in custody
of the sheriff until otherwise directed by the court

Lawson Goodwin)   The Defendant having been hereto-
   Vs)   fore arrested on a Casa and now
Christopher Prick)   on this day the Defendant comes
   into open court and took the in-
solvent debtors oath and is thereupon discharged by the
court from the custody of the sheriff

(P.271) It is therefore considered by the court that the
Defendant recover against the Plaintiff the costs of this suit
and that the plaintiff may be in mercy &c.

William Carter Sheriff returned the states writ of Veniri Facias Executed from which the following persons were selected
towit. John Ward, Foreman, John K. Insor, Saml. Montgomery,
John Lyons, Caldwell Brown, Elijah Hardin, David Wagner,
David Brummit, Anderson Kite, Reuben Brooks &Caleb Smith
Peter Rasor, John Fletcher, then and there standers by (viz)
Coleb Smith, Peter Rasor,& John Fletcher summoned by the
sheriff impanneled sworn and charged to enquire for the body
of the county Carter and withdrew to enquire of thier presentment

Abraham Tipton a constable was sworn to attend the Grand
Jury

Robert K. Preston & com) The defendant by his atto James
   Vs) P. Taylor comes into open court
Elisha Williams) and confesses Judgement for two
   hundred forty one Dollars &six
cents. Therefore it is considered by the court that the
Plaintiff recover against the Defendant the aforesaid sum
of two hundred and forty one dollars and six cents together
with the costs in this behalf expended and that the Defendant be in mercy &c.

(P.272) On motion of James F. Taylor Esqr. Joseph
McCullough Esqr. was qualified as an attorney and admitted
to practices

Joseph Slimp assignee &c) For reasons appearing to the
   Vs) court an afft. of the Defend-
J. Cornet & J. Hickory) ants It is ordered by the
   court that a commission issue
to any Justice of the peace for any county state of Kentuckey
to take the deposition of Madison Reno Defendants giving
twenty days notice of the time and place

J. Slimp Assignee) For reason appe aring to the court
   Vs) It is ordered that a commission Is-
J. Cornet & J. Hickory) sue to take the deposition of Eli
   Rasor Plaintiff giving the Defend-
ants two days notice of time and place of taking the same

Samuel Howard Exhibited his petition praying that he may
be admitted to keep an ordinary It is therefore ordered
that the said Samuel be admitted to keep and ordinary
and the said Saml. entered into bond with Saml. W. Williams
& Abner McLeod securities in the penal sum of five hundred
dollars (sec bond)

(P.273)   Ordered by the court that the sheriff bring into
court the body of Lewis Kade who was ordered in custody of
the sheriff and the said Kade be discharged and pay the costs
of entries & comment - It is therefore considered by the
court that the state recover of said Kade the costs aforesaid
and that Execution Issue therefore

John Jobe   )   The defendant being arrested on a
     Vs   )   Casa came into open court and took
Joseph E. Roberts)   the Insolvant debtors oath and is
                             therefore discharged by the court

Enoch Duncan   )   The Plaintiff dismisses his suit and There-
     Vs   )   fore it is considered by the court that De-
Stephen Cooper)   fendant recover against the plaintiff his
costs and charges put to about his defence and that Defendant go hence without day and that the Plaintiff may be in
mercy &c

State   )   Continued on aft of the atto General
  Vs   )
Polly Scott)

State   )   The Defendant comes into open court and
  Vs   )   acknowledges herself indebted to the state
Polly Scott)   in the sum of fifty Dollars and Jesse Cole
                     her bail came into court and acknowledges
himself indebted in the sum of fifty dollars to be levied
 of there goods and chattles lands and tenements & Void on
condition that the sd. Polly Scott appear before the justices
of our court of Please and quarter sessions to be held at
the court house (P.274) in Elizabethton on the second
Monday in February next, towit Tuesday second day of said
session then and there to answer to a charge of the state
and not depart the said.court without leave first had
obtained

Nave & Carriger)   Refferred to William B. Carter &
    Vs)   Alfred M. Carter if they cannot
C. Lewis & P. Lewis)   agree to choose an umpire and their
& H. Lewis)   award to be a judgment of court

State)   The defendant being charged on
    Vs .)   the bill of presentment of the
George Smithpeter).   Grand Jury and he for plea thereto
saith that he is not guilty and
puts himself upon his country and James P. Taylor attorney
General who prosecutes on behalf of the state doth the like
whereupon came a Jury towit Solomon Ellis, Joseph Slimp,
Howel Lewis, Manuel Jenkins, Elisha William David Bowers,
William O'Brian, Owen Edwards John C. Helm, Andrew Wilson,
Richard Dunlap and John T. Bowers, chosen Elected tried
upon there oaths say do find the deft is guilty in manner
and form as charged in the Bill of presentment Therefore it is
considered by the court that the defendant be fined ten
dollars and be in custody of the sheriff until the fine and
costs be paid or give security for the same

(P.275)
Nave & Carriger)   Allen Royston a witness in this cause
    Vs)   proves one days attendance
Lewis & Lewis)

A deed of conveyance from Samuel Garland to Moses Estep for
fifty three acres of land proven in open court by John
Richardson & William Garland two Subscribing witnesses thereto and admited to record let it be registered

The assignment of a plat and certificate of survey from
Joseph Wilson to Thomas Burger acknowledged in open court by
Ezekiel Smith atto in fact

The assignment of a plat and certificate of survey from
Joseph Wilson to Thomas Burger for twenty five acres of
land acknowledged in open court by Ezekiel Smith atto in
fact

    And then the court adjourned till tomorrow 9 oclock,
                       W. B. Carter,
                       G. W. Greenway,
                       Geo. Emmert.

(P.276)   Wednesday November 12th 1828 court met according to adjournment Present the Worshipful

                            George Greenway,
            Esquires.   William B. Carter,
                            George Emmert.

Joshua Jobe) This cause continued by consent
    Vs) and a commission awarded to the plff
James J. Tipton &) to take the testemony of Thomas
George Lacy Admr. of) Tipton Thomas J. Tipton Rebecca
Isaac Tipton dec'd) Tipton & Susannah Tipton all of
    Blount county an giving the De-
fendants ten days notice of the time and place of taking
the said deposition it is further agreed that at February
court eighteen hundred & twenty nine it shall be continued
untill May court 1829 and that the deporetions aforesaid
taken and time between this & that time shall be read on
the trial of the about cause

Abial C. Parkes prays he may be admited to keep and ardinary
and Granted on complying with the Law and entered into Bond
with Jeremiah Campbell and James I. Tipton his securities
in the sum of five Hundred Dollars (sec. bond)

(P.277)
State) It is ordered by the court that
    Vs) the fine of ten dollars entered
George Smithpeter) against him at this court be remitt-
    ed to twenty five cents and that
the state recover the same and that Execution Issue

Joshua Jobe) Thomas Tipton & Thomas J. Tipton
    Vs) proven there attendance for three
James J. Tipton &) days each and travaeling to & from
George Lacy admr.) two hundred and sixty miles each
of Isaac Tipton decd.)

John Stuart) The plaintiff suffers a non
    Vs) suit Therefore it is consid-
Michael Massengill admr. & &) ered by the court that the
    defendant may go hence with-
out day & recover of the plaintiff his costs about his defence
in thatbehalf expended and the plaintiff in mercy & &.

Thomas Crutchfield) Now at this day came a Jury and the
    Vs) Jury towit, Michael Hyder, Owen Ed-
Henry H. Have) wards, John Have, Jesse Jenkins, E-
    John Powers, Pleasant Profit Eli
Rasor, Mordacai Williams, Abner McLeod, Hugh Jinkins &
Jonathan Range chosen elected tried upon their oaths say do
find the defendant hath not paid the debt in the plaintiffs
declaration mentioned and by reason of the detention thereof assess the plaintiff damage to six dollars Therefore it
is considered by the court that the plaintiff recover against
the defendant the debt in the declaration mentioned and
(P.278) also the damage of six dollars assessed by the

jury in manner and form aforesaid and his costs and charges
put to about his suit in this behalf expended and the defendant in mercy & &

James Estep) The plaintiff dismisses his suit and the
   Vs) defendant comes into court and assumes
Isaac Estep) upon himself one half of the court It is
  .   therefore considered by the costs that
plaintiff and defendant recover over against each other
the one half of the costs in this behalf expended & &
and that the plaintiff & Deft be in mercy to each other & &.

Samuel Maxwell) And now at this day comes the plaintiff
   Vs   ) by his attorney James Taylor and there-
Elija Hathaway) upon came a jury to enquire of the plain-
tiff damage and the Jurors of that Jury towit,
Michael Hyder, Owen Edwards, Solomon Ellis, John Nave, Jesse
Jenkins, John Bowers, Pleasant Profit, Eli Rasor, Mordacai
Williams, Abner McLeod, Hugh Jenkins and Jonathan Range,
chosen elected tried upon thier oaths say do find for the
plaintiff and assess his damage to sixty seven dollars and
eighty cents It is therefore considered by the court that
the plff recover of the defendant the damage assessed
(P.279) as aforesaid by the Jury aforesaid and also the
costs and charges which he hath about his suit in this behalf expended and that the Defendant be in mercy & &

Robert Burrow for the use) And now at this day came the
of Netherland   ) parties aforesaid by thier
   Vs   ) attorneys and thereupon came
John Rasor   ) a jury

Michael Hyder, Owen Edwards, Solomon Ellis, John Nave, Jesse
Jenkins, John Bowers, Pleasant Profit, Eli Rasor, Mordacai
Williams, Abner McLeod, Hugh Jenkins and Jonathan Range
Chosen Elected tried upon thier Oaths say do find for the
plaintiff and assess his damage to fifty five dollars and
seventy cents therefore it is considered by the court that
the plaintiff recover over against the defendant the said
sum of fifty five dollars and seventy cents assessed as
aforesaid by the Jury aforesaid his damage and also the
costs and charges put to about his suit in this behalf expended and the Defendant in mercy

Jarrett Arnold) Rule to shew cause why the certoionari
   Vs   ) should be dismissed on argument of coun-
Peter Rasor) sel is discharged and rule to quash the
        Judgement and Execution as to Peter
Rasor is made absolute It is therefore considered by the
court that the said Peter Rasor recover of the plaintiff
his costs in this cause and that execution issue

(P.280)
Johnson Hampton) Defendant and James I. Tipton assume the
   Vs   ) costs of this suit and the Plaintiff dismiss-
Thomas Carver) es his suit It is therefore considered by
             the court that the plaintiffs recover of th
the Defendant and James I. Tipton The costs which he hath
a bout his suit in this behalf expended and defendant be in
mercy. & &

Elizabeth Croughn appointed guardian of Uriah Croughn who
came into open court and entered into Bond with James I.
Tipton her security in the sum of five hundred dollars
sec. bond

The Defendant Wilson Sams having been taken on a Casa Leroy
Sams having entered into bond with the said Wilson in persuance to act of assembly and the sd. Sams having failed
to comply with his bond according to act of assembly therefore

Peter Rasor   ) On motion of plaintiff by attorney for
  Vs   ) Judgment against the defendants It is
Wilson Sams &) therefore considered by the court that
Leroy Sams   ) the Plaintiff recover over against the
            defendant the sum of twelve dollars
ninety seven cents & five mills and also the costs of this
motion

A Power of attorney from William Gott and Jane G. Gott
formerly Jane G. Britton and Hannah Britton to James
Britton in the words and figures following towit.
Know all men by these presents that We William Gott
Jane G. his wife formerly Jane G. Britton & Hannah Britton
all of carter county State of Tennessee (P.281) having
full faith and confidence in our brother James Britton
of Sumner county west Tennessee do hereby nominate constitute and appoint the said James Britton our attorney in
fact for us and in our names to ask sue for and recover of
one Crutcher the Executor or administrator of Abraham Britton
decd. all sum or sums of money or other valuable things
which may be due us as legators or destributes of the said
Abraham Britton decd. furthermore we do empower him
Should it become necessary to make any other attorney or attorneys it fact to carry into effect or aid in executing
the trust hereby intended to be vested in the said James
Britton. Furthermore we do impower his on the recient of
any sum or sums of money or other Valuable thing in consideration aforesaid for us and in our names to execute reciepts
acquitance or other discharges In short we do fully authorize
our said attorney to take all lawful*and means to recover of
the said Crutcher or any other person or persons our shares
of said Estate in as ample a manner as if we were personally
present hereby ratifying and confirming whatsoever our said
 *ways

attorney may lawfully do in the premises In testemoney whereof we have hereunto subscribed our hands and seals this elev-
enth day of November eighteen hundred and twenty eight

> (Seal) William Gott,
> (Seal) Jane G. Gott,
> (Seal) Hannah Britton.

Was acknowledged in open court by the signers admitted to record and ordered to be certified

(P.282)   A deed of conveyance from James P. Taylor to
Enoch Duncan for twenty five acres of Land was acknowledged
in open court by James P. Taylor the maker thereof and was
thereupon admitted to record let it be Registered

A deed of conveyance from William Brummit to David Brummit
for one ninth of one hundred and fifteen acres of land was
acknowledged in open court admitted to record Let it be registered

A deed of conveyance from Joseph Tipton to Nathaniel Taylor
for ninety nine & half acres of land was proven in open
court by Thomas Tipton one of the subscribing witnesses
thereto left open for the probit of the other witnesses

A deed of conveyance from Jesse Smith and Mary Smith his
wife, Caleb B. Cox, Anna Cox his wife, William A. Harris &hiswife
Elizabeth Harris to Benjamin White for two hundred acres of
land acknowledged in open court by the said Jesse Smith
Caleb B. Cox & William A. Harris and the said Mary Smith
wife of the said Jesse Smith Anne Cox wife of Caleb B Cox
Elizabeth Harris wife of William A Harris being examined
seperately and appart from there said husbands by the court
touching thier free consent of signing sealing & executing
the same say they executed the same freely voluntarily and
of thier own accord without fear threat or persuation of
thier said husbands and admitted to record let it be registered

(P.283)   Reuben Miller proved his attendance as a constable for three days for which he is allowed agreeable to
law

Court adjourned till tomorrow morning 9 oclock

> W. B. Carter,
> William Gott,
> Geo. Emmert.

Thursday Morning 13th Novr. 1828
Court met according to adjournment present the Worshipful,
W. B Carter, Wm Gott, & Geo. Emmert, Sequires.

A power of atty from Elizabeth Croughn guardian of Uriah
Croughn to James I. Tipton was acknowledged in open court
by the said Elizabeth Croughn and admitted to record and
ordered to be certified for registration a suit said power
of atty is in the words and figure following viz

Know all men by there presents that I. Elizabeth Croughn
guardian of my son Uriah Croughn Repososeing special trust
and confidence in my friend Col. James I. Tipton of Carter
county & state of Tennessee have this day nominated constituted and appointed and by these present do nominate the
said James I. Tipton

(P.284) Thursday Novr. 13th 1828
My atto. in fact for me and in my name as guardian to call
upon Joseph Croagh Executor administrator of Fergison
Croughn dec'd for such of the Estate of the said Uriah
Croaghn leagacy or distribution shear of said Estate as may
be due my said word and if the same is not promptly paid I
do empower him to institute any suit or suits that is his
openion be necessary to secure the legacy or Distribution
shear of said Estate due my said ward
Furthermore when he shall have obtaind the same by settlement
suit or otherwise I od impower him in my name as guardian of
said Uriah Croaghn to execute any reciept acquitances or other
instruments of writing necessary to discharge the person or
persons of whom he may recieve said money of all further liability therefore in short I do hereby invest him with as
full power to do and tranact said bussiness with all manner
of persons in any county in Virginia in as full and ample a
manner as I could do myself were I personally present hereby
ratifing and confirming whatsoever my said atto. may lawfully do in the premisses given under my hand & seal this 13th
day of Novr. 1828   her
                              (Seal) ElizabethX Croughn
                                                      Mark
Attest. J. P. Taylor.

Swinhill for Nathan Birchfield Junr. use)   James I. Tipton
                Vs   )   Dept shff re-
Nathfield Birchfield issu'd by G. Emmert)   tur'd hereinto
                                                court as exr.
Esqr. at the about suit for the sum of Eighty Dollars Debt &
fifty cents costs upon which the sheriff return'd that he had
made search for property of the Deft but could find none but

had levied this execution on a tract of land in the Limestone Cove adjoining Wm Baker and others as the property
of Nath. Birchfield Sr. Where said Birchfield now lives
Novr. 1st 1828 Jas. I Tipton D. shff which return appearing
to the court it therefore ordered by the court that the
(P.285) sheriff sell said land of so much thereof as will
be of value sufficient to satisfy said Execution and costs
of return order & &

A deed of conveyance from Felix Brown to Joseph Smith for
seventy acres of land proven in open court By Caleb Smith
& James Keys two subscribing witnesses thereto and admited
to record let it be registered

Samuel Howard) Wm Carter sheriff returned an Execution
    Vs   ) issued by a justice of the peace infavour
Joseph Scott) of Samuel Howard against Joseph Scott for
                 the sum of thirty three Dollars and forty
four cents with Interest from the 13th Augt. 1828 & legal
costs that may acerue search made no property found in my
county to levy this Fi Fa on but levied on thirty acres of
land in Carter county on Lick creek as the property of
Joseph Scott adjoining the widow Lacy land 4th of Septr.1828.
W. Carter shff For which return appearing to the court It is
therefore ordered that the shff sell said land or so much
thereof as will be of Value Sufficient to satisfy said Execution & costs

(P.286)   Thursday Nov 13th 1828

Ordered by the court that the sheriff of Carter county recieve of the people in payment of county taxes for all county
purpose North and South Carolina bank notes at par and that
the Trustee of Carter county recieve it of his in payment of
all such claimes Vs the sheriff

A. W. Taylor presents his petition praying for a jury of View
to inspect & lay off a road up Buffleao creek from the Mouth
of A. W. Taylors spring branch to the road near Archibald
Williams tan yard or to pass up by A. W. Taylors house & intersect the road near James Gourleys and on motion the court
ordered Archibald Williams Caswell C. Taylor Samuel W Williams
Charles Lizenby James Gourly Nicholas Payon Nich Daniels
(P.587) & Isaac Taylor Senr. be a jury of View to examine
both routs any five of them shall be sufficant to examine &
lay out a road on one a the other routs and report to next
court, Court adjourned untill court in course,
                          W. B. Carter,
                          Geo. Emmert,
                          William Gott.

State of Tennessee Carter county at a meeting of a court of
please and quarter sessions held for Carter county at the
Court house in Elizabethton on the second Monday of February
in the year of our Lord 1829 Present the Worshipful,
William B. Carter, Jeremiah Campbell, William Gott, John
J. Wilson, William Peoples, James Keys, John Richardson,
Johnson Hampton, George W. Greenway, Hampton Hyder, Lawson
White, Ezekiel Smith, and John L.Williams, Esquires.

For reasons appearing to the court It is therefore ordered
that John Hampton and Thomas Hampton be released of a poll
tax each for the years 1821 & 1922

Samuel E. McQueen resigns the office of constable

(P.288)   Ordered by the court that Moses Banks be appoint-
ed overseer of the public road from Fishers old fields on
Doe River to the Limestone Cove to the road that passes from
Reeves Iron works over the Iron Mountain

Ordered by the court that Wyley Edwards be appointed to the
office of constable and came into open court and entered into Bond with Owen Edwards and John Helm his securities in
the sum of one thousand Dollars with condition sec bond and
took the several oaths required by law

Ordered by the court that Thomas J. Stokes be appointed to
the office of constable and came into open court and entered
into bond with William Donally and James B. Mourley his security in the sum of one thousand dollars with condition sec
Bond and took the several oaths required by law

Ordered by the court that Rebecca Shawley wife & relict of
James Shawley dec'd be appointed administratrix and William
Barton Holt administrator of the said James Shawley dec'd
and the said Rebecca Shawley & William B. Holt come into
open court and entered into Bond with Jacob Holt thier security in the sum of one thousand dollars with condition sec
bond and the s'd Rebecca & the said William were qualified
as administratrix and administrator as the law directs set
letters of administration issued

(P.289)   Elisha Smith constable returned an Execution
Issued by a justice of the peace in favor of Lawson Goodwin
against Larkin L. Wilson for the sum of seven dollars and
twenty five cents and legal costs search made no goods nor
chattles found in my county but levied on one tract of land
containing fifty acres supposed to be the property of Larken
Wilson lying on Mill creek known by the name of Groons creek
lying between John Wilsons land & Barnabas Oaks land November

the 12th day 1828   For which return appearing to the court
It is therefore ordered that the Sheriff sell said Land or
so much thereof as will be of Value sufficient to satisfy
said Execution and costs & &.

Ordered by the court that the hands living on the following
farms towit Thos McQueens,Joseph Jinkins Andrew Arnold,
Thomas Berrys, Johnston Kiks, Worleys Charles Andersons
Montgomerys, place and all the hands living in said bounds
be the hands to work the*road from Andrew Wilson of Little p
Doe to where it intersects the public road near Dorans Mill
under Andrew Arnold overseer *new

Abner McLeod exhibited his petition praying that he may be
permited to keep an Ordinary in Elizabethton and granted on
complying with the requisites of the law

Ordered by the court that John Potter be appointed overseer
of the public stage road from where John Musgrove Junr path
leaves it to the state line & have all the hands near said
road East of Mill creek including Matthias Wagner Junr.
Jaret Arnold

(P.290)   Ordered by the court that Godfrey Dun be appointed overseer of the stage road from Showns crossroads to where
John Musgrove Junr. path leaves it and have all the hands giv-
en heretofore to said road West of Mill Creek except Matthias
Wagners Junr

Ordered by the court William Bowman be appointed overseer
of the public road in the room of Edward Henry & that John
Haun, Geo. Williams J. L. Williams hands and Edward Henry &
P. Moorhead and have the same hands that Henry had to work
said road

Nathan Baughman)   The defendant being arrested on a Ca Sa
         Vs   )   came into open court and took the in-
Thomas Gillis   )   solvent debtors oath and returned a
                         schedule of his property in the follow-
ing words and figures towit Schedule of Thomas Gillis property one bed and furniture three knives ; one or two forks four
plates one oven & lid & Hooks ten or twelve bushels of corn
one flax Wheel one reel one young cow which property except
what is secured to this Defendant by act of assembly
I do hereby transfer to William Carter sheriff for sd.
Baughmans benifit February 9th 1829
                                        Thomas Gillis.

It is therefore ordered by the court that the sheriff sell
said property Except the property Deft by law for the benefit of the Plaintiff and make return to next court and that
the Defendant Gillis be discharged from cusdody & & recover
agt. plff costs & &. *allowed, *deft

(P.291)   Ordered by the court that the hands on the following farms towit Almun Oaks Absolem Loyd Edward Austins Charles Anderson Peter Wills Lewis Wills & & be released from working the new road under Andrew Arnold and return back to thier former road to work under William Michael overseer of the public road from the widow Dorans to the lime kiln near Hughs Wardens-

Ordered by the court that Andrew Taylor Solomon Hendrix Joel Cooper Isaac Taylor Michael Hyder Saml. W Peoples Samuel Lacy Samuel Lusk and John L. Lusk or any five of whom be a Jury to View mark and lay off a road from the ford of the creek near John L. Williams up past David Pughs dwelling house thence to the dividing line between sd Pugh & Nathaniel McNabb thence along sd. line into the main road that passes from Elizabethton to Reeves Iron works and make report to the next court the nearest and best way should they believe it better & less to the prejudice of the public & endividuals that the nearest way

Ordered by the court that the hands on the following farms towit Benjamin Wilson John Minks William Donallys Alexander Wilson Adam Winsels Richd. Donally William Wilson Andrew L. Wilson Thomas Johnson & all hands in said bounds subject to work publicroads be the hands to work under Alexr. Wilson overseer of the public road from the widow Dorans to where it intersects the stage road near John Wagners *living

(P.292)   Ordered by the court that David C. Moody be overseer of the public road leading from Leonard Harts to Hannah Lacys in the room of Reuben Lacy and have the same bounds and hands that the sd. Lacy had

Ordered by the court that William Grason be appointed overseer of the public road from the long bridge on the south fork of Roans creek to the state line and work one half the hands that worked under Jacob Reece and ordered that the others half work under Augustin Cook overseer and work from Wagners Forge to the long bridge on the south fork of Roans creek

Ordered by the court that John Wright be appointed overseer of the road from David Hains fince to John Wrights lane and that the hands living within the bounds of said road runing on east & west line from the extreme point be the hands to work said road with the exception of Peter Holt Jesse Maddux Christopher McInturf John McInturf and Henry Johnson

Ordered by the court that Jacob Snider be appointed overseer of the public road from the ford of the River about the widow Smiths to the state line at Averies turnpike road and work the following hands

John Shuffield Daniel Cable Barnabas Oaks Isaac Snider
Jesse Sizemore Barnabas Bowman Michael Snider William
Snider James Bradley James Polk Jacob Smith James Hunt
John Vance & Robert Vance & Benjamin Purkins

(P.293)   Ordered by the court that the Public road
run as Joseph Renfro has opened it through his farm

Ordered by the court that James Range, William Smith,
Andrew Taylor John Inman, James Clark, John . Bowers,
William Nave, Joseph Obrian, Michael Lyon, James Hetherly,
Jacob Cammeron, Daniel Campbell, Daniel Smith, William Whaley
Isaac Anderson, Samuel Bogart, John Bennet, Andrew L. Wilson
Richd Arnold, Jonathan Pugh,   Lewis Morgan, John Roe Aaron
Owen, Samuel S. Patton, Owen Edwards and John Glover be
jurors to May session 1829

William Peoples Esqr. returned a list of the taxable property
and polls in Captain McInturfs distric for the year 1829

Ordered by the court that Elizabeth Cooper be appointed guardian for the minor heirs of Joseph Cooper dec'd towit Andrew
Cooper Nathaniel W. Cooper Patience Cooper Frances Marion
Cooper Barsheba Cooper Joseph Cooper Isbell Cooper Mary Cooper
and William Jones Cooper enters into bond with security
in the sum of one hundred dollars

(P.294)   For reasons appearing to the court It is therefore
ordered that Charles Lewis be released from the payment of
poll tax for the year 1821 & 1822

Samuel E. McQueen)   The Plaintiff dismisses his suit and
        Vs   )   the Defendant William Clawson assumes
William Clawson &)   the costs therefore It is considered
Charles Anderson)   by the court that the plaintiff recov-
                       er of the Defendant William Clawson h
his costs and charges put to about his suit in this behalf &
the defendant be in mercy

On motion for an appropreation of one hundred and thirty
dollars for maintainance of the following paupers towit
William Netherley the sum of twenty five Dollars Elizabeth
Humphreys twenty dollars Matthias Keen fifty five dollars
Ann Morgan Taylor daughter of Stephen Taylor fifteen doll-
ars George Williams Clerk calling each Justice present by name
those voting in favor of the sd appropriation John L. Wilson
Yea Lawson Whith Yea William Peoples Yea Hampton Hyder Yea
George Emmert Yea Green Moore Yea Ezekiel Smith Yea George
Greenway Yea John L. Williams Yea William B. Carter Yea
William Gott Yea and James Keys Yea except as to the appro-
priation of twenty five dollars to William Netherley he was
na from which there appearing a majority in favor of the
appropriation It is thereupon ordered by the court that the

aforesaid sums be appropriated for the maintainance of the said paupers

(P.295) for the following periods of time towit William Netherly for the year 1829 Elizabeth Humpherys for the term of one year from the time of the last allowance Matthias keen from Novr. Session 1827 to Novr. Session 1828 Ann Morgan Tw for one year from this time Taylor for one year from this date.

Ordered by the court that a certificate Issue to Hugh Jenkins in the room of one lost by the said Hugh for thirty five dollars for the maintainance of Naomi Hetherly one of the poor from Novr. session 1821 up to Novr. session 1822

The assignment of a plat and certificate of Survey from Martin Fares to Absolem Loyed for twenty five acres of Land was proven in open court by Samuel E McQueen & William Donalley two subscribing witnesses thereto & ordered to be certified

The assignment of a plat and certificate of survey from Martin Fares to Absolem Loyd for fifty acres of Land was proven in open court by Samuel E. McQueen & William Donalley two subscribing witnesses thereto and ordered to be certified

The assignment of a plat and certificate of survey from James Primmer to Lawson white for fifty acres of land was acknowledged in open court by the maker thereof James Primmer and ordered to be certified

(P.296)   The assignment of a plat and certificate of surve voy from James Primmer to Lawson White for one Hundred acres of land was acknowledged in open court by the James Primmer the Maker thereof & ordered to be certified

A deed of conveyance from William Bridges & Elizabeth Bridges his wife to Aaron Stalcup for twenty five acres of land was acknowledged in court by the said William Bridges and the sd. Elizabeth Bridged wife of the sd William being examined by the court seperate and apart from her sd. Husband saith that she executed the same freely voluntarily and of her own free will without the persuasion threat or fear of said husband and admited to record let it be registered * open

A deed of conveyance from William Carter shff to Leonard Shown for three hundred acres of land acknowledged in open court by the sd. William Carter maker thereof and admitted to record Let it be registered

A deed of conveyance from Vaut Heaton Elizabeth Heaton Joseph Heaton William Roberts and Tadosha Roberts to

Peter Rasor for two acres of land proven in open court by
James B. Mourley and William B. Carter on the part of Vaut
Heaton Elizabeth Heaton & Joseph Heaton and acknowledged by
William Roberts Tadosha Roberts and sd. Tadosha Roberts wife
of the said William Roberts being examined by the court seperate and apart from her said husband saith she executed the
same freely voluntarily & of her free will without fear
threat or persuasion of her said husband & admited to record
let it be registered

(P.297)   A deed of conveyance from Arther Pierce to Michael
Pierce for two hundred acres of land was proven in open court
by Christian Carriger and Griffin Pierce two subscribing
witnesses thereto and admitted to record Let it be registered

A deed of conveyance from John McEfee to Lazarus Innmon for
sixty eight acres of land was   proven in open court by
James P. Taylor & Abiel C Parks two subscribing witnesses
thereto admitted to record let it be registered

A deed of conveyance from Lazarus C. Innman to Joshua
Swanger for sixty eight acres of Land was acknowledsged in
open court by the said Lazarus Innman maker thereofwas admitted to record let it be registered

A Bill of sale from Valuntine Bowers to John Range for a
negro woman named Rebecca about twenty eight years of age
was acknowledged in open court by the maker thereof and admitted to record Let it be registered

A release from William Hardin and Christian Carriger to John
Range for the negro mentioned in the about stated Bill of
sale was acknowledg'd in open court by the William & Christian
the makers and was admitted to record let it be registered

(P.298)   A Bill of sale from Arthur Pierce to Michael
Pierce for two negroes Jim & Hannah was proven in open court
by Christian Carriger and Griffin Pierce two subscribing
witnesses thereto was admitted to record let it be registered

Ordered by the court that a contingent tax be laid levied
and collected for the year 1829 on each hundred acres of land
                                                            12½
On each town lot--- 25
On each free poll---12 ½
On each slave--- 25
On each stud horse or Jack the season of one mare--------
On each Maechant--$5.00
On each Hawker or Peddler------------------------------------- 2.50
Ordered, by the court that an additional county tax be laid
levied and collected for the year 1829   cts

on each hundred acres of land----------------------------- 12½
On each town lot--- 25
On each free poll--- 12½
On each slave--- 25
On each stud or Jack-- 25
On each Merchant---$2.50
On each Hawker or pedler---------------------------------- 1.25
Ordered by the court that apoor tax be laid levied andcollect-
ed for the year 1829

On each hundred acres of land---------------------------$00.18 3/4
On each town lot--- 00.37½
On each free poll--- 00.18 3/4
On each slave-- 00.37½

Ordered by the court that a additional tax be laid for the
work done & to do on the courthouse
On each hundred acres of land---------------------- 6¼
Each town lot--- 12½
Each slave--- 12½
Each white poll--- 6¼
Each stud horse--- 25
Each Merchant--- 50
Each hawker or   pedler----------------------------- 25cents

(P.299) The court proceeded to elect from amoung themselves a quorum court for the present year towit Geo. Emmert
Geo. Greenway, Ezekiel Smith Wm B. Carter & John I. Wilson
were chosen to constitute and hold the court for the present year

Court adjournad until tomorrow morning ten oclock
W. B. Carter, Geo. Emmert, G. W.   Greenway, Ezl. Smith,
John Williams, John I. Wilson , L. White,William Gott,
Jereh. Campbell, J. Keys

(P.300)   Tuesday February 10th 1829

Court met according to adjournment present the Worshipful
             1-James Keys
             2-John L.Williams
             3-William Gott
             4-George Greenway
             5-Ezekiel Smith
             6-Green Moor
             7-George Emmert
             8-John I.Wilson
             9-Lawson White &
             10-william B. Carter.   Esqures.

William Carter sheriff returned the states writ of Venire
executed from which the following persons were drawn as
Grand Jurors towit and the court appointed Godfrey Nave
foreman Isaac Carroll, Valuntine Bowers James Bradley Benjamin
Hyder, Philip Shell, Ruse Wardin John Nave, William Perry
Charles M.D. Gourley William Stover, Andrew wilson &
Joseph Wagner Impanneled sworn charged and withdrew to en-
quire· of thier presentments

Thomas Gourley constable sworn to attend the grand Jury

State)   The Defendant comes into court and be-
  Vs   ) - ing charged   on   the Bill of Indietment
Sarah Shaver) pleads guilty whereupon the court having
             heard evidence fined the said Sarah six
and one fourth cents It is therefore considered by the
court that the state recover of the sd. Sarah the fine
aforesaid and the costs of this prosecution and that the
Deft be in mercy and that execution issue therefore

(P.301)
State)   The Defendant being charged on the bill of
  Vs   )   Indietment and she for plea thereto saith
Nancy Bowers) that she is not guilty thereof and puts her
             self on the country and James P. Taylor at-
torney General does the like. Whereupon came a jury and the
Jurors of that Jury towit, Jonathan Poland,George Smith David
Moody, Squire Estep David Hays, John Berry,Alfred Sams, Enoch
Estep, Reuben Lansdown, Daniel Stout, Caleb Cox & John Keehn
being empanneled tried and sworn the truth to speak on the
issue Joined on thier oath do say they find that the Defendant is guilty in manner and form as charged in the Bill of
indietment. It is thereupon considered by the court that the
Defendant be fined the sum of ten dollars and remain in custody of the sheriff until fine and costs be paid or security
be giving for the same. It is therefore considered by the
court that the state recover of theDefendant the fine aforesaid and also the costs of this prosecution and the Defendant be in mercy & &.

Samuel Tipton) The defendant comes into court and confesses*
    Vs   ) the sum of ninety seven dollars & thirty six
Brian Obrian) cents debt and all costs It is therefore con-
              sidered by the court that the plaintiff recov-
er of the Defendant the sd. sum of ninety seven dollars and
thirty six cents debt and also his costs and charges in this
behalf expended and the defendant in mercy*Judgment for the &&
Execution stayed six months

(P.302)

Joseph Slimp Assignee & &)	The plaintiff comes into
Vs)	open court and dismisses
John Cornut &)	his suit and the Defendant
James Hickey)	comes into court and assumes
	the costs. It is therefore
	considered by the court that t

Plaintiff recover of the Defendant the costs and charges
which he hath in this behalf expended and the Defendant be
in mercy & &

Eli Rasor proves 2 days attendance as a witness

Garland Wilson for the use of)	The plaintiff comes in-
R. Clawson)	to court and dismisses
Vs)	his suit and the Defend-
Aaron Stallcup)	ant comes into court
	and assumes the costs

It is therefore considered by the court that the plaintiff
recover of the defendant his costs and charges in this behalf expended and the defendant be in mercy & &.

Henry Earnest)	The plaintiff comes into court and
Vs)	dismisses his suit and the defend-
George W. Greenway)	ant comes into court and assumes
	the costs. It is therefore consid-

ered by the court that the plaintiff recover of the defendant
his costs and charges in this behalf expended and the defendant be in mercy

Hambleton Hampton is rea pointed constable gives Johnson
Hampton and William B. Carter securities and is qualified as
the law directs sec bond

Robert McLin & Thomas Crow summoned as Jurors to the Veniri
are released from serving as Jurors

(P.303)   The assignment of a plat and certificate of survey from Peter Rasor to Joseph Robeson for fifty acres of land
acknowledged in open court by the maker thereof & admitted
to record

The assignment for a plat and certificate of survey from Jacob
Loe to Josep Roberson for fifty acres of land was acknowledged in open court by the maker thereof was admitted to record

A deed of conveyance from Alfred W. Taylor to Joseph Robeson
for fifteen acres of land was acknowledged in open court by
the maker thereof admited to record let it be registered

William Gott Esquire returned a list of the taxable property
and polls in Captain Courleys company for the year 1829

A deed of conveyance from Rolling Jinkins to Emanuel Jinkins
for one hundred acres of land proven in open court by Christian
Carriger one of the subscribing witnesses thereto and that
the said Christian Carriger believes that the other subscribing witness Godfrey Carriger is dead and that he believes it
to be the hand writing of the said Godfrey Carriger and admitted to record let it be registered

A deed of conveyance from William Roberts & Theodocia Roberts
to Joseph Heaton for eighty two acres was acknowledged in
open court and thesd. Theodocia Roberts wife of William
Roberts being Examined by the court seperately and apart
from her sd. Husband saith that she executed the same freely
Voluntarily and of her own free will without the persuasion
fear or threat of her said (P.304) Husband and admitted to
record let it be registered

A deed of conveyance from Samuel Howard to William Tompkins
for fifty acres of Land acknowledged in open court by the
maker thereof was admitted to record let it be registered

A deed of conveyance from James Edins Sr. to James Edins
Jur. for seven acres & one half acre of Land was proven in
open court by James Clark and Nathaniel T. Edins two subscribing witnesses thereto was admitted to record let it
be registered

Ordered by the court that James B. Mourley be appointed overseer of the public road up little Doe from Joseph Robesons
to Caspers forge on little Doe and work the hands that formerly worked under Samuel Howard and the same bounds

Ordered by the court that David R. Kinnick be appointed overseer of the public road in the room of Hambleton B Hampton
and have the following hands to work the same towit all the
hands on John Duggers farm Johnson Hampton farm Elias Vine
William Vine William Dugger Junr. farm be the hands to work
the road from Johnson Hampton to Joseph Ashers old house

(P.305) Ordered by the court that William B. Carter late
sheriff & Collector of the public and county tax for the
year & 1822 be released of the tax laid on the following per-
sons they being insolvants towit Isaac Cooley 90³/4 cents
John Delasmit 93³/4 cents Joshua Fincher 93³/4 cents John Ma
Maddin same George Nustin same Jonathan Price same Greenberry
Coren same Benjam Donathans heirs $1.87½ Joseph Cal 93³/4
John Lucky same David Clark same Joel Dunlap same Daniel
Glover same Levi Hardin same Andrew P. Hazlet same Richd. Hun
same Richd. Kite same Benjamin Peters same Micahah Rust same
George Rust same Richd. Roberts same John D. Scotch same
James Lewis same Joseph Sanders same Edge Comb Merrt same
Edward Reeves same Isaac Smith same William Smith same and

Joshua Hall.

Green Moore Esqire returned a list of the taxable property
and polls in Captain A.M.Wilsons district for the year 1829

James P.Taylor attorney General called on George Williams
clerk for the Treasurers reciept for the year 1828 which
is in the following words towit Recd. of George Williams
clerk of the county court of Carter county his return from
the first day of October 1827 up to the first day of October
1828 together with the sum of one hundred and thirty dollars
& thirty five cents the amount of Revenue by him collected
for said term as Pr. commissioners certificate 13th October
1828   Miller Francis Treasurer of East Tennessee

(P.306)   Recd. of George Williams clerk of the county of
Carter county a list of the Revinue which the sheriff of
Carter county is chargable for the year 1828 13th October
1828
                    Miller Frances
Treasurer of East Tennessee

24th December 1828 Recd. of George Williams clerk of Carter
county a Statement the fines for the year 1828 also fourteen
dollars & forty four cents in part of a certificate No131
which is filed in my office the 24th Decr.1828 recd. by me &

Ezl. Smith Trustee for Carter county
N.B. as pr commissioners report

Court adjournd untill tomorrow nine Oclock
                         Geo. Greenway,
                         John I. Wilson,
                         Geo. Emmert,
                         John L.Williams,
                         Julius Dugger.

Wednesday 11th day of February 1829 Court met according to
adjournment present the Worshipful
                         George Emmert,
                         William Gott,
                         John L.Williams,
                         Geo. Greenway,
                         John Wilson,
                         Julius Dugger,
            Esquires.   Johnson Hampton &
                         William B. Carter.

(P.307)   February session 1829 We do certify that Christian C. Nave an applicant for a Leave to practice Law is a
young man of good moral character has resided in Carter county all his life and that he is of the age of twenty one years
                              John L.Williams,
                              George Emmert,
                              George Greenway,
Ordered by the court that a copy of the above be furnished
to Mr Nave by the clerk of this court

John L.Williams returned a list of the taxable property and
polls in Captain Greers District for 1829

John M.Preston)   On argument of counsel and for reasons
    Vs   )   appearing to the court The demurrer is
John Ward   )   overruled It is agreed by & between the
                    parties that the plaintiff may amend
his declaration and that Defendant plead to issue whereupon
the proceedings are continued until next court

State   )   The Defendant being charged on the Bill of
    Vs   )   Indictment and she for plea thereto saith
Polly Scott   )   she is not guilty thereof and puts herself
                    on the country and James P. Taylor attorney
General who prosecutes on behalf of the state doeth the like
whereupon came a Jury towit, Jonathan Poland, George Smith,
John C. Helm, Squire Estep, Silas Helton, Reuben Lansdown, H
John T. Bowers, Henry Lowdermilk, Michael Lyon Leonard Bowers
Thomas Nave, N. William Garland, chosen elected tried &
sworn on thier oaths do say they find the Defendant is not
guilty in manner & form as charged in the Bill of Indictment

(P.308)   It is therefore considered by the court that the
Defendant go hence without day and it is further considered
by the court that James Lovelace the prosecutor be taxed
with the costs and that the state recover of the sd. James
the costs of this prosecution and that the sd. James may be
in mercy & &

State   )   The Defendant being charged on the Bill
    Vs   )   of Indictment and he for plea thereto
Henry McKelyea)   saith he is not guilty thereof and puts
                    himself upon his country and James P.
Taylor attorney General who prosecutes on behalf of the state
doeth the like whereupon came a Jury towit Jonathan Poland,
George Smith, John Fletcher, Squire Estep, Silas Helton,
Reuben Lansdown, J.F. Boren, Henry Loudermilk, Michael Lyon
Leonard Bowers, Thomas Nave, N.W. Garland
Chosen elected tried and sworn on thier oath do say they find
that the Defendant is not guilty It is therefore considered
by the court that the Defendant go hence without day and
that the county be taxed with the costs and that the county
Trustee pay the sd. costs out of any moneys not otherwise
appropreated

State	)	The attorney General with leave of the
Vs	)	court enters a nole prosequi and the De-
John McInturff	)	fendant assumes upon himself the costs.

It is therefore considered by the court
that the state recover of the defendant the costs of this
prosecution and that Execution may issue for the same

(P.309)

State	)	The attorney General with leave of
Vs	)	the court enters a nole prosequi
Polly Carter now	)	and John McInturff assumes upon
Polly McInturff	)	himself the costs. It is therefore

considered by the court that the
state recover of the said John McInturff the costs of this
prosecution and that Execution may Issue for the same

State	)	The defendant being charged on the bill
Vs	)	of Indietment for plea thereto saith that
Sherrod Furr	)	he is not guilty thereof and puts himself

upon his country and James P. Taylor at-
torney General who prosecutes on behalf of the State doeth
the like. whereupon came a Jury towit Jonathan Poland,
George Smith, John Fletcher, Squire Estep, Silas Felton
Reuben Lansdown, J.T. Boren, Henry Loudermilk, Michael Lyon,
Leonard Bowers, Thomas Nave and N.W Garland
Chosen elected tried and sworn on thier oath do say they
find that the defendant is not guilty It is therefore considered by the court that the defendant go hence without day
and that the county be taxed with the costs and that the trustee pay the same out of any money not otherwise appropreated

State	)	The attorney General with leave of the court
Vs	)	enters anole prosequi and the defendant as-
John Edwards	)	sumes upon himself the costs It istherefore
		considered by the said John Edwards

The costs of this prosecution and that execution may issue
for the same * the court that the state recover of

(P.310)

State	)	The defendant being charged on the bill
Vs	)	of Indietment for plea thereto saith
Thomas Snodgrass	)	that he is not guilty thereof and puts
		himself upon his country and the attor-

ney General on behalf of the state doeth the like whereupon
came a Jury towit, Godfrey Nave, Isaac Carrol, Valuntine Bowers
James Bradley, Benjamin Hyder Philip Shell, Huse Wardin John
Nave, William Perry Charles M.D. Gourley, William Stover &
Andrew Wilson chosen elected tried and sworn on thier oath
do say they find that the Defendand is not guilty
It is therefore considered by the court that the defendant
go hence without day and that the county pay the costs and
that the trustee pay the same out of any money not otherwise
appropreated

State) The attorney General with leave of the
Vs). court enters a nole prosequi
Alexander Wilson) It is therefore considered by the cou/ court that the defendant go hence without day and that the county pay the costs and that the Trustee pay the same out of any money not otherwise appropreated

State) The attorney General with leave of the
Vs) court enters aNole prosequi It is there-
William Michael) fore considered by the court that the Defendant go hence without day and that the county pay the costs and that the Trustee pay the same out of any money not otherwise appropreated

State) The attorney General with leave of the court
Vs) enters a nole prosequi and thereupon
E. Snider) Whitney Sheffield comes into court and assumes upon himself the costs of this prosecution It is therefore considered by the court that the state recover of the said Whitney Sheffield the costs of this prosecution and that Execution may issue against him for the same

(P.311)

State) Moses Estep prosecutor. The defendant Squire
Vs) Estep and Enoch Estep his security came in-
Squire Estep) to open court and acknowledged themselves indebted to the State of Tennessee that is to say the said Squire Estep in the sum of two hundred dollars and the said Enoch Estep his security in the sum of one hundred dollars to be levied of thier goods and chattles Lands and Tennements to the use of the state yet to be Void on condition the said Squire Estep make his personal appearance before the circuit court on the third Monday of March next at a court to be then held for the county of Carter at the court house in Elizabethton then & there to answer a charge of the state laid against him of Larency Moses Estep Prosecutor and stand to and abide the Judgment of the said court in that behalf and not depart the said court without leave of the sd. court first obtained

Moses Estep comes into court and acknowledges himself Indebted to the state of Tennessee in the sum of one hundred dollars to be levied of his goods and chattles lands and Tennements to the use of the state yet to be void on condition the said Moses Estep make his personal appearance before the circuit court at the court house in Elizabethton on the third Monday of March next and from day to day until discharged by the court then and there to prosecute and give evidence on behalf of the state against Squire Estep on a charge of Larceny

A deed of conveyance from Joseph Gentry to David Gentry
for one hundred and ninety three acres of Land proven in
open court by John Ward & William Ferris two subscribing
witnesses thereto and admitted to record let it be regis
tered

(P.312)   Ordered by the court that William B. Carter
sheriff and collector for the year 1821 be released of
the following insolvent taxable persons towit Isaac Cooley
56½ cents
George Moor--- -------------------------------------- 56½ cents
Harris Privit-- 56½ cents
John Almony-- 56¼ cents
Josiah Adams--- 56¼ cents
Walter Blevins-- same
Elijah Crow-- same
Joel Dunlap-- same
Andrew P. Hoslep-------------------------------------- same
Edgecomb Merit--- same
Edward Reeve--- same
Micajaj Rust-- same
George Rust-- same
Dempsey Richie--- same
Thomas Taylor-- s.me
Thomas Denton ----------------------------twelve dollars twenty five
cents
Lucus Emmert---56½ cents
Jno. Gray-- 56¼ cts
Hugh Morris -- 56¼ cts
John Delashmit--------------------------------------- 56¼ cts
Danl. Glover--- 56¼ cents

State of Tennessee)   Be it remembered that heretofore
Carter county   )   towit. At a court of pleas &
quarter sessions holden forsaid
county at the court house in Elizabethton on the second
Monday in February in the year of our Lord one thousand Eight
hundred and twenty nine a notice was returned in the following words and figures towit Andrew Taylor esqr. late sheriff
of Carter county Alfred M. Carter James P. Taylor and securities Take notice that on Wednesday of the next county
court of pleas and quarter sessions to be held for Carter
county at the court house in Elizabethton on the second
Monday of February next I mean to move The court for a
Judgment against you for the failure of sd. Andrew Taylor
late sheriff and collect of Carter county to pay over to
the county Trustee of Carter county the county taxes due
sd. county for the year one thousand eight hundred and
seventeen and one thousand eight hundred & eighteen attend
and oppose the same if you think proper 10th of Novr.1828
* and Archibald Williams Esq. his   B'z'l Smith.
Trustee of Carter Co.

(P. 313)   Which notice was returned marked thereon "recd.
11th November 1828 delivered a copy of the within notice
to Andrew Taylor and James P. Taylor 11th Novr. 1828
and to A. M. Carter 12th and to Archabald Williams 13th
November 1828 W. Carter Sheriff
    And afterwards towit during the sd. session of the said
court continued and held the same day & year aforesaid towit Wednesday third day of sd. session came the said Ezekiel
Smith county Trustee of Carter County by his attorney James
Rhea Esqr. and on motion of the said Ezekiel by his attorney
aforesaid moved the court for a Judgment against the sd.
Andrew Taylor Alfred M. Carter James P. Taylor and Archabald
Williams his securities for the failure of the said Andrew
Taylor collector as aforesaid to pay over the county taxes
to the county Trustee of said county for years aforesaid ... r
whereunto it is considered by the court that Samuel Juston
Govr. for the time being in and over the state of Tennessee
recover over against the aforesaid Andrew Taylor ... Alfres
M. Carter James P. Taylor and Archabald Williams his securities the sum of two hundred & twenty dollars thirty cents
and three mills for the failure of said Andrew Taylor collector of the county taxes for the years aforesaid to pay
over to the Trustee aforesaid the aforesaid sum of two hundred and twenty dollars thirty cents and three mills the
balance of the taxes due to said county for the years aforesaid and also costs of this motion and that execution may
issue therefore from which sd. Judgment the said Andrew
Taylor Alfred M. Carter James P. Taylor & Archabald Williams
by thier (P. 314) attorneys John Kennedy & Alfred W. Taylor
Esqr. pray an appeal to our next circuit court of Law to be
held for Carter county at the court house in Elizabethton
on the third Monday in March next which appeal is granted
by the court and the said Andrew Taylor, Alfred M. Carter,
James P. Taylor & Archibald Williams by thier attorneys
aforesaid entered into bond with John Kennedy & Alfred W.
Taylor there securities in the following wards & figures
towit

State of Tennessee)   Know all men by these present that
Carter County   )   we Andrew Taylor Alfred M. Carter,
                            James P. Taylor and Archabald
Williams are held and firmly bound unto Samuel Huston Covr.
for the time being and his successors in office in the sum
of five hundred dollars to be paid to the said Samuel Houston
his heirs Executor administrator or assigns to the which
payment well and truly to be made we bind ourselves heirs
Executors or administrators Jointly and severally firmly by
there presents sealed with our seal & dated this 11th day
of February 1829 The condition of the above obligation is
such that whereas in the suit brought by Samuel Houston

Govr. for the time being against Andrew Taylor A.M. Carter
James P. Taylor and Archd. Williams in the county court of
pleas and quarter Session held for the county aforesaid on
the second Monday of February last Judgement was recoverd.
by the said Saml Huston for the sum of two hundred and twenty Dollars thirty cents and whereas the sd. A. Taylor A.
M. Carter James P. Taylor & Archd. Williams have prayed
for and abtained an appeal from the said Judgment to the
next circuit court of Law to be held for Carter county at
the court house in Elizabethton on the third Monday of March
next now in case the said (P.315) Andrew Taylor A.M. Carter
James P. Taylor & ArchdMonday Williams do well and truly prosecute thier said appeal with effect or in case they fail or
he cost therein shall well and truly pay all such damage costs
and charges as shall be awarded against them by sd. circuit
court and also fulfill the sentence Judgment & Decree of said
court then the above obligations to be void or else to be in
full force and virtue ,
                              A. Taylor (seal)
                              J.P. Taylor (seal)
                              A Williams (seal)
                              A. M. Carter (seal)
                              by J. P. Taylor attorney
                              John Kennedy (seal)
                              A.M. Taylor (seal)

Ordered by the court that IsaacAnderson Calwell Brown Joseph
Brown, William Brown John McInturf & Ephraim Buck be a Jury
of View to lay off mark & report to next court a change in
the road leading from Elizabethton to Reeves Iron works on
N McNabbs land to change the Jonesborough road so as to let
the said run with the Carter road to D. Pughs line then to
turn with Pughs line till it intersects the original road
otherwise for both road to run together on about middle
ground to Pughs line- Ordered that said Jury inspect the
proper change and routs & report to next court & &

(P.316)   Ordered by the court that Joel Voan be one of
the hands of Smith Campbell to work in his bounds

Court adjourn'd untill tomorrow morning nine oclock,
                              Geo. Emmert,
                              Geo. Greenway,
                              John I. Wilson.

Thursday February 12th 1829 ,court met according to adjournment present the Worshipful John Wilson, George Greenway
and George Emmert Esquires

A deed of conveyance from William Carter Sheriff to George Lacy for one hundred and fifty acres of land was acknowledged in open court by the said William Carter shff the maker & was admitted to record let it be registered

Ordered by the court that William Gott be a commissioner to settle with Alfred W. Taylor Entry taken for Carter county according to act of assembly in such case made and provided

Eliza W. Carter) The Plaintiff by attorney dismiss-
   Vs) es this suit and the defendant
James B. Mourley) comes into court and assumes the
                costs It is therefore considered
by the court that the plaintiff recover of the defendant her costs in this behalf expended and the Defendant be in mercy&&

(P.317)
J. Nave & C. Carriger). For reasons appearing to the court
   Vs) it is ordered that the rule of re-
C. Lewis & others) ference heretofor entered in this
                cause be set aside and the cause is
ordered to stand for trial in the regular way

Robert Burrow) The Demurrer of the Defendant to the fourth
   Vs) court in the plaintiffs declaration was bro
John Nave) ught before the court and the court having
                heard argument thereon It is considered by
the court that the demurrer be sustained to which opinion of the court the plaintiff by attorney tenders a Bill of Exception & prays that it may be signed & sealed & made a part of the record of this cause which is done accordingly

Jacob Drake) The plaintiff comes into court and dismisses
   Vs) his suit and assumes the costs It is there-
Jeremiah Boyd) fore considered by the court that the defen-
                dant recover of the plaintiff his costs and
charges about his defence in this behalf expended and that the plaintiff be in mercy for his clamor &.

State) The defendant comes into court and
   Vs) confesses that he is guilty of the
Benjamin C. Harris) charge alledged against him where-
                upon the court having heard the
circumstances of the case fine the defendant one dollar It is therefore considered by the court that the state recover of the defendant the fine aforesaid and also the costs of this prosecution and that execution may issue for the same

(P.318)
State) The defendant comes into court &
   Vs) for plea to the charge alledged
James B. Mourley) against him saith that he is
                guilty & submits to the court

Whereupon the court having heard evidence and duly considered the same fine the defendant fifty cents It is therefore
considered by the court that the state recover of the defendant the fine aforesaid and also the costs of this prosecution and that Execution may issue against his for the
same

State ·) The defendant comes into court and pleads
Vs) that he is guilty of the charge alledged
Abner McLeod) against him whereupon the court fines the
defendant One dollar It is therefore considered by the court that the state recover of the defendant
the fine aforesaid and also the costs of this prosecution
and that execution may issue for the same

State) The defendant comes into court and pleads
Vs) guilty & submits to the court whereupon
Jesse Adams) the court fines the Defendant one dollar
It is therefore considered by the court
that the state recover of the defendant the sum of one dollar the fine assessed by the court as aforesaid and also
the costs of this prosecution and that Execution may issue
the same

James B. Mourley) On motion and for reasons appear-
Vs) ing to the court the plaintiff is
John Atkins) permited to amend his writ by
changing the letter T in the de-
fendants name for the letter D so as to read, Adkins, in-
stead of Atkins

(P.319)   William B. Carter returned to court a list of
the taxable property and polls in Captain McLeods district
for the year 1829

Abner McLeod) It is ordered by the court that certior-
Vs ads) ari and supersideas issue to John
J. Dugger) Richardson Esqr. upon A. McLeod on com-
plying with legal prereqursites

James B. Mourley
Vs
Reuben Miller
Constable

James B. Mourley) Whereas a capias adsatesfaccendum
Vs) was issued by Julias Dugger Esquire
John Rasor Senr.) in favor of the plaintiff against
the Defendant for the sum oftwenty
one dollars and ninety/cents debt and the further sum of fifty cents costs which Ca Sa came into the hands of Reuben
Miller constable and the said Reuben Miller constable as afore-

said having failed to take bond and security as in such
case made and provided on motion of the plaintiff by his
attorney and for reasons appearing to the court
It is therefore considered by the court that the said
James B. Mourley recover over against the said John Rasor
Senr. & Reuben Miller constable the aforesaid sum of twenty
onedollars and ninety cents debt & fifty cents costs with
Interest from the second day of June eighteen hundred and
twenty seven until paid together with the costs of this motion and that execution may issue therefore

(P.320)   Rueben Miller constable proves his attendance
at this session of the court as constable for four days

State	)
Vs	)
Wm Harvey	)

John McInturff proves four days attendance
as a witness in this cause

Ordered by the court that the clerk issue a copy of or order
in pursuance to a petition of A. Taylor issued at last court
returnable to next court

Thomas Gourley constable proves his attendance at this session
three days for which he is allowed agreeable to Law

And then the court adjourned till court in course,
                                        W. B. Carter
                                        Geo. Emmert,
                                        G. W. Greenway,
                                        William Gott.

(P.321)
State of Tennessee   )   At a meeting of a court of please
Carter county   )   and quarter sessions held for the
                              said county at the court house in
Elizabethton on the second Monday of May in the year of our
Lord one thousand eight hundred and twenty nine present the
Worshipful,
                         Richard Donally,
                         Jesse Cole,
                         George W. Greenway,
                         William Gott,
                         John Richardson,
                         George Emmert,
                         William B. Carter,
                         William Peoples,
                         John L. Williams &
                         Jeremiah Campbell   Esquires.

On motion for a appropriation for the support and maintainance of James Graves for the sum of seventy five dollars
and John Shaver for the support of a pauper Omey Heatherley
seventy five dollars William Carter shff fifty dollars for
his exofficio services and George Williams clerk fifty
dollars for his exofficio services George Williams clerk
fifteen dollars for making out the tax lists for the year
one thousand eight hundred and twenty nine and James Rhea
twelve dollars and fifty cents for prosecuting a suit
Samuel Houston Governor for the time being against Andrew
Taylor late sheriff & collector of Carter county and his
securities and the said George Williams clerk calling each
Justice present by name and those voting in favor of said
appropriation Richd. Donally, Yea Jesse Cole Yea George
Greenway yea William Gott yea, John Richardson yea
George Emmert yea William B. Carter yea William Peoples
yea John L. Williams yea and JeremiahCampbell yea and there
appearing a majority of the acting Justices of sd. county in
favor of said appropriation It is therefore ordered by the
court that the clerk issue certificates to the respective
claimants for the aforementioned sums

James Rhea Isud. the 13 Jany. 1841 by J.L. Bradley clerk

For reasons appearing to the court It is therefore ordered
that John Whitehead and Elijah Hathaway be realeased of a
Poll tax for the year one thousand eight hundred & twenty
nine

Christian C. Nave exhibited in open court a Licence under
the signiture of Edward Scott Samuel Powel two of the Judges of the circuit courts of law and Equity in & for the
state of Tennessee to practice law as an attorney in the
several courts of law and Equity in the state of Tennessee
and took the several oaths required by law for an attorney
and admitted to Practice

John Richardson Esquire returned a list of the taxable property and polls in Captian Naves District for the year 1829

State   )   The Defendant being charged upon
   Vs   )   the bill of Inditment submited to
Elizabeth Heaton)   the court therefore it considered
                        by the court that the Defendant
be fined six cents and a fourth of a cent Thereupon Washington
Heaton comes into court and assumes upon himself the fine
aforesaid and the costs of this prosecution
It is therefore considered by the court that the state recover of the Defendant and the said Washington Heaton the sd.
fine and the costs of this prosecution and the defendant in
mercy

(P.323)   The last will and Testament of Jesse Humphreys
decd. was presented for probate by Polly Humphreys his widow
which was opposed by George Humphreys and Elisha Humphreys
Whereupon it is ordered by the court that a Jury come to
enquire whether the said Instrument offered for probate by the
sd. Polly be the last will and Testament of Jesse Humphreys
decd. or not
For reasons appearing to the court from the affidavit of
Elisha Humphreys it is ordered by the court that a commission issue to any justice of the peace for Monroe county

State of Tennessee to take the deposition of Cleming Love
of Monroe county to be read as evidence on the trial of
the validity of the instrument of writing purporting to
be the last will and testament of Jesse Humphreys decd.
on giving ten days notice to the said Polly widow of the
said Jesse Humphreys decd.

Five Justices present towit Richd. Donally Jesse Cole
George W. Greenway William Gott John Richardson & George
Emmert John Taylor produced in open court the Scalps of two
Wolves adjudged by the court over four months old and the
said John being sworn on his oath saith that he Killed the
said Wolves in the county of Carter since the first day of
January 1811 and it appearing to the satisfaction of the
court that the sd. John Killed the said Wolves in the county
It is therefore ordered by the court that the said John
Taylor be allowed six dollars for Killing the said two Wolv-
es to be paid out of state Treasury

(P.324)   On motion of Peter Parsons Esquire it is ordered
by the court that Tennessee Carriger be appointed Guardian
of the minor heirs of Godfrey Carriger decd.

Samuel Scott returns one stud horse at two dollars the season of one mare

Ordered by the court that the Trustee recieve and pay over
the amounty of a certificate of an allowance made to Ann
Morgan a pauper at February session 1829 for fifteen dollars
to and for the use of Jeremiah Cates who entered the body
of said Ann Morgan decd.

Jesse Cole prays that he may have his mark recorded which
is a hole in the left ear and two slits in the right ear

Ordered by the court that John Wright and Saml. W. Williams
be appointed commissioner to settle with the county Trustee
and collector of county moneys & &

State   )   The attorney. General by leave of the cou-
   Vs   )   rt enters a nole prosequi Defendant and
Richard Taylor)   William Clawson Junr. assume the costs.
                    Therefore it is considered by the court
that the state recover of the said Richd. Taylor and the said
William Clawson Junr. the costs of this prosecution and the
defendant in mercy & &

A deed of conveyance from Enoch Dunkin to Abel Guin for twenty five acres of Land acknowledged in open court by Enoch
Dunkin the maker thereof and admitted to record let it be registered

(P.325) Ordered by the court that a Jury of View be ap-
pointed to examine the road leading from John L Williams
up the Buffeloe creek by David Pughs to the fork of the
Jonesbora road towit, William Simerly, Caleb Smith, William
Jones,Nathan Birchfield Senr. Thomas P. Insor, John Bryles,
James I. Tipton, John C. Helm, Jacob Range, William Baker,
John Shields, Henry Simmerly.
Whose duty it shall be or any five of them to examine the
new contemplated road leaving the old road by John L Williams
and also the old road in doing which they shall examine and
report according to law and say which rout shall be the es-
tablished road

Ordered by the court that Adam Loudermilk, Henry Loudermilk,
Thos. P. Insor, Jonathan Taylor John Williams Andrew Taylor
Junr. and John C. Helm or any five of whome be a Jury to
view the main road beginning near the house of Jonathan
Taylor to make alterations and run again into the main road
near John C. Helms Mill

Ordered by the court that Joseph Cable, Emanuel Jenkins,
David Nave, John T. Allen, Matthias Wagner, Peter Wills,
Jacob Smith, James Campbell, William Brown, Isaac Carrol,
William Greer, John Carriger, William Stover, William Hardin,
Valuntine Bowers,Bayles Miller, William Shown, Isaac Shown,
Andrew Wilson,Boneyparte Blevins, Samuel Lacy, Samuel Lusk
James Gourley, Nicholas Pain, Jonathan Range & John T. Boren
be appointed Jurors for our next circuit court of law to be
held for Carter county on the third Monday of September next
at the court house in Elizabethton & &

(P.326) Ordered by the court that William Peoples be
allowed twenty five dollars for his back rearages as
trustee for Carter county for the year 1822 when settlement made whith him by Christian Carriger Joseph Renfro
& David Pugh commissioners appointed by the court and
the said Peoples made oath to the satisfaction of the
court that they told him it was the aforementioned sum

Ordered by the court that Joseph Obrian overseer of the
road leading from Obrian Gott & Obrians forge to enter-
sect the Jonesborough road by William Simmerleys, have
all the hands belonging to the forge above mentioned together with James Morgan to work on sd. road

Ordered by the court that Daniel Cable, John Sheffield,
George Sheffield Daniel Shell, Jacob Snider, Isaac Snider
Jacob Smith, Elijah Smith, James Jones, Barnabas Oaks,
Johnson Hampton and Robert Vance, be a Jury of view to examine the road passing through John Wilsons plantation and
that they report to our next court what damages said Wilson
sustains by said road passing through his plantation

Ordered by the court that Able Dugger be appointed overseer
from Duggers ford to Vanhus and have the following hands towit Thomas Dugger, Michael Pierce, Vanhus,s hands James Miller
Hugh Wilson William Perkins Jeremiah Whaley, and all the
hands on Samuel Burns farm. Abraham Whaley, Joseph Vaun &
Hardy Pierce

An artical of agreement between William Ingram & John Ingram
acknowledged in open court by John Ingrim & proven in open
court on the part of William Ingrim by Jabez Murry one of
the subcribing witnesses (P.327) thereto and thereupon
admited to record let it be registered

A deed of conveyance from John Wilson to Thos. Johnson for
thirty two acres & half of land proven in open court by
Taylor McNabb and Richd. Donally two subscribing witnesses
thereto and admited to record let it be registered

A deed of conveyance from Thos. D. Love to John Wright for
fifty acres of land was acknowledged in open court by Thos
D. Love the maker thereof admited to record let it be registered

A deed of conveyance from Vaut Heaton to James B. Mourley
for three hundred and sixteen acres of land was acknowledged
in open court by the maker thereof Vaut Heaton was admited
to record let it be registered

Ordered by the court that the following persons be a Jury to serve at the August session of the court of pleas and quarter session held for Carter county namely (1) John Glover, (2) Thomas Crow, (3) John Grindstaff, (4) Arthur Pearce, (5) William Snider (6) Henry Smith, (7) Hugh Jenkins (8) Henry Colbough, (9) Archabald Vest (10) Richard Dunlap, (11) Henry Nave, (12) David Bowers, (13) Jacob Stover, (14) Samuel Tipton Junr (15) Lazarus C. Inman,(16) Joseph Renfro (17) Lewis Morgan (18) Samuel McKeehen (19) Wm Taylor, (20) Charles Lisenby (21) Tobias Hendrix (22) John Crosswhite, (23) Joseph Robinson, (24) Armsted Cooper, (25) David Brummit (26) James W. Clawson

Ordered by the court that Henry Loudermilk be appointed overseer of the road leading from the fork of the road at the top of the hill at J. Williams to the county line the direct road to the factory in the room of John Williams and have the same hands and same bounds

(P.328) Ordered by the court that Clabourn Justice be appointed overseer of the public road in the stead of William Obrian and have the same hands and bounds

Ordered by the court that John McInturff be appointed overseer of the public road on Buffeloe at the uper corner of David Hains fence to the forks of the road below Saml Lacys and that Austin Guin William McNabb Alfred McNabb Samuel Pugh Alfred Bishop John Mourland Samuel Lacy Taylor McNabb and Ephraim H Buck be the hands to work said road

Ordered by the court that John Wright be appointed overseer of the public road from the cornor of David Hains fince by McInturffs shop to where it intersects the other in said Wrights lane and that the hands living on the lands of John Wilcox John Carroll William Peoples Christopher Price Jesse Mattox John Wright Thomas D. Love on Buffeloe Creek and David Grant be the hands to work on said road

Ordered by the court that Thomas Greer be appointed overseer in the room of Thos. Snodgrass and work on the same road and have the same hands that Snodgrass had

Ordered by the court that A. L. Wilson be appointed overseer of the public road in the room of A. Wilson and have the same hands and bounds that A. Wilson had

Ordered by the court that Matthias Broyles be appointed overseer of the stage road leading from Elizabethton to John Williams and have the same hands Lucas Emmert had to work on said road

(P.329)   Ordered by the court that J. Campbell J. Keys
W. Carter J. Hampton and A. M. Carter commissioners heretofore appointed for the superentending of the building of
the new court house be and are hereby requested to lay before this court now in session the statement of the amount
of the taxes laid for the purpose of building said house
the amount collected for each year the amount paid over by
the collectors for each year and that the chairman thereof
will report the said matters to this court instanter and
that the sheriff deliver a copy of the above order to the
said Chairman immediately

Ordered by the court that Moses Banks be appointed overseer
of the Public road from the Limestone Cove to the Buckeye
springs on the top of the Iron Mountain and have all the
hands from Geo. Hains's up that worked under Jno. Britt &
Nathan Birchfield and the hands under David Guinn and then
the court adjourned till tomorrow nine oclock

                              Jesse Cole,
                              Geo. Emmert,
                              L. White,
                              John J. Wilson,
                              Geo. Greenway,
                              John Richardson,
                              R. Donally,
                              William Gott,
                              J. H. Hyder

(P.330)   Tuesday May 12th 1829
Court met according to adjournment Present the Worshipful
                 George Emmert,
                 Richard Donally
                 William B. Carter
                 Lawson White
                 John J. Wilson

Joseph Wilson   )   J. Wilson exhibited his petition in
      Vs   )   court praying writs of certiorari &
John Wilson   )   supersedeas & & and for reasons ap-
                      pearing to the court from said petit-
ion It is ordered by the court that writs of certiorari and
supesedeas issue on the petitioner complying with the pre-
requisites of the law relative to the issuance of said writs

State   )   The attorney General with leave of
      Vs   )   the court enters a nole prosequi
Samuel Overholse)   in this case and Samuel Overholse
                      and Wm Vaun his security come into
court and assumed the costs It is therefore considered by
the court that the state recover of the said Samuel Overholes
and Wm Vaun his security the costs of this prosecution and
the Defendant in mercy & &

State	)	The defendant being charged pleads
Vs	)	guilty and submits to the court and
Isaac Garland	)	the court having heard and under-
		stood the circumstances of the case

fine the Defendant six cents and the fourth of a cent thereupon William Garland comes into court and assumes with the defendant the costs It is therefore considered by the court that
the state recover of the defendant and his security William
Garland the fine aforesaid and the costs of this prosecution
and the Defendant in mercy & &

Joseph Obrian being one of the original Veniri and an overseer
of the public road is therefore released from service as a
Juror

(P.331)

State	)	The defendant being charged pleads
Vs	)	guilty and submits to the court and
Samuel Garland	)	the court understanding the circum-
		stances of the case fine the Defend-

ant six cents and the fourth of a cent thereupon William   *
Garland comes into court and assumes with the defendant the
costs It is therefore considered by the court that the state
recover of the Defendant and the said William Garland the
fine aforesaid and also the costs of this prosecution and
the Defendant in mercy & & * fine aforesaid and the

State	)	The defendant being charged pleads guilty
Vs	)	and submits to the court and the court
John Oliver	)	having heard and understood the circumstan-
		ces of the case fine the Defendant six cents

and the fourth of a cent thereupon Samuel Garland comes into court and assumes with the Defendant the fine aforesaid
and the costs of this prosecution It is therefore considered
by the court that the state recover of the Defendant and
the said Samuel Garland the fine aforesaid and also the costs
of this Prosecution and the Defendant in mercy & &

William Carter Sheriff & & returned the Venire Facias ex-
ecuted from which were drawn thefollowing persons for grand
Jurors towit, (1) Samuel Bogart, (2) Samuel E. Patton,
(3) Owen Edwards, (4) James Heatherly, (5) John Inman (6)
William Nave, (7) Aaron Owens, (8) Jacob Cammeron, (9)
Andrew L. Wilson (10) Lewis Morgan, (11) John I Powers (12)
John Rowe (13) Isaac Anderson and the court appointed
Samuel Bogart foreman of sd. grand Jury

Wyley Edwards constable sworn to attend the grand Jury
Stephen Tilson who was a constable for the county of Carter
tendered to the court his resignation of the office of constable as follows May session Tuesday May 12th 1829 Stephen
Tilson a constable in Captain McInturfs company resigns his

commission as constable in said company in open court.

Stephen Tilson
Which was accepted by the court & made a record

William Gott Esquire tendered to the court the following
resignation of the office of Justice of the peace for
Carter county (Viz) To the Worshipful the court of please
& & for Carter county I do hereby resign the office of
Justice of the peace for Carter county May 12th 1829 which
was accepted by the court and made of record,
W. Gott

Rebecca Shawley administratrix and William B. Holt administrator of the goods chattles & & of James Shawley decd. returned to court an Inventory of the goods and chattles
rights and credits of James Shawley dec'd.

A deed of conveyance for ninety acres of land more or less
from Elizabeth Heaton to George W. Heaton was acknowledged
in o pen court by Elizabeth Heaton the maker thereof was
admited to record let it be registered

A deed of conveyance from Vaught Heaton Joseph Heaton William
Roberts and his wife Theodocia Roberts formerly Theodocia
Heaton Meredy Dugger & Hannah Dugger formerly Hannah Heaton
and Washington Heaton and Elizabeth Heaton to Peter Rasor
for three acres of Land acknowledged in open court by the
makers thereof Elizabeth Heaton Vaut Heaton William Roberts
Joseph Heaton George W. Heaton & Teolocia Roberts wife of
William Roberts Meredy Dugger and the sd. Teodocia Roberts
wife of sd. William Roberts being examined by the court
touching her free consent of signing sealing Executing the
same Seperate & apart from her Husband saith she executed
the same freely Voluntarily and of her free will without
fear threat (P.333) or persuasion of her said Husband an
admited to record let it be registered*Hannah Dugger

The court proceeded to the election of a sheriff and on
counting the ballots it appeared that William Gott was
duly and constitutionally elected who came into court and
took the several Oaths require'd by law for a sheriff and
entered into bond with William B. Carter Caleb Smith John
Obrian & Alfred W.Taylor his securities in the following
words and figures towit

State of Tennessee   )   Know all men by there present
Carter county   )   that we William Gott, William
                          B. Carter, Caleb Smith, John
Obrian and Alfred W. Taylor are held and firmly bound unto his excellency William Hall Governor for the time being
and his sucessors in office in the full & Just sum of
eight hundred dollars to the which payment well and truly

to be made we bind ourselves our heirs Executors and administrators Jointly and sevirally firmly by there present
signed sealed with our seals and dated this 12th day of
May 1829 The condition of the above obligation is such
that where as the above bound William Gott is constituted
& appointed sheriff in & for the county aforesaid for and
during the day of the above date now. It therefore the
said William Gott do and shall well & truly collect and
recieve all the state taxes in the county aforesaid for
the year one thousand eight hundred and twenty nine and
one thousand eight hundred and thirty and account for and
pay the said taxes into the Treasurers office of East
Tennessee on or before the first day of December in each
and every year then the above obligations to be void and of
no effect else to be and remain in full force and Virtue
* term of two years from the

William Gott (seal)
William B. Carter(seal)
C. Smith (seal)
Jno. Obrian (seal)
A.W. Taylor (seal)

(P.334)   William Gott Sheriff and collector of county
taxes enters into Bond with William B. Carter, John Obrian
Caleb Smith & Alfred W. Taylor his securities in the
following wards and figures towit

State of Tennessee   )   Know all men by these present
Carter county   )   that we William Gott William B.
                             Carter John Obrian Caleb Smith
& Alfred W. Taylor are held and firmly bound unto Jeremiah
Campbell chairman of the county of pleas and quarter session
of the county aforesaid for the time being and his successors in office in the full and Just sum of five thousand dollars to the which payment well and truly to be made we bind
ourselves our heirs Executors and administrators Jointly
andseverally firmly by there presents signed and sealed with
our seals and dated this 12th day of May in the year of our
Lord 1829 * court
The condition of the above obligation is such that whereas
the above bounds William Gott is constituted and appointed
sheriff and collector of the county taxes in and for the
county afroesaid for and during the term of two years from
the day of the above date now if therefore the said above
bound William Gott do and shall well and truly collect and
recieve all the county taxes in and for the county aforesaid for and during the term aforesaid account for and pay
the said taxes into the county Trustees office of the county
aforesaid on or before the first court to be held for the
county aforesaid after the first day of January in each and
every year then the above obligation to be void and of no
effect else to be and remain in full force & virtue

William Gott (seal)
William B. Carter (seal)
John Obrian (seal)
C. Smith (seal)
A. W. Taylor (seal)

(P.335)   William Gott Sheriff entered into Bond with
William B. Carter, John Obrian Caleb Smith & Alfred W.
Taylor his securities in the penal sum of ten thousand
dollars for the preformance of his duty in office as sheriff
sec bond

Abraham Tipton appointed constable

George Emmert elected coroner

Ezekiel Smith elected court Trustee and sd. E Smith entered
into bond with Richard Donally and Lawson White his securities in the sum of two thousand Dollars with condition &c %
sec bond

James B. Mourley appointed constable entered into bond with
his securities William Donally & Johnson Hampton in the sum
of one thousand dollars with condition sec bond

And then this court adjourned till tomorrow nine oclock
                              W. B.   Carter
                              Geo. Emmert
                              G. W. Greenway

(P.336)   Wednesday May 13th 1829

Court met according to adjournment present the Worshipful
William B. Carter George Emmert & George W. Greenway

State   ) The defendant being charged on the Bill
  Vs   ) of Indietment pleads not guilty
John Hinkle   ) Thereupon came a Jury towit (1) John Nave
               (2) Henry H. Nave, (3) James I. Tipton,
(4) Ewin Heatherly (5) Squire Estep (6) William Overby,
(7) Joseph Cable, (8) Thomas Heatherly (9) Thos. Ellit,
(10) Valuntine Bowers (11) Nehemiah Harley and (12)
Vincent Kelly Who being elected tried and sworn the truth
to speak on thier Oath do say they find that the defendant
is not guilty in manner and form as charged in the Bill
of Indietment It is therefore considered by the court that
the defendant go hence without day and that county pay the
costs of this prosecution and that the Clerk issue certi
ficates to those persons entityled to costs thereon

State   ) James Lovelace who being summond in this
  Vs   ) case to give evidence on behalf of the
John Hinkle) state being Solemnly called came not but
             made default therefore It is considered
by the court that James Lovelace forfeit according to act
of assembly

State   ) The defendant being charged on the bill
  Vs   ) of Indietment he for plea thereto saith
Solomon Church) he is not guilty Thereupon came a Jury
             towit John Nave Henry H. Nave James I. Tipton
Squire Ester William Overby Joseph Cable Thomas Ellit Valuntine Bowers Nehemiah Harly Vincent Kelly Anderson Kite John
Hinkle who being sworn the truth to speak on the issue Joined on there Oath do say thay find the defendant is not guilty as charged in the bill of Indietment It is therefore considered by the court that the defendant go hence without day and on motion of the defendants counsel to tax the costs to Thomas Heatherly the prosicutor it is ordered that Thos. Heatherly be taxed with the costs It is therefore (P.337) considered by the court that the state recover of Thomas Heatherly the Prosecutor the costs of this prosecution and that Execution Issue against him for the same

State   ) The Defendant being charged on the bill
  Vs   ) of Indietment pleads guilty and submits
William Beard) to the court Thereupon the court having
             heard evidence and fully understood the
circumstances of the case fine the Defendant five dollars It is therefore considered by the court that the state recover of the defendant the sum of five dollars the fine assessed as aforesaid together with the costs of this prosecution and that the Defendant be in custody untill the fine and costs be paid or security given to secure the same

State   ) Thos Heatherly Prosecutor The defendant being charged on the bill
  Vs   ) of Indietment for plea thereto
Alexander Fracure) saith he is not guilty Thereupon
came a Jury towit 1-John Nave 2- Henry H. Nave 3- James I. Tipton 4- William Overby 5- Thomas Ellit 6- Valuntine Bowers 7- Nehemiah Harley 8- Vincent Kelly 9-Anderson Kite 10- John Hinkle 11-Samuel Tipton 12- Lazarus C. Inman Who being sworn the truth to speak on the issue Joined on their oath do say they find that the Defendant is not guilty as charged in the Bill of Indietment It is therefore considered by the court that the defendant go hence without day thereupon the counsel for the Defendant moved the court to tax Thomas Heatherly the Prosecutor with the costs and for reason appearing to the court it is ordered by the court that the costs be taxes against Thomas Heatherly

The Prosecutor and that the clerk may issue execution against him for the same To which opinion of the court taxing the
the prosecutor with the costs the said Thomas Heatherly by
his counsel executs and tenders a Bill of exception and prays
that it may be signed and sealed and made a part of the record of this cause which is done accordingly and prays an ap
appeal in the nature of a writ of Error to the circuit court
to be held for the county of Carter at the court house in
Elizabethton on the third Monday of September next & enters
into recognizance for the prosecution of the same and thereupon the appeal is granted

(P.338)

John Nave & Christian Carriger Vs Peter Lewis Charles Lewis & Howel Lewis	The plaintiff by thier counsel came into court and dismiss thier suit and also the defendant came into court and assumes upon themselves the costs It is therefore consider- ed by the court that the Plaintiffs recover of the defendant the costs

which they have about thier suit in this behalf expended and
the defendants in mercy & &

State Vs Samuel Garland	The attorney General with leave of the court enters a nole Prosequi in this cause and Ewins Heatherly the Prosecution comes into court

and assumes the costs It is therefore considered by the court
that the state recover of the said Ewins Heatherly the costs
of this prosecution and that execution may issue for the same

State Vs William Heatherly	The defendant being charged on the Bill of Indietment for plea thereto saith he is not guilty thereupon came a Jury towit Lorenses

Richardson, Peter Emmert, Samuel Tipton,Robert Stuart, James
Range Henry Little, Benjamin Hyder, Lucas Emmert, Henry
Grindstaff, Richard Dunlap, Charles Lewis & Jesse Jenkins
Who being sworn the truth to speak on the issue Joined on
thier Oath do say they fine that the defendant is guilty in
manner and form as charged in the Bill of Indietment thereupon the court fine the Defendant six cents & one fourth of
a cent Ewins Heatherly comes into court and assumes with the
defendant the costs It is therefore considered by the court
that the state recover of the defendant and Ewins Heatherly
the fine aforesaid together with the costs of this prosecution and the deft in mercy & &

(P.339)

State   )   The defendant being charged on the bill
  Vs   )   of .Indietment pleads guilty and sub-
William Beard)   mitts to the court and the court having
                      heard evidence on the case and fully
understood the circumstances of the case fine the defendant
ten dollars and order that he be imprisoned in the jail of
Washington county ten days because of the insufficuncy of
the Jail of Carter county and there to remain untill he
gives security for the fine and costs of this prosecution
or be otherwise legally discharged and that he gives security to keep the peace towit the good people of this state
and particularly James Harvey for twelve months in t'e pen-
alty of five hundred dollars and that the sheriff of Carter
county carry this order into effect

State   )   Thomas Heatherly prosecutor comes
  Vs   )   into open court and acknowledges
Alexander Frasure)   himself indebted to the state in
                          the sum of one hundred dollars
to be levied of his goods and chattles lands and Tennements
and John Hinkle & Mecklin Nicholson his securities came into
court & acknowledged themselves severally indebted to the
state in the sum of fifty dollars each to be levied of thier
goods and chattles lands and Tennement to the use of the
state yet to be void on condition the said Thos Heatherly
make his personal appearance before the circuit court to be
held for Carter county at the court house in Elizabethton on
the third Monday of September next then & there to Prosecute
and give evidence on behalf of the state in prosecution the
state against Alexander Frazure and stand to and abide the
Judgement of the said court and not depart the same without
leave first had and abtained which appeal is granted by the
court

(P.340)

State   )   The defendant being charged on the bill
  Vs   )   of Indietment pleads not guilty and puts
Enoch Estep)   himself upon his country and the attor-
                    ney General doeth the like Thereupon
came a Jury towit Samuel Burns, Jonathan Range John Nave,
Vincent Kelly, Thomas Ellit, John Hinkle, Joseph Cable,
James I. Tipton, Valentine Bowers, William Overby, Anderson
Kite, Nehemiah Harley, Who being sworn the truth to speak on
the issue Joined on thier oath do say they find that the
defendant is not guilty as charged in the bill of Indietment It is therefore considered by the court that the defendant go hence without day and that the county pay the
costs and that the clerk issue certifiates to such persons
are entitled to the same

(P.341)   William Gott Esquire who was heretofore appointed a commissioner to settle with the Entry-taker of Carter
county made the following report towit.To the Worshipful
court of please & & for Carter county at May session 1829
The undersignd represents to your Worshipful that in obed-
ience to an order made at Febuary session 1829 I have proceeded to settle with Alfred W. Taylor Entry- taker of
Carter county & find that said Taylor has recieved entries
commencing with Nol and ending with No 1316 made on the 24th
day of March 1829 amounting to thirty five hundred and one
dollars fifteen cents and six mills after deducting two per
cent given to him by act of asembly and find that said Taylor
has paid over to A. M. Carter Bank agent for Carter county
thirty four hundred and thirty six dollars sixteen cents and
seven mills leaving said Taylor indebted to the public sixty four dollars ninety eight cents and nine mills and have
furthermore examined the Location of said office and find
them recorded as required by act of assembly & & In testimoney whereof I have hereunto set my hand & seal this 31st
day of March 1829,

                     William Gott (seal)
                     Commissioner

Rec'd of Alfred W. Taylor Entry taker for Carter county
sixty dollars ninety eight cents & nine mills school
funds this 8th day of May 1829
Duplicated reciepts signed
                     A. M. Carter.
                     Agent.

Recd. of Alfred W. Taylor four dollars for two days services
appointed by the court of please & quarter sessions to settle
with him as entry taker for Carter county which settlements
was agreeable to said order effected this 31st March 1829
A Duplicate,   Wm Gott

And then court adjourned till tomorrow 9 oclock
                     W. B. Carter
                     Geo. Emmert
                     G. W. Greenway

(P.342)   Thursday May 14th 1829 court met according to
adjournment present the worshipful George W. Greenway
George Emmert & William B. Carter.

Robert Burrow   )   Ordered by the court that a commiss-
     Vs   )   ion Issue to any Justice of the
John Nave   )   peace for Sanquace county state of
Illenoise to take the deposition of Solomon Gibson on behalf of the defendant to be read as evidence on the trial of
this cause on giving thirty days notice of the time and place
of taking the same to the Plaintiff

John M. Preston)   In this cause came the parties
    Vs   )   by thier attorneys and thereup-
John Ward)   on came a Jury towit. Michael
    Lyon, Larensa Richardson, Daniel
Chance, Mecklin Nicholes, Charles Bassendine, Nehemiah Harly
Edmon Sams, William Renfro, William Overbee, James Jinkins,
John Insor, Isaac P. Tipton who being empanneled and sworn
the truth to speak on the issue Joined between the parties
on thier Oath do say they find the Defendant has not Kept
his covenant as in pleading be alledged and assesse the plaintiff damage to ninety nine dollars and sixty cents It is the
therefore considered by the court that the plaintiff recover of the defendant the sum of ninety nine dollars and
sixty cents assessed as aforesaid by the Jury aforesaid for
the plaintiff damage together with the costs which he hath
about his suit in this behalf expended and the defendant in
mercy & &

Wyley Edwards constable proves three days attendance on the
court and it ordered that the clerk issue to him a certificate
therefore

(P.343)
Joshua Jobe   )   Ordered by the court that com-
    Vs   )   missions issue towit a commiss-
George Lacy &   )   ion to any Justice of the peace
James I. Tipton admrs of)   for Giles county to take the de-
Isaac Tipton decd.   )   position of Samuel Watson with
    twenty days notice one commiss-
ion to any Justice of the peace for Sanqueman county State
of Illonoise to take the deposition of John Dunlap with
thirty days notice one to any Justice of the peace for Blount
county to take the depositions of Wm Hendrix, Martin Wiseman
& Thomas Jones with ten days notice one to any Justice take
the deposition of Samuel Tipton Senr. of Carter county five
days notice to be debeneisse one other to any Justice of the
peace for Washington county to take the deposition of John
Tipton Senr.Abraham Jobe with ten days notice all on behalf
of the defendants all which to be read as evidence on the
trial of this cause

William Overbee)   In this cause came the parties by
    Vs   )   thier attorneys and thereupon came
Robert Burrow)   a Jury towit. Michael Lyon, Daniel
    Chance, Edmon Sams, William Renfro
Owen Edwards, Jacob Cammeron, John Ihsor, Isaac P. Tipton,
Alfred Sams, Benjamin Hyder, John Inman and John T. Bowers
Chosen elected tried and sworn the truth to speak on the matter of controversy between the parties on thier oath do
say they find the plaintiff the sum of seven dollars eighty
two cents Therefore it is considered by the court that the
*for

plaintiff recover of the Defendant the sum of seven dollars eighty two cents found as aforesaid by the Jury aforesaid together with the costs which he hath about his suit
in this behalf expended and the defendant in mercy & &

(P.344)

Wm Overbee	)	On motion of the defendant counsel and
Vs.	)	for reason appearing to the court a
Robert Burrow	)	rule is granted to shew cause why a new
		trial should be granted in this cause

James Harley assignee & &)For reason appearing to the
Vs   ) court it is ordered that a
George W. Carter   ) commission issue to any Jus-
) tice of the peace for
Washington county State of Virginia to take the deposition of John H. Fulton on behalf of the plaintiff to
be read as evidence on the trial of this cause on giving
twenty days notice of the time and place of taking the
same to the defendant

James B. Mourly   )   With & by the agreement of the
   Vs   )   parties these three causes are
John Atkins   )   ordered to be transfered to the
John Atkins   )   circuit court to be held for
   Vs   )   Carter county on the third
James B. Mourly   )   Monday of September next there
   Same   )   to be tried & determined and
   Vs   )   that the clerk make out tran-
   Same   )   scripts of the Records thereof

George Emmert Esquire who was elected coroner came into
court and took the oaths required by law and entered into
Bond with securities with condition sec bond

(P.345)

Isaac Williams for the use of)   The Plaintiff comes
A. C.   Parks   )   into court and dis-
   Vs   )   misses his suit and
Daniel Odoneal &   )   John Obrian comes in-
William Obrian   )   to court and assumes
)   upon himself with the
Defendant the costs It is therefore considered by the court
that the Plaintiff recover of the Defendant and John Obrian
the costs which he hath about his suit in this behalf ex-
pended

Tennessee L Carriger &) The Plaintiff by thier atton-
Godfrey Nave Admr.) ey came into court and dis-
of Godfrey Carriger decd.) miss thier suit and John Obrian
Vs) comes into court and assumes
William Obrian &) upon himself with the Defend-
Joseph Obrian) ants the costs It is therefore
) considered by the court that
the plaintiff recover of the Defendant and John Obrian the
costs which they have about thier suit in this behalf expended and the Defendants in mercy & &

Tennessee L. Carriger &) The Plaintiffs by thier
Godfrey Nave Admr.) attorney came into court
of Godfrey Carriger decd.) and dismiss thier suit
Vs) and John Obrian came in-
William Obrian &) to court and assumes up-
Joseph Obrian)) on himself with the De-
) fendants the costs and
charges. It is therefore considered by the court that the
Plaintiffs recover of the defendants and John Obrian the cos
costs and charges which they have about thier suit in this
behalf expended and the defendants in mercy & &

(P.346)   Court adjourned untill tomorrow 9 oclock,
Geo. Emmert,
W. B. Carter,
G. W. Greenway.

Fryday 15 May 1829 Court met according to adjournment present
the Worshipful, Wm. B. Carter George Emmert & George Greenway
Esqr. The minutes of yesterday proceedings were read and signed

Henry Simmely) The Defe Grindstaff presented his
Vs) petition for a certiorair & & which
Benjamin Grindstaff) was granted on his giving bond & se-
curity

Wm Overby) The rule entered for a new trial in this case
Vs) this day on argument of counsel is made
R. Burrow) absolute and a new trial granted

A deed of Mortgage executed by Mark Reeve Casper W. Reeve
Robert Reeve & Job Whitall Reeve to Wm B. Carter on the
thirteenth day of February 1823 writ issud by Nathaniel
Kelsy & James Roberts was produced in court for probate as
to the execution thereof by Mark Reeve & Jobe Whitall Reeve
and thereupon James P. Taylor proven that James Roberts a
witness tosaid deed of mortgage is void & that the signature
thereto is in the proper hand writing of said Roberts to the
best of his knowledge & belief on which proof & the proof of
Nathaniel Kelsy the other subscribing witness thereto made

at the former term of this it is (P.347) admitted to record and ordered to be registered

State   )   The attorney General with leave of the court
  Vs   )   enters a nole prosequi in this cause and
Eli Campbell)   Zachariah Campbell comes into court and as-
               sumes upon himself with the defendant the
costs of this prosecution It is therefore considered by the
court that the state recover of the Defendant and Zachariah
Campbell the costs of this prosecution

Ordered by the court that Wm B. Carter, George Greenway &
George Emmert Esqr. be a committee to settle with Tennessee
L. Carriger & Godfrey Nave administrators of Godfrey
Carriger decead. and report to next court

Ordered by the court that Wm B. Carter, George Emmert &
Ezekiel Smith Esqr. be appointed a committie to settle with
Wm. Carter & Reuben Miller administrator with the will ex-
amind and report to next court

Ordered by the court that Wm. B.Carter George Emmert &
George Greenway Esqrs. be a committie appointed to settle
with James I. Tipton & George Lacy admrs. of Isaac Tipton
decd. and report to next court

(P.348) It appearing to the satisfaction of the court
that Susan Bowman & Louisa Reno orphan children heretofore
bound to Wm Messick said heirs stolen & taken away from
him by thier mother It is ordered that his bond entered int
to with the chairman of the county court of Carter be can-
celld and for nothin sold

Ordered by the court that Wm Beard confined in the jail of
this county have the ballance of his imprisonment remitted

Wm Beard & A. W. Taylor A. C. Parks Michael McCann his securities came into court & jointly acknowledged themselves
indebted to the state of Tennessee one hundred Dollars to
be levied of thier goods & chattles rights & credits and
void on condition that the said Beard for the term of
four months keep the peace and well and truly remain himself toward the good people of this state & particutarly
towards James Harvy then this recognizance to be void &
of no effect otherwise to remain in full force and vertue

State)   In this cause the deft being detaind
  Vs)
Wm Beard)

Same)   In prison for the costs of this suit & the
  Vs)   attorney General having waivd. motion was
Same ')   brought into court & took the insolvent
              debtors oath & was there upon discharged

(P.349)   Court adjournd. until court in course
                      Geo. Greenway,
                      Geo. Emmert,
                      Wm B. Carter.

     The end.

www.ingramcontent.com/pod-product-compliance
Lightning Source LLC
Chambersburg PA
CBHW072118020426
42334CB00018B/1636